America's Dates With Destiny

Pat Robertson

America's Dates With Destiny

THOMAS NELSON PUBLISHERS
Nashville • Camden • New York

Published in Nashville, Tennessee, by Thomas Nelson, Inc., and distributed in Canada by Lawson Falle, Ltd., Cambridge, Ontario.

Printed in the United States of America.

Unless otherwise noted Scripture quotations are from THE NEW KING JAMES VERSION. Copyright © 1979, 1980, 1982, Thomas Nelson, Inc., Publishers.

Scripture quotations noted NIV are from The Holy Bible: New International Version. Copyright © 1973, 1978, International Bible Society. Used by permission of Zondervan Bible Publishers.

Library of Congress Cataloging-in-Publication Data

Robertson, Pat.
  America's dates with destiny.

  1. United States—Politics and government. 2. United
States—Politics and government—Moral and ethical
aspects. 3. Christianity and democracy—United States—
History. I. Title.
E183.R625 1986   973   86–23654
ISBN 0-8407-7756-6

To the memory of
my distinguished father,
the late United States Senator A. Willis Robertson
of Virginia, whose life spent in the service
of the American people taught me
a love of our history and
respect for our institutions of government,
as well as instilling in me a desire
to protect and preserve
those institutions that guarantee
all our freedoms

CONTENTS

PART TWO **LOSING OUR WAY**

IF THE FOUNDATIONS
ARE DESTROYED,
WHAT CAN THE RIGHTEOUS DO?

PSALM 11:3

INTRODUCTION

During the past twenty-five years, early American history has been rewritten. This generation of public school students can go through twelve years of elementary and high school and another four years of college without one lesson featuring the central role of America's Judeo-Christian heritage in the founding and later history of the nation.

In a 1986 study of public school textbooks in America, the role of religion in history was found to be "largely excised." Education Secretary William J. Bennett denounced this "assault of secularism on religion." The survey illustrates how the "liberal bias" of the courts and the publishers' desire to "skirt controversy" have created a generation of school textbooks that fail to mention God, let alone give any "serious positive treatment to conservative views."[1] And the religious faith and biblical heritage of our forefathers have been eliminated from the record almost altogether.

The study, financed by the United States Department of Education, discovered that in the textbooks your children or grandchildren might be studying at this very moment, the Pilgrims' first Thanksgiving Day is often described "without any reference to their thanking God for their survival in the new land."[2] And the central role of Christian faith and biblical truth in shaping the charters of our original colonies, the curriculum of our original schools and universities, even the Declaration of Independence and the Constitution, has been censored from the historic record.

World history, too, has been scissored by these self-appointed censors. In today's muddle-headed textbooks, Joan of Arc, for example, is discussed without any mention of her faith in God, her religious commitment, or her elevation to sainthood by the Catholic Church. How could modern "historians" forget the heroic contributions to the exploration and settling of the world by Christian missionaries, ministers, priests, and laity over the past two thousand years? How do publishers dare to censor from the record the courageous, self-sacrificing efforts of those early missionaries to plant churches, schools, hospitals, orphanages, clinics, and every kind of spiritual and social service throughout the world? Lies, half-truths, and silence have replaced the facts about religious faith and its importance to the history of our nation and our world. Yet understanding the facts of our history is the only way we can wisely chart the nation's future.

To help in one small way to correct this imbalance, I have written *America's Dates with Destiny*. Every chapter presents a dramatic moment in the life of this nation. From all the thousands of dates worth remembering, I have chosen just twenty-three. These fascinating days occurred over a period of almost four centuries. They represent major national choices that will influence our history forever.

A Lifetime Fascination with History

I was born and lived most of my life surrounded by memories of this nation's past. My birthplace and childhood home were in Lexington, Virginia, a historic Blue Ridge Mountain town nestled in the southeastern Shenandoah Valley. When I was just learning to read, my father and I walked by the old cemetery on Main Street where the great General "Stonewall" Jackson is buried. The old marble headstones recall the names and short histories of the soldiers who gave their lives in the Revolutionary and Civil wars, and of the colonial and early state leaders, remembered and forgotten, who are buried there.

My mother, Gladys Churchill Robertson, was typical of many Southern women committed to understanding, appreciating, and keeping alive her own family's history. She was an heir to the heritage and traditions of the great English family that produced Sir Winston Churchill and generations of honorable, hard-working Britons and Americans. Carefully she uncovered the roots of her family and of my father's forebears, the Robertsons and the Harrisons. Through the Jamestown Society we traced eleven generations directly to the first permanent English settlement at Jamestown; to Benjamin Harrison, a signer of the Declaration of Independence; to Captain A. Robertson, one of George Washington's officers in the Revolutionary War; and through the Harrison line to two American presidents. My mother took great delight in our heritage deep in Virginia's colonial history, and she insisted that our family take seriously the responsibilities endowed on us by that heritage.

My dad, A. Willis Robertson, represented Virginia in the United States House of Representatives until I was sixteen and in the United States Senate until I was thirty-seven. During those thirty-four years my father spent in Congress, our family commuted between our home in Lexington and our temporary residences in the nation's capital. I grew up in two very different worlds, both alive with history.

In Lexington, my boyhood friends and I rode our bicycles up Jefferson Avenue to the great, grassy, tree-lined campus of Washington and Lee University, founded as Liberty Hall Academy twenty-seven years before the signing of the Declaration of Independence. George Washington established the college with his endowment gift in 1796, and Robert E. Lee saved the school from obscurity after the Civil War by serving as its president from 1865 until 1870. One year after World War II ended, I entered Washington and Lee to study for a liberal arts degree with a major in American and European history.

In Washington, D.C., as a young boy surrounded by history and fascinated with it, I wandered beneath the ornate rotunda of the United States capitol building fascinated by the statues honoring heroes of the then forty-eight states. I stood in wonder before the giant paintings of the great battle scenes of our nation's history, and I read stories from the nation's past in the Library of Congress and the Smithsonian Institution. As a teenager I accompanied my father on visits to various presidents in the White House, and during my childhood and young adult years, I sat in the Senate gallery watching my father and his colleagues make history, and after crucial votes and debates, I joined them in the exclusive Senate dining room for their exciting times of repartee and fellowship.

My father promised me that if I graduated Phi Beta Kappa from Washington and Lee, he would send me to Europe for graduate studies. The prize was so alluring that I reached that distinction my junior year. Upon my graduation in 1950, I spent a summer studying British culture in London. Two weeks after my return from England, I was called to active duty with the Marines and seven months later found myself in Korea with the 1st Marine Division. Questions about the meaning and purpose of life that had begun to gnaw at me at Washington and Lee only grew with these experiences in Europe and Asia. Something was missing in my life, and I longed to find it.

It was after returning to civilian life that I entered Yale Law School, determined to be a lawyer and eventually a statesman like my father. But at Yale, my questions about the meaning and purpose of life remained unanswered. In my classes I began to experience personally what happens when history is rewritten and the spiritual dimension of man is ridiculed, caricatured, or ignored entirely. That great university, founded by ten Congregational clergymen "to plant and propagate in this Wilderness, the blessed Reformed, Protestant Religion, in the purity of its Order, and Worship" had moved away from its original Christian charter and had virtually written God out of its curriculum. The academic standards were rigorous and admirable, but the real questions of life and death were seldom answered there.

I became disillusioned with law even as I studied it. Like the universities, the legal system of this nation had forgotten its history. The courts had drifted away from their historic moorings in the Constitution. And the great directions for law and government as outlined by the Declaration of Independence had been forgotten by a legal community dedicated not to the biblical principle that all men are created equal[3] but to a manipulative, often cynical use of the law.

During law school I worked one summer as staff investigator for the Senate Appropriations Committee, of which my father was a member. When the committee sessions were over, he and I would sit in his office sipping glasses of bourbon and branch water, discussing the issues troubling Congress and the nation. America's political system, like its universities and courts, seemed to be drifting, without any real direction. I found myself more and more discontented with becoming a lawyer or a politician and more and more determined to find answers to the questions that haunted me.

At Yale I met and married another Yale graduate student, Dede Elmer. Before graduation from law school, I was hired by W. R. Grace, Inc. Immediately after graduation I began work as an executive trainee and trouble shooter in their South American manufacturing operation. I had been bitten by the entrepreneurial bug and making big deals in business and a lot of money were my principal goals.

I should have been happy in the business world. There was unlimited opportunity. I had a lovely wife, a growing family, and an apartment overlooking New York Harbor. I represented W. R. Grace in projects in South America. Temporarily, I stayed active in politics. I even chaired the Stevenson for President Campaign Committee on Staten Island.

As time went by, however, I found that living to make dollars didn't make sense. The underlying questions about life and its purpose began to haunt me once again. I felt restless and confused. Careers in law, government, and business came to seem meaningless. I was a successful graduate from an Ivy League law school, but I had become disillusioned with law long before graduation. And with a secure business career guaranteed by my position with W. R. Grace, Inc., I studied for the New York bar exam only halfheartedly. I raced through it and failed. Looking back now, I wonder if it could have been my way to register a protest against what had happened to the historical roots of the entire legal system. Nothing really mattered to me then but finding a solution to my emptiness.

Then, one day in April 1956, a pastor-missionary friend of my mother took me to dinner. We talked about my search for God's purpose in my life. He took out his Bible and began to show me the answers.

That night in a plush hotel dining room after years of searching, I rediscovered my own spiritual roots. That night I confessed Jesus Christ as my Savior and Lord. I felt God's salvation in my life for the very first time. I could see why evangelical Christians called the experience "new birth."[4] What happened that night was a new beginning for my life, a chance to start again. Two years later, God blessed me with another kind of spiritual experience. His Spirit entered my life, and suddenly I knew what millions of people around the world are discovering, that God is not remote. He is an ever-present source of comfort, power, and strength. In those two rather orthodox, biblical experiences, my life was changed forever.

I left business and entered New York Theological Seminary. Dede and I moved into a rundown house in the Bedford-Stuyvesant section of Brooklyn to raise our family and begin our ministry. Then armed with a law and business background, and satisfied that through the Bible my questions about life and death were being answered at last, I bought a television studio in Virginia Beach, Virginia . . . but that's another story.

For twenty-seven years, I have been a professional broadcaster and a committed Christian. Our network has grown from one dilapidated television station in Virginia Beach to the fifth largest cable network in the nation with 31 million households (89 million people) connected. A. C. Nielsen estimates that 29 million people watch my 700 Club program every month. Now our CBN network, our CBN University with its five graduate schools and a law school, and our extensive humanitarian outreach program—including Operation Blessing and the Heads Up Literacy Campaign, our Freedom Council, and our Legal Foundation—employ thousands of full-time and volunteer personnel around the world and operate with a combined budget of more than $200 million annually. And from the beginning of it all, one of the primary goals has been to call America once again to its spiritual heritage.

America's Spiritual Roots

The real history of the founding of this nation does not lie. Our forefathers, almost to a man, believed in God. They were students of the Old and New Testaments and were deeply influenced by the life and teachings of Jesus. They founded the nation on principles basic to our Judeo-Christian heritage. And they feared for the future of this nation if the people ever turned from those principles.

Now, the day they feared has come. Our nation's spiritual heritage is being systematically eliminated from the historical record. A whole generation of American students is being cheated of an honest, thorough, uncensored look at our nation's past. But here and there, the truth is beginning to surface. Private and public lives are being transformed by it. Across the nation, new winds are blowing. What will happen to America and to the world if the people of this generation rediscover our spiritual heritage and commit their lives and the life of this nation to it?

I have written *America's Dates with Destiny* to help bring us one step closer to that great goal. The book is divided into three sections. The first includes eleven exciting days in early American history when our forefathers clearly demonstrated the early spiritual directions of this nation. The second section includes nine tragic dates from our own times that show how far the nation has wandered from its original goals. And the last section includes three dates that give us hope that our nation is finding its way back to its spiritual heritage.

This year, the school board of Los Angeles was sued to prevent any mention of God in the students' graduation speeches. A settlement was announced between the school board and the American Civil Liberties Union that in the graduation ceremonies of that huge school system, "no prayers or any mention of God will be allowed." That day, June 5, 1986, was another date with destiny. The parent who brought the suit against prayer, the ACLU lawyers who supported and defended it, the courts, the school board, the students, and the general public who remained silent were all players in a historic tragedy. Perhaps if they had known the past better, they could have made a wiser decision about the future.

Remember, even as you read the stories behind these twenty-five dates with destiny, the clock is ticking. Each new day becomes a great stage on which the drama of this nation's future is being played. You and I are players, too. We can sit in silence and watch our nation stumble forward into an uncertain future, or we can remember the past and act with courage and determination to set our nation on the right path once again.

PART ONE

BEGINNING
OUR
JOURNEY

1

THE CAPE HENRY LANDING

APRIL 29, 1607

Rediscovering Our Nation's Spiritual Heritage

Three tiny sailing ships—the *Susan Constance,* the *Godspeed,* and the *Discovery*—rode at anchor in Chesapeake Bay just a few hundred yards off Cape Henry, Virginia. Most of the 149 men of the Virginia Company lined the railings, squinting restlessly into the late afternoon sun as it silhouetted the distant dunes and sparkled off the sea. This was the end of their third long, impatient day anchored on the fringe of the New World. Crew and passengers together were waiting for the return of Captain John Smith's scouting party before they clambered down rope ladders off their small, full-rigged ships into longboats for the last hundred yards of their four-thousand-mile journey from England to America.

After land was first sighted on April 26, handpicked sailors and Smith's small party of militia explored "the fair meadows ablaze with wild flowers" that embraced the bay with its great, navigable river and its many feeder streams, brooks, and marshes. They found a campfire deserted by startled Indians and sampled the freshly roasted oysters abandoned there. They picked and ate wild strawberries "four times bigger and better than ours in England." They even sailed their hastily assembled longboat several miles up the James River, searching for a suitable place for a permanent settlement.

For those still unable to disembark, impatience grew with each new report. Finally, Captain Smith and his scouting party appeared on the dunes and signaled the men to join them. As our forefathers were being ferried to the beach at Cape Henry, John Smith, his soldiers, and the ship's carpenter were erecting in the sand a rough wooden cross they had carried from England just for this day.

The men on shore and the ship's company rowing toward the beaches must have seemed a strange and motley crowd to the Indians spying from a safe distance on the dunes. The settlers' faces were windburned and leathery; their hands, calloused; their bodies, thin, weak, and pale. Only one man had died, but the journey had taken a terrible toll on the survivors.

Imagine what that midwinter crossing of the stormy North Atlantic had cost them. Day and night for four and one-half months, their little boats had plunged down the back side of one giant wave, wallowed in a dark and noisy trough of wind and water, struggled gamely up another mountainous breaker, then plunged back down again.

They had survived 131 days crowded in damp, cold, foul-smelling holds in the darkness beneath the decks. They had survived endless seasickness, broken bones from falls from the icy masts and wind-whipped rigging, illnesses and fevers of all sorts, and terrible bouts of depression and fear. But they had survived. The journey had ended. In just moments they would stand on wobbly legs in the fabled New World. One by one the longboats scraped against the beach, and one by one the men of the Virginia Company—the founders of the first permanent settlement in North America—waded ashore and collapsed onto the sand.

Suddenly the exhausted, lonely, dispirited crowd noticed their chaplain, the Reverend Robert Hunt, wading toward them through the surf, dressed in full clerical vestments. He wore a silver cross around his neck and carried a rare, much-treasured Bible in his hands. I imagine that he walked through his little congregation of weary travelers and stood for a long, silent moment before the cross.

As he faced the rough-hewn wooden cross, were his eyes wet with tears? Did his hands tremble? Did his lips move in silent, heartfelt prayer? Even without a photograph, it isn't difficult to imagine what happened next. Up and down the sand dunes, men quit their noisy chatter and their groans of relief. One by one they rose from their places in the sand to join Chaplain Hunt there at the foot of the cross.

Finally, with only the cries of sea birds drifting on the silence above them, Robert Hunt began to lead the first public prayer of the first permanent settlement in America. Together, the men of the Virginia Company thanked God for their safe journey and recommitted themselves to God's plan and God's purpose for this New World.

On the second floor of our CBN Center is an original oil painting that captures that moment on April 29, 1607, when our forefathers gathered on the beach to claim this land for God and His cause. In *The Landing at Cape Henry,* sailors and gentleman merchants kneel side by side with soldiers in steel armor. Masons and carpenters, farmers, cooks, and deckhands remove their caps and stand or kneel in quiet reverence.

To understand the spiritual commitment of these men and of those who followed them to establish each of those first thirteen American colonies is to understand better why God has blessed this nation in the past, as well as the choices we must make now if we are to receive His blessings in the future.

Darkness was just one hour away. A young soldier waved me past his sentry post at the west entrance of the Fort Story Military Reservation. I drove up Atlantic Avenue through a cluster of drab, gray barracks and parked beneath a wooden observation tower looking out across the sand dunes toward Chesapeake Bay. The late afternoon sun silhouetted the eighteenth-century lighthouse behind me and cast long shadows across the sand and gravel road on which I walked.

I love to visit that spot just twelve air miles from my office at CBN Center in Virginia Beach. As nations go, ours is young. Our history is short and storm-tossed. But what history we do have as an English-speaking people living on these shores began just twenty years short of four hundred years ago on that almost-forgotten beach. A marker placed on the spot by the Department of the Interior tells in eloquent simplicity what happened here: "Act 1, Scene 1, of the unfolding drama that became the United States."

Modern historians have a tendency to forget this act of worship by our forefathers, to discredit the significance of their spiritual goals to our nation's past, and to minimize the relevance of those same goals to our nation's future. Once again we see how the deep Christian convictions of our nation's founders have almost been written out of American history.

To understand the men who risked their lives to plant the cross on a windswept beach in Virginia is to understand better who we are as a people and how and why we have prospered as a country. To turn back the clock almost four hundred years, to kneel beside our English ancestors in the sand, to feel what they felt that day, and to remember what gave them confidence to face their future in this New World is to understand better what can give us confidence to face our own future in the troubled days ahead.

The Dream Behind the Cape Henry Landing

The landing at Cape Henry began as a dream planted in the heart of Richard Hakluyt, an Anglican clergyman and one of England's great Renaissance geographers during the last half of the sixteenth century. It was Hakluyt's lifelong passion to see the North American continent explored, settled, and evangelized by England. His commitment to the development of the New World came directly from two primary biblical truths, one from the book of Genesis in the Old Testament and one from the gospel according to Matthew in the New.

The Old Testament Charter

In the beginning, God commanded Adam and Eve to "have dominion . . . over all the earth."[1] By all reports of explorers who had visited North America and by Richard Hakluyt's own eyewitness account, the New World was a kind of paradise, a second Garden of Eden. Hakluyt believed God was calling European Christendom to take dominion over this New World and all its creatures.

Since the Reformation, especially in John Calvin's work in Geneva beginning in 1536, business (the creation and exchange of goods) was seen as God's way to have dominion over the earth, to develop and share its vast resources. But business was to be carefully regulated by biblical command for the good of all humanity. The rule of love was to be the rule of business, and the life and teachings of Jesus were the model by which businesses were to be run.

Richard Hakluyt dreamed of villages, towns, and cities in North America where Indians and settlers could live in peace and prosperity. He envisioned new factories to hire England's unemployed, new clientele for English trade, and new prosperity and happiness for all. Material prosperity for everyone was a Christian goal to Hakluyt, and the resources of the New World were God's gift to bring all people closer to that objective.

The New Testament Charter

The New Testament commission was even more significant to Christians like Richard Hakluyt. Just before Christ ascended into heaven, He issued another kind of command, a spiritual commission to all believers. That New Testament charter to men and women of faith is called the Great Commission. It reads simply:

> Therefore go and make disciples of all nations, baptizing them in the name of the Father and of the Son and of the Holy Spirit, and teaching them to obey everything I have commanded you. And surely I will be with you always, to the very end of the age.[2]

Hakluyt had heard the stories of the uncivilized Indian peoples of North America who lived and died without any knowledge of God or of God's love in Christ. He had gathered heartbreaking accounts of the misery of those people who lived in bondage to pagan practices, to constant tribal rivalry and warfare. He had read the letters of Cortez with their frightening tales from the New World of human sacrifices to gods of wood and stone.

Hakluyt sincerely believed that people with no knowledge of God or of the Christian faith were imprisoned by the forces of death and darkness and needed to be set free by the power of Christ's life, death, and resurrection. He believed, too, that government based on biblical teaching was the best way—if not the only way—to gain and maintain liberty in the land.

Finally, in 1606, Richard Hakluyt's efforts to establish a permanent settlement in Virginia resulted in the Virginia Charter from King James I. That charter reflects the Christian faith both of King James— who authorized the English translation of the Bible published in 1611 which became the greatest treasure of the English language—and of Richard Hakluyt, who believed his real authority for building a plantation in North America came from the Bible, not just from king or council. At the heart of this charter were these words:

> We would vouchsafe unto them our Licence, to make Habitation, Plantation, and to deduce a colony of sundry of our people into that Part of *America* commonly called VIRGINIA . . . .

We greatly commend . . . so noble a work, which may by the Providence of Almighty God, hereafter tend to the Glory of his Divine Majesty, in propagating of *Christian* religion to such People, as yet live in Darkness and miserable Ignorance of the true Knowledge and Worship of God, and may in time bring the Infidels and Savages, living in those Parts, to human Civility, and to a settled and quiet Government.[3]

In Elizabethan prose, King James was giving our forefathers power to accomplish four goals in the New World:

First, "habitation." Under God, they were to take dominion, or control, over family and civic life together.

Second, "plantation." Under God, they were to take dominion over the land.

Third, they were to share Christian faith with the Indians.

Fourth, they were to introduce Indians and settlers alike to life and government under God.

Thirteen Colonies Share the Dream

During the next 125 years, thirteen colonies were established on the Atlantic coastline of North America. The charter of each new plantation colony reflected goals almost identical to those of the company that landed first at Cape Henry, although the men and women who founded each of the original colonies were different in many ways.

The Reverend Robert Hunt and the men of the first English settlement at Jamestown were faithful members of the Church of England and loyal supporters of the king. But the Plymouth Colony was founded by a little band of religious dissenters from the Church of England who were known by king and clergy as "separatists."

These Pilgrims had fled England for Holland in 1608 to find religious freedom. In 1620 they sailed on the *Mayflower* with patents from the London Company authorizing their settlement in northern Virginia. But they were blown off course by the treacherous and unpredictable Atlantic winds. On November 11, 1620, they landed at Plymouth Rock on Cape Cod in New England. Before landing, forty-one Pilgrims wrote and signed the Mayflower Compact. See how it, too, reflects the spiritual goals of the charter of the Virginia Company:

IN THE NAME OF GOD, AMEN. We . . . the Loyal Subjects of our dread Sovereign Lord King *James,* by the Grace of God . . . Having undertaken for the Glory of God, and Advancement of the Christian Faith, and the Honour of our King and Country, a Voyage to plant the first Colony in the northern Parts of *Virginia;* Do . . . in the Presence of God and one another, covenant and combine ourselves together into a civil Body Politick, for our better Ordering and Preservation, and Furtherance of the Ends aforesaid.[4]

It is interesting to note here that though King James I had given them a charter to establish a plantation in northern Virginia, when God fixed their course to land hundreds of miles to the north, William Bradford and his Pilgrim brothers appealed to God's Great Commission as an adequate new charter to replace the charter of their king.

Eight years after the Mayflower Compact, some Puritans obtained a charter from King James's successor, King Charles I, to build their own plantation in the New World. This was the Massachusetts Bay Colony, the second permanent English settlement in North America. These Puritans, though members of the Church of England, were critical of the church, demanding "purer" doctrine and worship and stricter religious discipline. The Puritans would find themselves in serious disagreement with Anglicans and Pilgrims alike; yet, their charter, too, rested squarely upon the authority of the Great Commission and echoed the goals of the first settlers of Virginia and Massachusetts. The Puritans set out to create a people in the New World who would be "soe religiously, peaceablie, and civilly governed, as their good Life and orderlie Conversation, maie wynn and incite the Natives of Country, to the Knowledg and Obedience of the onlie true God and Sauior of Mankinde, and the Christian fayth."[5]

On June 20, 1632, the Charter of Maryland was issued by King Charles to Lord Baltimore of Ireland. A Catholic, Lord Baltimore shared the same zeal for the cause of Christ and the establishment of civil government under God as did his Anglican, Puritan, and Pilgrim brethren:

Our well beloved and right trusty Subject Caecilius Calvert, Baron of Baltimore . . . being animated with a laudable, and pious Zeal for extending the Christian Religion . . . hath humbly besought Leave of Us, that he may transport . . . a numerous Colony of the English Nation, to a certain

Region . . . in a Country hitherto uncultivated . . . and partly occupied by Savages, having no Knowledge of the Divine Being.[6]

In January 1636, Roger Williams was banished from the Colony of Massachusetts Bay for his outspoken support of complete religious freedom. In that same year, he purchased land from the Narragansett Indians and settled the town of Providence. An Anabaptist, the forerunner of the Baptist movement in America, and later a Seeker, or Quaker, Williams was constantly in disagreement with his Anglican, Puritan, and even Pilgrim brothers. Nevertheless, his charter for Rhode Island, granted by King Charles II on July 8, 1663, was at its heart almost identical to the charters of Virginia and Massachusetts: "Pursueing . . . their sober, serious and religious intentions, of godlie edifieing themselves, and one another, in the holie Christian ffaith and worshipp as they were perswaded; together with the gaineing over and conversione of the poore ignorant Indian natives . . . to the sincere professions and obedienc of the same faith and worship."[7]

Twenty years after Roger Williams founded Rhode Island, the Carolinas were colonized under a 1663 charter issued by King Charles II to Sir William Berkeley and seven other Englishmen. That colony eventually attracted a large number of Presbyterians from Northern Ireland, as well as Huguenots from France, who came to the New World not only to escape persecution, but also to help spread the gospel in the new land. King Charles II described the goals of these new settlers as follows: "Being excited with a laudable and pious zeal for the propagation of the Christian faith . . . [they] have humbly besought leave of us . . . to transport and make an ample colony . . . unto a certain country . . . not yet cultivated or planted, and only inhabited by some barbarous people, who have no knowledge of Almighty God."[8]

In 1681, Quaker William Penn obtained a charter to build his plantation in the New World. Notice how remarkably similar are the goals of Quaker Pennsylvania to the aims of the Anglican, Puritan, Pilgrim, Presbyterian, Baptist, and Catholic settlers who came before: "To reduce the savage natives by gentle and just manners to the Love of Civil Societie and Christian religion."[9]

Of the remaining five original colonies, three—Connecticut, New Hampshire, and New Jersey—were originally part of New England, colonized under the Massachusetts Bay Charter. These colonies, too, reflected Richard Hakluyt's original dream for the New World by simply restating the original charters or adding their own restatement of those earliest Christian purposes.

The Price They Paid To Keep the Dream Alive

It is time once again to remember those original charter goals of our forefathers, to tell the stories of the settlers who kept those goals and the price they paid to do it. I get defensive when we refuse to look backward at our spiritual past—for example, at the cross, the prayer, and the settlers on their knees at Cape Henry—because that refusal keeps us from looking forward into the future with enough wisdom and direction to make the hard decisions facing us today.

I admit I have another, more personal reason to get defensive about that prayer meeting and its historical significance. My own blood relative John Woodson, the surgeon of the Virginia Company, was there that day. He later joined those who were kneeling on the beach. So I am responsible to my own heritage to keep alive what really happened there.

In fact, in 1985 I shared a banquet speaker's table with the Reverend Robert Hunt, an Episcopal clergyman whose own roots go back four centuries to his namesake, the chaplain of the Virginia Company. During the festivities honoring his namesake, Mr. Hunt leaned over and whispered to me, "Hello, Cousin." Apparently the Hunts and the Woodsons intermarried during those early Jamestown years, making me related to Chaplain Hunt himself. So, I hope I can be forgiven for finding it difficult to let history rob this date of its real significance. The truth would not be served by the continued confusion about Cape Henry and the spiritual roots of this nation. And my ancestors would certainly not be pleased by my silence.

When I walk alone on that historic beach, I think about my own ancestor, Robert Hunt, and the price he paid to come to this new land. In this age, when travelers can cross the Atlantic on the *Concorde* in three hours or on a luxury liner in five pampered days, it is almost impossible to imagine the difficulty of Hunt's and the other settlers' getting across that huge ocean to the New World, let alone surviving the unfriendly environment once they landed here.

Richard Hakluyt had felt too old and infirm to lead the expedition and so had encouraged his friend Hunt to be chaplain in his place. Hunt had come aboard at Blackwall with his library and personal supplies. For six weeks their three small ships had to remain anchored in a storm just twenty miles from his home. Trapped by those raging seas, Chaplain Hunt became so ill that few expected him to recover. Still, nothing would persuade him to give up the journey. Like Hakluyt, Hunt was determined to carry out this great commission. When at last he could stand against the winter storm, he walked among the seasick, frightened, lonely settlers, reminding them of their calling and restoring to them the vision they pursued.

When finally they set sail for Virginia, winter gales and headwinds continued to cause "much dissension and discontent." Many wished they had never set out upon this journey. But Hunt encouraged the settlers through that stormy Atlantic crossing. By his prayers and words of wisdom, he convinced them to continue. His determination to endure hardship served as an example to his countrymen, and they praised him and his ministry among them.

After landing at Cape Henry, sailing up the James River, and establishing their rough log fortress at Jamestown, the settlers faced a new round of trials: bad weather, short supplies, unfriendly Indians, inadequate and rotting foodstuffs. In one settler's words, those next months were filled with "endless and cruel discomfort." Then, as the men were locked behind the log walls of their fortress, terrified by the natives, rationed "to half a pint of wheat and half a pint of wormy barley boiled in water per day," sickness struck.

"Scarse ten amongst us coulde either goe or well stand; such extreame weaknes and sicknes oppressed us," one settler wrote in obvious despair. Finally, with their food almost gone, Captain Newport sailed back to England for help, leaving 104 men to build that first permanent settlement in Virginia and to keep the dream alive. By September 10, half the settlers were dead.

In the midst of the suffering the settlers experienced during their first winter in Jamestown, in January 1608, the wooden church and many of the log homes of the settlers burned, including the home of Chaplain Hunt. Captain John Smith, reporting later on that fire during their first year in America, wrote, "Good Master Hunt, our preacher, lost all his library, and all that he had (but the clothes on his back) yet none ever saw him repine at his loss."

According to those early records, Hunt led the settlers in daily worship, preaching and teaching them to keep the commission that Christ Himself had given them. Captain Smith described the worship in

Jamestown with these words: "We had daily Common Prayer morning and evening, every Sunday two sermons, and every three months the holy Communion, till our minister died." Of Hunt's life among them he concluded, "Till he could not speak he never ceased to his utmost to animate us constantly to persist."

During that winter of death, Robert Hunt was buried in Jamestown with dozens of the men he had pastored on the long Atlantic journey and during their first year in America. Would the search "for gold, adventure and natural resources," as a placard placed at Cape Henry by the Department of the Interior puts it, have been a sufficient motivation to see Robert Hunt through those terrible trials? I don't believe so. The settlers remembered his reading from the Bible for two hours every morning and walking alone into the woods to pray. Robert Hunt, and in varying degrees all those men who sailed with him, had a commission from God, and at that landing at Cape Henry we are reminded once again of how seriously they took it.

I like to remember the dedication and determination of this company of men who volunteered to leave their wives and families to build what Hakluyt called "God's plantation in the New World." I like to think about them and their commitment as I stand alone on the beach at Cape Henry and try to picture them, kneeling in the cold, wet sand before that hastily erected cross shortly after their long voyage ended in Chesapeake Bay.

That handful of men at Cape Henry who were the first to put down permanent roots in this soil were given solemn words of counsel by the king before they began their journey. James I ended his charter to the men of the Virginia Company with this prophetic warning: "The way to prosper and achieve good success is to make yourselves all of one mind for the good of your country and your own, and to serve and fear God the Giver of all goodness, for every plantation which our Heavenly Father hath not planted shall be rooted out."

As a nation, we have almost forgotten King James's words of warning. We rewrite our history with man at the center, and we forget that a wooden cross planted on Cape Henry that day caused them all to kneel.

Just twenty-six years ago, I bought a little Christian television station a few miles from Cape Henry. God has blessed that first station and transformed it into a giant network. The Christian Broadcasting Network has the same goals that brought our forefathers to this land: to obey the Great Commission in sharing the life and teachings of Jesus with those who don't know about Him, and to do our part to help build a nation under God that offers peace and prosperity to all.

Of course, our forefathers and those who followed them here did not live up to the life and teachings of the Man who died upon the cross. The stories in our nation's history about cruelty to the Indians, misuse of the land, racial and class prejudice, and bigotry and injustice are often true. But those moments that illustrate our forefathers' failures happened not because those men *kept* Christ's commission, but because they *wandered* from it.

Injustice and cruelty in the land have existed not because our forefathers took their charter too seriously but because they did not take it seriously enough. Keeping to our Christian goals didn't cause suffering, but not keeping to them. Following Christ didn't lead to injustice or cruelty or loss of human rights and freedom, but not following Him.

What would have happened here if no cross had been planted on the beach at Cape Henry? What would have become of this nation if our forefathers had never tried to obey Christ's Great Commission or follow His example? What will become of this people today if we forget the example of the Anglicans, Puritans, Pilgrims, Baptists, Catholics, and Quakers who went before us? What principles will guide us as a nation if we simply ignore the Dominion Mandate of the Old Testament and the Great Commission of the New Testament that directed and empowered our forefathers' life together?

We must not forget that day when the men of the Virginia Company knelt in the sand at Cape Henry to thank God for His faithfulness and to seek His guidance for this nation's future. Instead, let us renew our commitment to their stated goals. Let us kneel in the sand beside them to pray our own prayers of confession, thanking God for His blessings in the past and seeking His direction for the future.

2

THE MASSACRE
AT HENRICO COLLEGE

MARCH 22, 1622

Rediscovering the Higher Purpose of Education

An hour before sunrise on March 22, 1622, the English settlers who had left Jamestown and were building plantations along the upper James River awakened to face another wintry working day. Women were getting dressed or preparing fried eggs and pork sausage over open, wood-burning fires. Children were breaking thin sheets of ice from outdoor wooden tubs and howling with mock horror as they splashed the night's sleep from their eyes. After breakfast, men and boys worked from sunrise to sunset preparing the earth for spring planting, tending the grape arbors, or weeding among the tender new mulberry trees. Women and girls washed, cleaned, and cooked together.

Those merchants, traders, and officials of the Virginia Company who lived on one of the three major streets of the new city of Henrico were probably still asleep, enjoying the warmth and comfort of their wood-framed homes. After years in the primitive North American wilderness, Henrico seemed a kind of paradise. Living in Jamestown, the settlers had been surrounded by foul-smelling, mosquito-infested waters. An easy sail up the James River from the Chesapeake Bay, they had felt vulnerable to attack by ships from Spain or by bands of marauding Indians. The new city of Henrico had been built on a high promontory above the James River. Abundant freshwater springs and verdant fields were protected on three sides by the river and on the fourth by Dutch Gap, a long, deep moat the settlers had constructed against invaders.

Just two miles away from Henrico, on a ten-thousand-acre grant of land, brickmasters and masons, carpenters and blacksmiths, machinists, potters, and farmers who had been hired and shipped to Virginia to build Henrico College were dressing in their sleeping quarters or eating breakfast in their communal dining hall. King James I, the Archbishop of Canterbury, the London and Virginia Companies, and the people of England and Virginia shared a dream that one day on this clearing in the woods near Henrico a great university would rise in the New World to rival Oxford or Cambridge in the Old. And acre by acre, brick by brick, that dream was taking shape.

No one suspected that the dream for Henrico and its university would die that same Good Friday morning.

As the settlers awakened to that last day in Henrico, Indian warriors under the command of Chief Opechancanough were moving into position around the city and preparing for a surprise attack against it, the settlement at Henrico College, and the major plantation homes up and down the river. Before the day ended, those same Indian braves would launch their swift and bloody assault.

Then suddenly a young Indian Christian pounded on the gates of Henrico City. The warning was sounded. Armed militia led the settlers on a hurried exodus from Henrico. Runners were sent to Henrico College and to the large plantations nearby.

Although they had prepared fortifications for just such an emergency, the people panicked. They stumbled from their houses and into boats just moments before the Indian attack began. Leaving everything behind, riding anything that would carry them, the settlers fled downriver toward Jamestown. As they departed, Indians appeared from the forests dressed in war paint and feathers and carrying torches, bows, arrows, spears, and a few long rifles.

What happened next is a mystery, lost to the annals of history. Did Chief Opechancanough himself provide the warning? Did he burn Henrico City to the ground, or did the buildings fall into ruin because no one returned to care for them? Was the superintendent at Henrico College, Captain George Thorpe, murdered and his body mutilated by the Indians? Or did he die of natural causes years later in the city of Jamestown?

Historians are not certain.[1] Five people died during the Indian attack on Henrico. Seventeen workers were massacred on the university campus. A few died in their plantation houses along the river. But most of the settlers from Henrico fled safely to Jamestown. Those who insisted on returning to rebuild their city and complete this first great university in America were forced to return to Jamestown by orders of the Jamestown Council. King James I died, and his successors were too involved in England to take up the project again. What the Indians didn't destroy of Henrico and its great university dream soon collapsed in ruin and has since disappeared under almost four centuries of weather and neglect.

Now, at Dutch Gap on Farrar's Island just ten miles south of Richmond, Virginia, overlooking the double *U* bends of the James River, there is a simple cross marking the site where a great university was to stand. The charter of Henrico College was a blueprint that reflected our forefathers' purpose and plan for education in the New World. It must not be forgotten. From the carefully preserved records of king and Parliament, archbishop and London Company, we can reconstruct a clear picture of their dream for that university and for education on every level throughout the land.

What we learn from those records is that the universities in America have departed from that vision for education in this country. As a result, too many of our school boards, principals, and teachers have no ultimate goals to direct them. Too many of our graduates leave America's classrooms with their most important questions still unanswered. Education in America has lost its way, and from this almost-forgotten dream buried in the fields and forests of Virginia we can find help in getting us back on the right trail.

No marker in the ruins of Henrico City guides us to that historic spot where "Rock Hall" once stood. No crumbling walls, no foundation outlines in the earth help us find even a trace of the parsonage home of Henrico's most esteemed citizen, the Reverend Alexander Whitaker, a Cambridge graduate and the Church of England's most effective missionary advocate in the New World.[2]

Because of his enthusiastic and effective attempts to mobilize England's support for bringing Christ to the Indians, Whitaker was affectionately called the "Apostle of Virginia." Parson Whitaker introduced Pocahontas, daughter of Indian Chief Powhatan, to the Christian faith and provided her and her people with the rudiments of a Christian education. And Alexander Whitaker's ministry helped launch a system of higher education, for Indians and settlers alike, that once was the model for all education in America.

In 1612 another clergyman, writing in England, published a paper entitled "New Life of Virginia." His definition of the purpose of education in the New World was the standard definition for Whitaker and his contemporaries. "Take their children," he wrote, "and train them up with gentleness, teach them our English tongue and the principles of religion."[3]

The Appeal To Support Education in America

The first surviving fund-raising letter in American history was written by Parson Whitaker in 1612 and published in England by the Virginia Company. In that letter the missionary built a New Testament case for generous financial support for the work of educating the Indians in North America. After an emotional appeal to help alleviate "the miserable condition of these naked slaves of the devil,"[4] Whitaker told his readers that the American Indians were also "very understanding . . . quick of apprehension . . . subtle in their dealings . . . exquisite in their inventions and industrious in their labor."[5]

From the beginning of England's colonization of the New World, Indians like Pocahontas were taken to England and introduced in the court of King James and to the cultural and religious centers of Renaissance England. Some Indian children who were educated in English schools seemed fascinated by the life of Jesus and were quick to accept the Christian faith after the briefest exposures to the Bible and its teaching. With these living examples of the effectiveness of Christian education in the New World, the people of England pledged their faithful support.

On February 28, 1615, James I issued a letter to George Abbot, then the Archbishop of Canterbury, suggesting that he was pleased with the "propagating of ye Gospell" in Virginia and suggesting that the good archbishop mobilize the church to build "Schooles [in Virginia] for the education of the children." The king carefully instructed the archbishop to collect offerings throughout the churches of the realm "in as liberall a manner as they may" for the purpose of building a college there.[6]

On April 15, 1616, the Archbishop of Canterbury, George Newman, requested that ministers and wardens take several collections in the next two years "to erect a Colledge [in Virginia] for the trayning vp of the Children of those barbarous people, in the true knowledge of God and other Ciuil instructions."[7] Offerings were taken in every church in England to begin a college and a series of free public schools to prepare children for enrollment in the college.

In the spring of 1617 Reverend Whitaker drowned in the James River. His successor, the Reverend Patrick Copeland, soon after his arrival in Virginia wrote back to England, "There is a greater want of schools rather than churches in this new land."[8]

The Charter for a College at Henrico

In 1618 the Virginia Company petitioned King James I for a charter for a full-fledged educational program in the New World. The king approved the charter and set aside ten thousand acres of land near Henrico to build a plantation that would support and endow Henrico College and provide it a campus home. The stated purpose for the new school system was "education for the training of the Indians in the true knowledge of God and in some useful employment and to educate the children of the settlers who are now deprived of formal education."[9]

On July 31, 1619, the first legislative assembly ever to convene in the New World met in the Jamestown church and petitioned the Virginia Company in London to send, "when they shall think it most convenient, workmen of all sorts for the erection of the university and college." It is noteworthy that one of the first items on the agenda of this first representative, elected lawmaking assembly in America was a petition to the Virginia Company to send workmen to begin a university in the New World.

From the various historical documents, it is not difficult to get a clear picture of the purpose of education in Virginia. "In addition to civilizing and christianizing young Indians," the schools "should also prepare some of them as missionaries to their own people." The civilizing of the Indians "necessarily included instruction in the fundamental principles of Christianity. By teaching them the arts of civilization, the Company thought the Indians would become producers and aid in subduing the vast American wilderness. With the arrival of the governor, Sir George Yeardley, in 1618, the Company enlarged the original design of the College by providing for the admission of the English also to its advantages."[10]

It is also noteworthy that the support of education in the New World was not from king or Parliament or even by royal taxation. Instead, schools in Virginia were supported by voluntary Christian giving. Gifts were received from school children and lords, from widows and scholars, from the king, from Parliament, and from the directors of the great London companies. Valuable libraries of Christian books and Bibles, other gifts, and special offerings were contributed by concerned clergymen and laity alike.

One anonymous Christian donor delivered a letter to Sir Edwin Sandys at a meeting of the London Company wishing the college founders, "Good luck in the name of the Lord, who is dayly magnified by the experiment of your zeale and piety in giving beginning to the foundation of the college in Virginia, the sacred work so due to heaven."[11] His letter was accompanied by the gift of a valuable silver communion set with cover, a silver gilt trencher plate for the bread, a crimson velvet altar cloth, and a fine linen tablecloth to serve the university's sacramental meal.[12]

The Plan for Henrico College

On November 4, 1619, Captain William Weldon arrived in Virginia with a party of fifty skilled craftsmen to begin building the campus and developing the surrounding plantation lands. In 1620 George Thorpe replaced Weldon as superintendent of Henrico College because of dissatisfaction with Weldon's progress.

Back in England, the Reverend Patrick Copeland was appointed by the Virginia Company to form a committee to design lower or feeder schools to prepare the settlers' children for their new university. The minutes of the Virginia Company, dated October 30, 1621, give eloquent simplicity to their purpose for education in the colonies: "They therefore conceaved it most fitt to resolve for the erectinge of a publique free schoole w'ch being for the education of children and groundinge of them in the principles of religion, Civility of life and humane learninge served to carry with it the greatest waight and highest consequence unto the Plantations as that whereof both Church and Commonwealth take their originall foundation and happie estate."[13]

Historian Gordon McCabe has found plenty of evidence that in this first colony, the settlers worked out a well-devised and well-rounded plan for graded education in the colony from elementary school to university.[14]

Between 1619 and 1623, George Thorpe and his staff of educators, architects, builders, and farmers worked to create a university in America. Thorpe had overseen the cultivation of three thousand acres of college plantation land with corn, grapevines, and mulberry trees (to supply the contemplated silk industry).

It is apparent that by 1622 campus buildings were in various stages of construction to house students, classrooms, and libraries. That same year, the Reverend Patrick Copeland was appointed rector of the college and was about to proceed to Virginia to take charge of Henrico when Chief Opechancanough and his braves mounted their surprise attack on Good Friday morning.

Those who survived the massacre only to see their dreams of building the first university in America delayed even longer by civil and religious conflict in Virginia and England could be comforted by these words of the Reverend William Crashaw, a friend and coworker of the Reverend Alexander Whitaker in Henrico: "This work is of God and will therefore stand . . . . It may be hindered, but it cannot be overthrown. If we, then were so base as to betray and forsake it, God's whose it is, will stir up our children after us and give them that good land to enjoy . . . that men shall say, God hath made His ways known upon the earth and His saving health among all nations."[15]

Harvard College in Massachusetts

The second and more successful attempt to create a college in the New World was initiated in 1636, just fourteen years after the massacre at Henrico. The Puritans launched the first North American college, Harvard, in Cambridge, Massachusetts, just six years after they landed at Massachusetts Bay. A priceless little pamphlet written in 1643 following the graduation of its first class describes in clear and fascinating detail the history, purpose, and plan of Harvard in those early years. The pamphlet begins:

> After God had carried us safe to *New-England,* and wee had builded our houses, provided necessaries for our liveli-hood, rear'd convenient places for Gods worship, and setled the Civill Government: One of the next things we longed for, and looked after was to advance *Learning* and to perpetuate it to Posterity; dreading to leave an illiterate Ministery to the Churches, when our present Ministers shall lie in the Dust. And as

wee were thinking and consulting how to effect this great Work, it pleased God to stir up the heart of one Mr. *Harvard* (a godly Gentleman and a lover of Learning . . .) towards the erecting of a Colledge, and all his library.[16]

The requirements for enrollment head the list of eight rules and precepts observed by the college that follow:

1. When any Schollar . . . is able to make [write] and speak true Latine in Verse and Prose . . . . And decline perfectly the paradigims of *Nounes* and *Verbes* in the *Greek* tongue . . . [he is capable] of admission into the college.

2. Let every Student be plainly instructed; and earnestly pressed to consider well the maine end of his life and studies is *to know God and Jesus Christ which is eternall life,* Joh. 17:3 and therefore to lay *Christ* in the bottome, as the only foundation of all sound knowledge and Learning.

And seeing the Lord only giveth wisdome, Let every one seriously set himself by prayer in secret to seek it of him *Prov.* 2,3.

3. Every one shall so exercise himselfe in reading the Scriptures twice a day, that he shall be ready to give such an account of his proficiency therein, both in *Theoreticall* observations of the Language, and Logick, and in *practicall* and spirituall truths, as his Tutor shall require, according to his ability; seeing *the entrance of the word giveth light, it giveth understanding to the simple,* Psalm, 119:130.

4. That they eshewing all profanation of Gods name, Attributes, Word, Ordinances, and times of Worship, do studie with good conscience carefully to retaine God, and the love of his truth in their mindes, else let them know, that (nothwithstanding their Learning) God may give them up to *strong delusions,* and in the end to *a reprobate minde,* 2 Thes. 2:11,12. Rom. 1:28.

5. That they studiously redeeme the time; observe the generall houres . . . diligently attend the Lectures, without any disturbance by word or gesture . . . .

6. None shall . . . frequent the company and society of such men as lead an unfit, and dissolute life.

Nor shall any without his Tutors leave, or without the call of Parents or Guardians, goe abroad to other Townes.

7. Every Schollar shall be present in his Tutors chamber at the 7th houre in the morning, immediately after the sound of the Bell, at his opening the Scripture and prayer, so also at the 5th. houre at night, and then give account of his owne private reading . . . . But if any . . . shall

absent himself from prayer or Lectures, he shall bee lyable to Admonition, if he offend above once a weeke.

8. If any Schollar shall be found to transgresse any of the Lawes of God, or the Schoole . . . he may bee admonished at the publick monthly Act.[17]

I have included almost the entire pamphlet describing education during those early years at Harvard because it shows in such clear detail the spirit of our colonial forefathers' approach to education from the earliest days before the Henrico massacre up through the founding of all the great colonial universities.

Critics say that Harvard was a seminary just for training ministers. It isn't true. John Adams, John Hancock, Samuel Adams, James Otis, and Josiah Quincy are just a few of the early graduates of Harvard's Christian education. Each of these men made an incredible contribution to the birth and early life of this nation.

Yale College in Connecticut

Consider also Yale College, founded in 1701 by ten Congregational ministers "in his Majesties Colony of Connecticut." Compare the goals at Yale to the goals for education at Harvard. From a meeting of the trustees on November 11, 1701, we learn the founders' original purpose for Yale: ". . . to plant and under ye Divine blessing to propagate in this Wilderness, the blessed Reformed, Protestant Religion, in ye purity of its Order, and Worship."[18]

The founders at Yale, like their fellow settlers at Harvard, went on to be specific about the rules:

Whereunto the Liberal, and Relligious Education of Suitable youth is under ye blessing of God, a chief, & most probable expedient . . . . we agree to . . . these following Rules:

1. The said rector shall take Especial Care as of the moral Behaviour of the Students at all Times so with industry to Instruct and Ground Them well in Theoretical devinity . . . and [not to] allow them to be Instructed and Grounded in any other Systems or Synopses . . . . To recite the Assemblies Catechism in Latin . . . [with] such Explanations as may be (through the Blessing of God) most Conducive to their Establishment in the Principles of the Christian protestant Religion.

2. That the said Rector shall Cause the Scriptures Daily . . . morning and evening to be read by the Students at the times of prayer in the School . . . Expound practical Theology . . . Repeat Sermons . . . studiously Indeavor[ing] in the Education of said students to promote the power and the Purity of Religion and Best Edification and peace of these New England Churches.[19]

The act of the General Court authorizing the new college at Yale called for an institution where "youth may be instructed in the Arts and Sciences who through the blesing of Almighty God may be fitted for Publick employment both in Church and Civil State."[20]

As late as 1748, all professors and students at Yale had to subscribe to the Westminster Confession of Faith. And what kinds of scholars did Christian Yale produce during those early years? Consider just three Yale graduates: the inventor Eli Whitney, the educator and author Noah Webster, and the patriot Nathan Hale, who just before being hanged by the British said, "I only regret that I have but one life to lose for my country."

The Early American Colleges

For those first 150 years, education in America and the Christian faith were inseparable. The Bible served as the standard by which all other truth was measured. The life and teachings of Jesus were at the heart of the curriculum.

William and Mary College, founded in Virginia in 1691 with studies in grammar, philosophy, mathematics, and divinity, had God, the Holy Scriptures, and Jesus at the heart of its curriculum. And among the school's early graduates we count Thomas Jefferson, James Monroe, George Wythe, and John Marshall, chief justice of the United States Supreme Court.

Princeton College was founded in 1746 by Presbyterian clergymen during the spiritual awakening that was then sweeping the colonies. Princeton was also a direct result of spiritual revival and the desire to place spiritual renewal and commitment at the heart of higher education. Early Princeton graduates include James Madison, Henry Lee, Aaron Burr, and six members of the first United States Congress.

Dartmouth was founded in 1775 by Congregational clergyman Eleazar Wheelock, a graduate of Yale, as Moor's Indian Charity School in

Columbia, Connecticut. In the beginning, Dartmouth, like Princeton, reflected the early settlers' zeal to share Christian faith with the Indians and to educate young people in the spirit of Jesus and the Bible.

Columbia was founded by royal charter on July 17, 1754, in the vestry room of the Trinity Church schoolhouse in New York City with no smaller Christian commitment than Harvard and the others. Columbia's early graduates include Alexander Hamilton, John Jay, Governor Morris, and William and Robert R. Livingston.

The University of Pennsylvania grew from the Charity School established in 1740 by Christian evangelist George Whitefield. Brown University was chartered as Rhode Island College in 1764 by the Baptist descendants of Roger Williams "to train ministers and to educate youth properly in the Christian faith."[21] Rutgers was established by royal charter in 1776 by members of the Dutch Reformed Church, with their published commitment being to provide the "strictest regard to moral conduct and especially that young men of suitable abilities may be instructed in divinity."[22]

Even a quick review of the charters of the early colleges and universities in this nation reveals those shared primary goals. And elementary education for children in the colonies simply meant that schools should prepare young scholars for entrance into those same colleges and universities.

The Deluder Satan Law

As early as 1642 the Massachusetts General Court compelled settlers to educate their children to read and understand Christian principles and civil laws. In 1647 the same court enacted the "Old Deluder Satan Law," which required towns of fifty or more families to appoint a teacher of reading and writing. The Old Deluder Satan Law is a classic milestone in the history of colonial education:

> It being one Cheife p[roj]ect of ye ould deluder, Satan, to keepe men from the knowledge of ye Scriptures, as in former times by keeping [the]m in an unknowne tongue . . . so at least ye true sence & meaning of ye originall might be clouded . . . [and the] learning may not be buried in ye grave of our fathers in ye church & comonwealth, ye Lord assisting our endeavors . . . .
> It is therefore ordered . . . [that] after ye lord hath increased [the]m to

ye number of 50 housholders, shall then appoint one within their towne to teach all such children as shal resort to him to write & reade . . . & it is further ordered [that] where any towne shall increase to ye number of 100 families or housholders, they shall set up a gramer schoole . . . to instruct youth so farr as they may be fited for ye university.[23]

The Bible in Elementary Education

Passages from the Bible and key truths of the church were used to teach reading and writing in those early colonial grammar schools. The hornbook, introduced in about 1650, was a covered single sheet of parchment that contained the alphabet, vowels, and syllables alongside the doctrine of the Trinity and the Lord's Prayer.[24]

By 1690 the *New England Primer* had been introduced containing twenty-six rhymes depicting Christian teachings, one for each letter in the alphabet. The first rhyme, "In Adam's Fall, We Sinned All," illustrates why this widely used primer was called the "Little Bible" of New England. This primer also contained the Lord's Prayer, the Apostles' Creed, the Ten Commandments, "An Alphabet of Lessons for Youth," "The Duty of Children Towards Their Parents," "The Dutiful Child's Promise," the names and order of the books of the Old and New Testaments, and a short version of the Westminster Catechism.[25]

Noah Webster, friend of George Washington and Benjamin Franklin, pioneer educator, political writer, lecturer, and compiler of the great *American Dictionary of the English Language,* had this to say about education: "To give children a good education in manners, arts and science, is important; to give them a religious education is indispensable; and an immense responsibility rests on parents and guardians who neglect these duties." About the Bible, Webster said: "The Bible should be the standard of language as well as of faith."[26]

For more than two hundred years of our history as a nation, God, the Bible, and the life and teachings of Jesus were at the heart of education in the United States. Upon these strong spiritual foundations, the greatest public educational system in the history of the world was built.

3

JONATHAN EDWARDS'S SERMON AT ENFIELD (AMERICA'S FIRST GREAT AWAKENING)

JULY 8, 1741

Rediscovering the Importance of Spiritual Renewal

The white, wood-framed Congregational meetinghouse in Enfield, Connecticut, was jammed with farmers, merchants, visiting clergymen, and frontier families. From eyewitness accounts of that Sunday morning worship service on July 8, 1741, we get a fascinating picture of the great spiritual awakening that swept the American colonies in the eighteenth century.

The congregation probably sang at least two traditional hymns with seven or eight verses each. Long passages from the Old Testament, the Gospels, and the Epistles were read. An offering was taken. Totally unprepared for what was about to happen, dozing parishioners had to be awakened after the pastoral prayer by an usher carrying a long pole with a feather used to tickle the slumbering sinner.

But everything changed the moment the guest preacher stood, walked quickly to the pulpit, opened his Bible, and looked out across the congregation. He was just thirty-six years old, tall and wiry. He wore a black robe with a stiffly starched collar. His powdered wig framed a long forehead, a rather prominent nose, a small mouth with tight lips, and deep-set, dark blue eyes.

For a moment he stood in silence, slowly scanning the faces in the congregation. Then he opened his Bible, straightened his notes, leaned down onto the pulpit, and began to speak in a calm, resonant voice: "The wrath of God is like great waters that are dammed for the present.

They increase more and more, and rise higher and higher, till an outlet is given; and the longer the stream is stopped, the more rapid and mighty is its course, when once it is let loose."[1]

If the congregation had been dozing, it was suddenly wide-awake. The listeners lived in the world of man, but the Reverend Jonathan Edwards was opening up another world to them, the world of God. And that world of heaven and hell, angels and demons, judgment and mercy was as real to him as the fields and farms of Enfield were to the farmers and their families in the pews. Television, motion pictures, and stereo sound were still centuries away. But this one man used words to paint pictures of God's final judgment that filled the congregation with terror and a sense of impending calamity.

One eyewitness described Jonathan Edwards's words that day as "a most awakening sermon." And he added, "Before the sermon was done—there was a great moaning and crying out through ye whole House."

Many historians claim that Edwards was the greatest preacher of his age. Yet he wasn't fiery and animated like so many television preachers today. His voice didn't shake the meeting house in great, pear-shaped tones. His arms didn't gesture wildly. He didn't pace or perform. One biographer says he simply leaned on the pulpit, stared at a distant point in the meetinghouse and spoke quietly of God's wrath and judgment.[2]

"If God should withdraw his hand from the floodgate," he said quietly, "it would immediately fly open, and the fiery floods of the fierceness and wrath of God would rush forth with inconceivable fury. . . . Thus are all of you that never passed under a great change of heart by the mighty power of the Spirit of God upon your souls; all that were never born again, and made new creatures, and raised from being dead in sin to a state of new and before altogether unexperienced light and life."[3]

This Jonathan Edwards was no ignorant farm-boy fanatic. At thirteen years of age he was reading history, poetry, and philosophy in Latin, Greek, and Hebrew. At sixteen he graduated from Yale. At twenty he was preaching in New York City. At twenty-one he was a teacher at Yale. He spent the heart of his lifetime preaching and pastoring in New England, and he died at fifty-five years of age, the newly appointed president of Princeton University.

"O sinner," his voice echoed over the congregation's growing concern, "consider the fearful danger you are in. . . . And let every one that is yet out of Christ and hanging over the pit of hell, whether they be old men and women or middle-aged or young people or little children, now hearken to the loud calls of God's word and providence."[4]

A witness reported that even as Edwards preached, members of the congregation "yelled and shrieked, they rolled in the aisles, they crowded up into the pulpit and begged him to stop."[5] Another commented that after the sermon, one "waited with the deepest and most solemn solicitude to hear the trumpet sound . . . and was deeply disappointed, when the day terminated, and left the world in its usual state of tranquillity."[6]

"Therefore," Edwards concluded his Enfield sermon that day, "let everyone that is out of Christ now awake and fly from the wrath to come."[7]

Stephen Williams, another eyewitness to that sermon, said that during the sermon members of the congregation cried out:

> What Shall I do to be Saved?—O, I am going to Hell!—Oh what shall I do for Christ? So . . . ye minister was obliged to desist . . . after Some time of waiting the Congregation were Still so [that] a prayer was made . . . and Amazing and Astonishing ye power o God was seen—& Several Souls were hopefully wrought upon [that] night. & o ye cheerfulness and pleasantness of their countenances [that] received comfort—oh [that] God would strengthen & confirm—we sung an hymn & prayed and dismissed ye Assembly.[8]

W hen Jonathan Edwards preached his famous sermon "Sinners in the Hands of an Angry God," 134 years had passed since the men of the Virginia Company landed at Cape Henry and dedicated this new land to God and His purposes. More than 1,500,000 settlers had journeyed across the Atlantic to begin their lives in the New World. Thirteen thriving colonies spread from Georgia in the South to Massachusetts and New Hampshire in the North. Cities were forming up and down the Atlantic coastline from Savannah and Charleston to Philadelphia, New York, and Boston. Settlers were pushing back the wilderness and planting farms, small villages, and country towns from the Appalachians to the Adirondacks. The settlers and the king's representatives were constantly at each other's throats. It had been a long and exhausting century of struggle to claim and tame the land.

Already trouble brewed in the cities. By 1729 Philadelphia had experienced a series of riots by mobs of poor colonists who broke into the homes of the rich to steal food and clothing. Africans were being transported into North America in such great numbers that by the time of the American Revolution, one out of every six people in the colonies was a slave. In 1740 in Greenville, South Carolina, fifty black men were hanged to put down a rumored slave uprising. On February 28, 1741, after a burglary and a series of fires, rumors swept New York City that poor black and white men were plotting to seize power. One hundred and one men were convicted. Four whites and eighteen blacks were hanged. Thirteen blacks were burned alive, and seventy more were banished.

The wilderness frontiers were no more idyllic than the growing cities. For most settlers, the living conditions were primitive, dangerous, and without the comforts and constraints of wives and family, government, or the church. The farmers, traders, and developers who risked their lives beyond the limits of civilization were often strong-willed, independent sorts who had no other law to live by than their own. Bawdyhouses and prostitution proliferated in the wild, sometimes-lawless towns at the wilderness borders, as well as in the cities. Drinking and gambling, brawling and whoring had become fairly common pastimes.

Colonial churches and their clergy were losing their power to affect an increasingly worldly society. In fact, the churches were having troubles of their own. A majority of those first colonists who settled in North America had come to these shores out of religious or moral convictions, but the second and third waves of settlers were less interested in moral and religious issues than in the practical, day-by-day struggle to survive. Church membership was in decline, and the Christian faith's impact on society was decreasing radically.

In the beginning of the colonial period, church membership was mandatory. Settlers had to attend worship services to be a member of the community. Not to attend meant losing the right to vote, paying a fine, and facing the judgment and condemnation of neighbors. Colonial churches may have been filled in those early years, but far too often ushers needed long poles with feathers or hard leather fists attached to awaken the bored and sleepy parishioners. Then, when the colonies lost their charters and the English kings reasserted power over the local church authorities, Sunday attendance enforced by town marshal or colonial governor was discontinued. Naturally church attendance declined. At the same time, other historical factors combined to cause the church to lose its influence in the life of the early American colonies.

This was the beginning of the Age of the Enlightenment in Europe. Where their ancestors found it appropriate to give an unseen God the credit for order in the universe, men of the Enlightenment began to credit the natural laws of gravity and motion. After long, dark ages locked in ignorance and superstition, man began to focus on himself and on the wonders of the universe and, at the same time, to lose sight of the God who created man and spoke the universe into being.

Descartes wrote: "Instead of that speculative philosophy that is taught in the schools, we may find a practical philosophy by means of which, knowing the force and the action of fire, water, the stars, heavens and all other bodies that environ us . . . we can . . . employ them in all those uses to which they are adapted, and thus render ourselves the masters and possessors of nature."[9]

During the Enlightenment, man put himself, not God, at the center of the universe. And that spirit of "enlightened" Europe traveled with settlers to the New World with the news that God wasn't really necessary anymore. An absentee landlord of a world held together by self-existing natural laws, He had abandoned that world without revealing any instructions for its care and preservation. In short, if God existed, He was irrelevant.

The Christian clergy maintained that God had preserved in the Bible His own revealed law to complement His laws of nature made manifest in His creation. These laws were sufficient to instruct mankind for salvation and the salvation of the world and to govern itself in civil society.

But to a growing number of the "enlightened," the Bible appeared to be just one more ancient book and the church one more ancient place where the unenlightened and superstitious gathered to practice rituals no longer relevant or particularly helpful. If God was distant and uncaring, why should one struggle to obey these ancient biblical teachings that appeared to have little or nothing to do with the real world anyway? So modern man set out to conquer nature on his own. God and His revealed laws in Scripture were simply ignored.

The church was also responsible in some ways for its own decline. Although the early colonists had fled to the New World to practice religious freedom, the churches established on this continent became as rigid in their ways as was their mother church in England. When the

Wesleys tried to introduce their new hymns and gospel songs to their brothers and sisters in Georgia, they were brought before a Savannah judge for inserting unauthorized music into the Anglican church service. Established clerics and church leaders in America rushed to oppose the itinerant preaching of Whitefield, the Wesley brothers, and Jonathan Edwards.

The effectiveness of the church in those days was also crippled by divisiveness. The pioneer Christians who settled this land proved to be a strong-willed, determined lot. The major church groups that landed on these shores soon found themselves divided into smaller and smaller splinter groups. And the major denominations developing here were in conflict with each other and within themselves. Christ's prayer for unity in the church was far from being realized in colonial America during its first century in the New World.

Our forefathers were forming a nation that even in its infancy was in need of spiritual renewal. Fortunately the first great spiritual awakening to sweep the land was already on its way. Pastors and priests were rediscovering the power of biblical preaching. Lay men and women were rediscovering the power of prayer and biblical study. And evangelists from England were riding horseback across the country, fanning revival fires to life with their sermons on sin and salvation.

Methodist preacher John Wesley was holding meetings in Georgia with his brother Charles. The formal liturgy transplanted to the New World from the high Church of England was being renewed by the unauthorized hymns and psalms the Wesleys were introducing across the colonies. George Whitefield, another English Methodist, was preaching a series of amazing and fruitful sermons in towns and villages across New England and in the South. And in Boston the brilliant young theologian, Jonathan Edwards, published *The Narrative of Surprising Conversions,* an account of the religious revival that seemed to be taking hold across the colonies, the revival he called the Great Awakening.[10]

A Time of Preparation

Colonial religion had grown dry. Worship was cold and formal. People had wandered away from the church or attended only because they had to. Church members seldom read or studied the Bible. Prayers at meals or vespers were chanted by rote, but few people had regular or personal times of prayer and devotion. With the secularization of society came self-indulgence, greed, injustice, and immorality. Many of the people believed that God was distant and uninvolved in their daily lives. They knew about God intellectually, but they had not experienced Him in their hearts.

In a letter to another clergyman, Jonathan Edwards described his congregation in Northampton just before the spiritual awakening there: "It had been their manner of a Long Time . . . to make Sabbath and lecture days to be especially times of diversion and company keeping." There were many in them "who scoffed and made a Ridicule of the Religion."[11]

Before the revival, Edwards's sermons on man's sin and God's judgment had no apparent success. In fact, his most famous sermon, "Sinners in the Hands of an Angry God," was first preached in his own church without a ripple of response. Apparently the congregation in Northampton was not ready for revival, but the people of Enfield were, and the sermon there resulted in a time of great repentance and forgiveness.

As Edwards continued to preach the Word to his congregation at Northampton, however, he noticed in the adults "less and less of a party spirit." And the young people, too, "by degrees Left off their frolicking, and have been observably more decent in their attendance on the Publick worship."[12]

Edwards continued to proclaim that God held every person responsible for his choices, right or wrong. Week after week, Edwards held up the Bible as God's law and reminded his people that one day they would be held accountable for breaking that law. Even as Edwards preached, a heightened sense of sin and personal responsibility began to grow within the congregation.

Edwards wrote a friend that he began to notice in his own community

> a lively Conviction of the Truth of the Gospel, & the divine authority of the Holy Scriptures . . . scarcely a single Person in the whole Town was Left unconcerned about the Great things of the Eternal World; Those that were wont to be the vainest and Loosest Persons in Town seemed in General to be siezed with strong convictions: Those that were most disposed to condemn vital & Experimental Religion, & those that had the Greatest Conceit of their own Reason: the highest Families in the Town, & the oldest Persons, and many little Children were afected Remarkeably.[13]

After this time of preparation, the revival that finally did occur in Northampton was typical of the revivals then flaring up in cities and towns across the colonies.

The Time of Awakening

At the heart of this Great Awakening was the people's new awareness of their own sinfulness. Edwards wrote: "They seem to be brought to abhor themselves for the sins of their Past Life, and to Long to be holy, and to Live holily, and to God's Glory."[14]

In response, the people began to confess their sins and seek God's forgiveness for them. Edwards described the change he saw among his people: "I believe there never was so much done at Confessing of faults to Each other, and the making up differences, as there has Lately been."[15] Then, after confessing their sinfulness and realizing God's forgiveness, the people of Northampton experienced a great change.

Edwards's church in Northampton was not an isolated instance. Throughout the colonies, the Great Awakening resulted in the spiritual renewal of tens of thousands of people and in the mobilizing of those people to missionary zeal and social action.

Although Jonathan Edwards was the primary homegrown evangelist of the great revival during the second quarter of the eighteenth century, the itinerant preacher most associated with the origins of the Great Awakening was George Whitefield. Born in Gloucester, England, on December 16, 1715, young Whitefield met John and Charles Wesley when he was a student at Oxford. He was an impassioned orator. His sermons were long and loud and demanding of repentance. When the churches of England closed their doors on him, he began to hold services outside in parks and open fields.

When the Wesleys invited Whitefield to join them in America, he agreed gladly. In 1738 when Whitefield was just twenty-three years old, he arrived in Savannah, Georgia. There, he read Edwards's account of the stirrings of revival in New England and was moved and inspired by it. From 1739–41, young Master Whitefield rode horseback from Georgia to Maine holding his own revivals in towns and villages along the way.

The great Colonial southern churches with their thick brick walls, their transepts and rear galleries occupied by servants and slaves, and their high-walled wooden pews (sometimes even curtained for privacy and fitted to the personal taste of the owners) were often closed to Whitefield and his controversial ministry. The northern churches, especially the whitewashed, unadorned meetinghouses of New England, also refused to welcome him. At first the clergy were suspicious of Whitefield and his fellow evangelists. The Reverend Charles Chauncey, for fifty years the pastor of Boston's venerable First Church, the New England clergyman second only to Jonathan Edwards in influence, wrote a scornful, angry condemnation of Whitefield's visit to New England:

> I could never see upon what warrant either from scripture or reason he went about preaching from one province and parish to another where the Gospel was already preache'd and by persons as well qualified for the Word as he can pretend to be . . . . Might he not at first take up this practice from a mistaken thought of some extraordinary mission from God? Or from the undue influence of too high an Opinion of his own gifts and graces . . . too much encouraged to go on in it, from the popular applauses, every where so liberally heaped on him?[16]

So, often uninvited by the clergy of a town or village, Whitefield appeared, took out an advertisement in the local paper, handed out flyers announcing the time and place of his meeting, and stayed in the homes of friendly clergymen or lay people where prayers and plans were made for the revival.

Early in the morning, from farms and nearby villages, the people came by foot, by carriage, or on horseback to a tree-lined clearing or an open field where they gathered to learn and sing new gospel hymns, hear testimonies of lives changed in various towns along the way, and listen as George Whitefield preached God's Word to them.

Picture him in his black clerical robe and white collar. A simple pulpit had been placed in the center of a wooden platform. The crowds sat on rough benches, on the backs of wagons and carts, on hay bales or stands in the shade of the trees that framed the field. At the close of the singing, Whitefield picked up his Bible and began to preach.

The Bible was at the center of the Great Awakening. To Whitefield it was the wholly inspired, totally trustworthy, revealed Word of God. In the middle of that Age of Enlightenment when Galileo, Descartes, and

Isaac Newton were opening up man's world by explaining the natural laws that control the physical universe, George Whitefield was opening the Bible to introduce farmers and merchants to the laws of God.

The people responded to Whitefield's preaching with the same great emotion that greeted the words of Jonathan Edwards. The people knew they were sinners. They felt the consequences of their sinfulness. They were overwhelmed by their feelings of lostness. They desired forgiveness and sincerely sought it. Whether to a crowd of several hundred farmers in the woods near an isolated country town or in Boston, where nineteen thousand people turned out to hear him in a three-day visit, Whitefield preached the Word of man's sinfulness and God's judgment, and the people hearing God's voice in the voice of the preacher cried out for forgiveness and were forgiven.

The Reverend Charles Chauncy heard rumors of these revival "terrors" and wrote hastily to condemn them: "Such a horible scene that can scarce be described in Words," he writes. "That terror so many have been the Subjects of; expressing it self in strange effects upon the body, such as swooning away and falling to the Ground . . . bitter shriekings and screamings, convulsion-like tremblings and agitations, strugglings and tumblings and . . . indecencies I shan't mention."[17]

Jonathan Edwards and the other revival preachers knew well of the problems and excesses that accompanied the Great Awakening. But to the critics, Edwards replied:

> There have been as I have heard many odd and strange stories carried about . . . and There have been several Persons that have had their natures overborn under strong Convictions, have trembled and hadn't been able to stand, they have had such a sense of divine wrath; but there are no new doctrines Embraced, but People have been abundantly Established in those that we account orthodox; there is no new way of worship affected. There is no oddity of Behaviour Prevails . . . . And this is a true account of the matter as far as I have opportunity to Know and I suppose I am under Greater advantage to know than any Person living. I leave this to you, and shall only say, as I desire always to say from my heart To God be all the Glory whose work alone it is.[18]

America's Great Awakening led by Edwards, Whitefield, and the Wesleys in the eighteenth century was not the first great awakening in the world, nor would it be the last.

Often these times of spiritual renewal come just before a great war.

The preaching of Timothy Dwight, Congregationalist minister and president of Yale, led to the Second Great Awakening in America just before the War of 1812. Charles Finney, a professor and later the president of Oberlin College, was also instrumental in the second Great Awakening in the years before the Civil War.

Sometimes these periods of spiritual awakening bind up the wounds of war and call a nation to repentance, as with the preaching of Dwight L. Moody and the songs of Ira D. Sankey following the Civil War or the preaching of Billy Graham and his team following World War II.

With the Great Awakening of the eighteenth century, spiritual renewal swept through the colonies, church people began to share their newfound personal faith with their neighbors, and local churches came to life again. A new commitment to Christian higher education resulted in the formation of Princeton, Columbia, Brown, Rutgers, and dozens of other private colleges and schools by the various Christian denominations. A new outburst of missionary zeal for the spiritual and temporal needs of the Indians caused Dartmouth College, for example, to be formed to minister to Indian youth in 1769. Orphanages, hospitals, and other charities sprang up across the colonies to minister to settlers and Indians alike.

With spiritual renewal came a new democratic spirit as well. Taxation without representation alone didn't lead to the Boston Tea Party and the eventual collapse of British rule in the New World. People were also tired of dull, ineffectual religion, forced upon them by their colonial forefathers or by the representatives of king and Parliament. Out of that time of spiritual awakening came a new commitment to personal and political freedom. And because of the new life and health in the churches during and immediately after that Great Awakening, the American church became the cradle of a revolution.

Jonathan Edwards's sermon that day in Enfield is perhaps the best-known sermon in the history of this nation, and it initiated the New England phase of the Great Awakening. The time is here to remember that half-century of spiritual revival, for out of the Great Awakening came the Declaration of Independence, the American Revolution, and a new, young nation committed to "Life, Liberty and the pursuit of Happiness." We have no way of knowing what good might come to this nation if once again we seek a great spiritual awakening in the land.

4

DECLARATION OF INDEPENDENCE SIGNED

JULY 4, 1776

Rediscovering God As the Giver of Our
Unalienable Rights

On July 4, 1776, in a serene, red-brick building on Chestnut Street in Philadelphia, our nation was given birth. A month earlier, on June 7, Richard Henry Lee had called for a resolution by the Third Continental Congress that "these United Colonies are, and of right ought to be, free and independent States." Some delegates, however, agreed with Pennsylvania's Joseph Galloway when he warned, "Independency means ruin. If England refuses it, she will ruin us; if she grants it, we will ruin ourselves."[1]

From June 7–10, the delegates argued for and against Lee's call for independence. The aye votes prevailed. On June 11, Congress appointed Benjamin Franklin, Thomas Jefferson, John Adams, Robert R. Livingston, and Roger Sherman to "prepare a declaration" in support of Lee's resolution. That committee asked Jefferson to write "A Declaration by the Representatives of the United States of America." On June 28 the document was received by the Congress. More debate on content and wording followed. On July 2, Lee's Resolution for Independence was approved.

Finally, on July 4 Charles Thomson, secretary to the Committee of the Whole, distributed copies of Jefferson's edited declaration to the approximately fifty delegates in attendance. Across the mellow, wood-paneled assembly room, the delegates, seated in twos at tables covered in green fabric and cluttered with documents, quill pens, and inkwells, shouted for the right to suggest final changes in the document. My own relative, Benjamin Harrison of Virginia, who was chairing the session that day, rapped his gavel loudly and called for order.

John Hancock, President of the Congress, had determined that the Declaration would be voted on that day. Upon his standing orders, the doors of their meeting room in the Pennsylvania legislative assembly hall were closed and locked. As he explained, this was "to keep the horseflies out and the disagreements within." One by one the delegates were recognized. And out of their debate that day, this nation's demand for freedom took its final form.

Jefferson's attempts to blame King George III for slavery and to end that practice in the new nation were roundly defeated. "His Majesty" became "the King of England." Where Jefferson had written "Deluge in blood," the Congress wrote "destroy us." "Subjects" became "citizens." A long and rather melodramatic passage by Jefferson grieving for the relationship that might have been between England and the colonies was summarized more simply as "Enemies in War, in Peace Friends."

Thomas Jefferson sat silently at his desk, crossing out his own precious words, phrases, and sentences and replacing them with the approved wording of the delegates. According to the record, sixty-eight changes were made. Four hundred and eighty words were cut from the document. Historian Jim Bishop reports that Jefferson's copy of the Declaration "was so ink-marked and tracked that in sections it became illegible."[2]

The afternoon summer heat grew stifling in that closed meeting-room as the debate proceeded to its close. Late in the afternoon, Harrison returned the gavel to John Hancock, who called for a vote of the delegates to approve the Declaration in its edited form.

Secretary Thomson called the roll. "New Hampshire?"

"Aye!"

"Massachusetts?"

"Aye!"

"Rhode Island?"

"Aye!"

Waiting for orders from its governor, only New York temporarily abstained. Georgia was the last colony to sound the "Aye!" for independence. John Hancock signed his name to the document with a dramatic flourish and ordered his secretary to record the vote as unanimous. The edited document was delivered immediately to Dunlap the printer with an order for one thousand unsmudged copies to be delivered by dawn.

Before the meeting could be adjourned, a letter from General George Washington reporting the arrival of British troopships in New York harbor was read to a Congress shocked silent by the news. The exhausted delegates hastily ordered supplies and reinforcements for the Continental Army. Plans were discussed to strengthen the defenses of Philadelphia. A committee was appointed to design a great seal of the United States of America, and two men were appointed to the Bureau of Indian Affairs.

Then Hancock slapped his hand down on the table and declared that session of the Continental Congress adjourned. Finally, the meeting-room door was opened, windows were raised, and evening breezes began to cool the room. The delegates, however, seemed unwilling to adjourn to local taverns for the evening meal or to their sleeping quarters across the town. In small clusters they gathered around well-marked copies of the edited Declaration to read and reread the document they had created to launch a nation already plunged into war: "We hold these truths to be self-evident . . . ," someone read again, "that all men are created equal, that they are endowed by their Creator with certain unalienable Rights, that among these are Life, Liberty and the pursuit of Happiness."[3]

At the very beginning of our nation's history, our forefathers made important assumptions about God and His laws. Those men of the Continental Congress risked their lives to proclaim that God, not king or Parliament, was the source of this nation's freedom. On that day in Philadelphia, they appealed to God's laws when they declared certain unalienable rights of humanity.

More than two centuries have passed since that hot July afternoon. What has happened to this nation's commitment to God and His law? What will happen if we continue to move away from those spiritual foundations upon which our nation's freedom was built? It is time we dust off this great Declaration and read it seriously once again.

Independence Hall in Philadelphia witnessed more early American history and echoed with the stirring rhetoric of more American patriots than any other building in the land. In 1753 a damaged, then recast, bell was hung in the belfry of that Pennsylvania State House. The words inscribed around the cracked, two-thousand-pound bronze bell are from the Old Testament book of Leviticus: "Proclaim liberty throughout all the land to all its inhabitants."[4] God first spoke those words to Moses on Mount Sinai. They signaled the year of Jubilee in which prisoners were returned to their families and lands were returned to their rightful owners. How fitting that, beneath that bell, our forefathers declared themselves free from the tyranny of King George III and created the government that would replace forever his tyrannical rule.

Unfortunately, most of us have forgotten what really happened behind the locked doors of Independence Hall during those twenty-four days in June and July of 1776 when the final words of the Declaration of Independence were hammered into place. Few people care about the original intent of those fifty-six men from thirteen British colonies who struggled with each paragraph, line, and word of that document before they agreed to risk their lives, their fortunes, and their sacred honors by signing it. Seventh-graders memorize those lines that begin, "We hold these truths to be self evident . . ." and then never think about them again. For generation after generation of Americans, the meaning and intent of the Declaration grow dimmer and dimmer. Little by little, most people have forgotten altogether the words' significance and utmost importance to us and to our future.

In that first paragraph of the Declaration, which begins "When in the Course of human events . . . ," the lines were clearly drawn. The battle charge was sounded. Our forefathers were telling King George III that they were cutting the umbilical cord that bound them to mother England and taking their place as a "separate and equal" member in the community of nations.

Imagine the king's rage when he sputtered to his lords and ladies at his summer palace, "What right have they to declare their separation from our royal crown?" The king's question is the first question we need to answer these two hundred years later. Upon whose authority did our forefathers act? Upon what grounds did they launch our nation?

Did the king and his advisers scan the Declaration's introductory paragraph for some clue about why our forefathers dared to end a 169-year relationship with British royalty? Perhaps a prince, a duke, or a court counselor, after a closer look at the Declaration of Independence, finally found it.

"The Colonists say they are entitled to their independence by 'the Laws of Nature and of Nature's God.'"

Did King George groan aloud that day as three times the colonists appealed to God as the source and protector of their liberty? Did he remember another document presented to his predecessor 561 years earlier on the field at Runnymede with three similar appeals to God as the source and protector of the constitutional liberties granted the people of England against the tyranny of another king?

The *Magna Carta*, presented to King John in 1215, established the rule of law in England five centuries before the Declaration of Independence. That document was an agreement drawn up between king and people. It set limits on the amount of arbitrary power a king could wield over his subjects. It articulated certain principles of liberty and provided for "due process" to protect those liberties. That document, like our own Declaration of Independence, began with the king's confession that his power, too, was granted him "by the grace of God."

It is easy enough, however, to appeal to God and not really mean anything by it. "Our forefathers were all deists, anyway," some people answer. "They saw God as a clockmaker who wound up the world and left it ticking." Was God mentioned gratuitously in the Declaration of Independence by a committee of unbelievers, or was it a serious appeal by men who in different ways saw themselves as Christians and who saw God's authority and protection as the only trustworthy basis on which to found a nation?

The Spiritual Heritage of Thomas Jefferson

Thomas Jefferson was the man assigned by committee to write the original document. Although the concepts were not really original with Jefferson, his eloquence and simplicity memorialized those truths forever. At the heart of Jefferson's document is that key phrase, the "Laws of Nature and of Nature's God." Jefferson acknowledged that man's unalienable rights were "endowed by their Creator" and protected by "Divine Providence." How serious was Jefferson when he talked about God's laws in the Declaration? Did he himself believe in God and, if so, how strong were his convictions about God's being at the heart of this nation's liberties?

Jefferson is often called a deist. In fact, during his life he called himself at various times a "deist," a "theist," a "unitarian," and a "rational Christian."[5] Anyone who has studied the biographies and writings of

Thomas Jefferson knows he began early in life to doubt various tenets of Christian orthodoxy but often surprised friend and foe alike with the depth of his underlying belief in the God of history and in the life and teachings of Jesus.

As this nation's third president, Jefferson refused to proclaim national days of prayer and thanksgiving, although Washington and Adams had before him. He took these actions not out of disbelief in God but because of his consistent view of the appropriate relationship of government and religion. Yet Jefferson wrote to John Adams in 1823, claiming that the evidences for the existence of God are "irresistible." And just before his death, he argued that it would be a good thing if all Americans believed in "only one God, and he all perfect," and that "there is a future state of rewards and punishments."[6]

Regarding the source of our liberty, Jefferson said, "Can the liberties of a nation be sure when we remove their only firm basis, a conviction in the minds of the people, that these liberties are the gift of God? that they are not to be violated but with His wrath?"[7]

Jefferson's views of the Christian faith changed many times during his long and productive life, but we must take seriously his own words about the matter: "I am a Christian, in the only sense in which he [Jesus] wished anyone to be; sincerely attached to his doctrines, in preference to all others."[8] To his old friend Benjamin Rush, Jefferson, then old and living in retirement at Monticello, wrote that his own religious beliefs were the "result of a life of inquiry and reflection, and are very different from the Anti-Christian system attributed to me by those who know nothing of my opinions."[9]

At another time, after assembling the teachings of Jesus in a volume of forty-six pages, he wrote his friend Charles Thompson, saying, "A more beautiful or precious morsel of ethics I have never seen; it is a document in proof that I am a real christian, that is to say, a disciple of the doctrines of Jesus."[10]

Whatever evidences we have for the personal faith of Thomas Jefferson and the other framers of the Declaration—and I am convinced there is more than satisfactory evidence to illustrate the sincere and serious Christian convictions of most of them—we must next deal directly with their references to God and what they meant by them.

Those fifty-six men were, after all, representatives of the people. The real title of the document is "A Declaration of the Representatives of the United States of America." Whatever the signers' personal religious convictions, they used words to represent the convictions of the various state legislative bodies who commissioned them, and they used words to represent the beliefs of the people who were citizens of those states. Those words about God used in three crucial places in the Declaration meant something quite specific to the framers and their constituents. It is our task to find out exactly what those words meant in 1776 and what they require of us two hundred years later.

The Source of Our Liberty

Picture King George III alone in his chambers that night after receiving the Declaration of Independence. Earlier that day, he had dispatched Admiral Lord Howe on an emergency mission to Staten Island with the royal demand that the Declaration be revoked. The king must have been furious. He was king, after all, and the king made the laws, not the people. He had a Parliament, of course, but the king was used to having his way in the kingdom. Then, suddenly, his subjects in America were refusing to obey the king's laws and were appealing to a higher law—the "Laws of Nature and of Nature's God."

Those words—the "Laws of Nature and of Nature's God"—had very specific meaning in the eighteenth century. John Locke (1632–1704), the British philosopher, said it quite simply: "The law of nature stands as an eternal rule of all men, legislators as well as others. The rules that they make for other men's actions must . . . be conformable to the law of nature . . . . i.e. to the will of God."[11]

Sir William Blackstone (1732–80), the great teacher of the English common law, wrote: "Man, considered as a creature, must necessarily be subject to the laws of his Creator, for he is entirely a dependent being . . . . And, consequently, as man depends absolutely upon his Maker for everything, it is necessary that he should in all points conform to his Maker's will. This will of his Maker, is called the law of nature.[12]

It was generally held in England and in the colonies that the "Laws of Nature and of Nature's God" were discovered in two ways: from the physical laws of the creation and from the revealed laws in Scripture. If King George had lost his temper that day and in a fit of rage accidentally fallen from his fourth-floor palace window, he would have broken his bones and wounded his royal pride. That's a law of nature. Sir Isaac

Newton called it gravity. For convenience, using Blackstone and Locke as our guides, we might call it the will of God revealed in creation. Gravity is a law written into the workings of this world by the Creator. You don't have to believe in God to understand the law or to witness its power, but the law is there nevertheless, and breaking it results in immediate and sometimes painful consequences.

But King George had broken God's revealed law. He had overstepped the limits of his authority established by God in the Scriptures and noted by the *Magna Carta*. Again using Locke and Blackstone as our guides, we might categorize those eternal laws that limit a ruler's power as the will of God revealed in Holy Scripture. Blackstone wrote, "Upon these two foundations, the law of Nature and the law of Revelation, depend all human law; that is to say, no human laws should be suffered to contradict these."[13]

The Unalienable Rights of Mankind

Now, let's look at the Declaration once again. In the first paragraph, the signers were telling King George III in no uncertain terms that one law is greater than the law of king or Parliament, and that is the law of God.

Then, in the second paragraph, they got down to some specifics of that law, beginning with these eight wonderful words: "We hold these truths to be self-evident . . . ."

Jefferson, Madison, Franklin, and the others were about to list the great truths that led to the birth of our nation and to the eventual creation of a better kind of government. Yet they told King George at the outset that those same truths with all their historic consequences were "self-evident"—that is, they were plain, widely recognized, and needed no further proof or explanation.

Then they listed these obvious truths:

> That all men are created equal,
> that they are endowed by their Creator with certain unalienable Rights,
> that among these are Life, Liberty and the pursuit of Happiness.
> That to secure these rights, Governments are instituted among Men,
> deriving their just powers from the consent of the governed,
> That whenever any Form of Government becomes destructive to these
> ends, it is the Right of the People to alter or to abolish it.

How could these magnificent assumptions upon which our nation was built seem so obvious to the signers of the Declaration? Dr. Henry Jaffa wrote: "Jefferson, in his unsophisticated innocence, said that in the Declaration, he was placing 'before mankind the common sense of the subject,' and that what he wrote was an 'expression of the American mind.' He did not, he said, aim at originality of any kind, but sought to give expression to the 'harmonizing sentiments of the day, whether expressed in conversations, in letters, in printed essays or in the elementary books of public right, as in Aristotle, Cicero, Locke, Sidney, etc.' "[14]

I believe the explanation for why this incredible truth that "all men are created equal" was such common knowledge can be found in the lives of the framers themselves.

From childhood, the men who wrote and signed the Declaration of Independence heard these truths from the Bible. They were read to them by their parents; they were taught to them in their schools and universities; and they were preached to them in their churches on Sunday mornings.

The truths come from the Old Testament history of the patriarchs Abraham, Isaac, and Jacob; of Moses and the prophets; and of kings Saul, David, and Solomon. They come from the New Testament life and teachings of Jesus and His disciples. They come from the history of God's relationship with His people, Israel, and what we learn about God's will for civil government from that story. Without that written, historical record of God's dealings with a nation, no Declaration of Independence would have been submitted, and we might still live in bondage to a king's tyranny.

Our forefathers knew well the story of the development of civil government in Israel. Describing those early days in our nation, one scholar wrote, "People then lived in constant face-to-face intimacy with Hebrew literature. The dramas of the Old Testament were their own dramas, the ordeals were theirs and the triumphs."[15]

The signers had read and studied the ancient stories, Old Testament and New. They had been taught the meaning and implications of those stories by John Locke, by Sir William Blackstone, and by Samuel Rutherford, a Presbyterian pastor who in 1644 had analyzed the authority of the English king in his classic biblical argument *Lex Rex*.

Even Thomas Jefferson, in his second inaugural address, made the comparison: "I shall need the favor of that Being in whose hands we are, who led our fathers, as Israel of old, from their native land and planted them in a country flowing with all the necessaries and comforts of life."

The Source of Man's Unalienable Rights

Therefore, to really understand the roots and the underlying assumptions of the Declaration, we begin at the beginning. We must hear again the words of Moses in the book of Genesis as our forefathers heard and echoed them in the Declaration, "that all men are created equal." From childhood, the signers had heard that magnificent story of creation when God "created man in His own image; in the image of God He created him; male and female He created them."[16] The signers did not hold to either ancient or current scientific theories that man "evolved" from lower species. They believed that every man, woman, and child in the universe was created by God, and that God, their Creator, loves each of them equally. "For God so loved the world" begins the most famous Scripture of all.

God's equal love for all creation caused the signers to affirm the second great truth in the Declaration: that all men "are endowed by their Creator with certain unalienable Rights, that among these are Life, Liberty and the pursuit of Happiness."

And where did our forefathers find this basic list of unalienable human rights? Again, they found them in the Bible. God is the giver of *life*. Moses said it in the Old Testament: "And the LORD God formed man of the dust of the ground, and breathed into his nostrils the breath of life; and man became a living being."[17]

God is the giver of *liberty*. The apostle Paul proclaimed it in the New Testament: "Now the Lord is the Spirit: and where the Spirit of the Lord is, there is liberty."[18]

And God is the giver of humanity's right *to pursue happiness*. King Solomon wrote about the pursuit of happiness in his ancient book of wisdom: "And also that every man should eat and drink and enjoy the good of all his labor—it is the gift of God."[19]

The framers believed those basic rights were God-given. They were not man-invented or state-granted. And because those rights were from

God, they were "unalienable." They could not be sold, traded, or taken away. Moses said it this way:

> "God is not a man, that He should lie, . . .
> Has He said, and will He not do it?
> Or has He spoken,
>   and will He not make it good?"[20]

And Jesus Himself promised, "Heaven and earth will pass away, but My words will by no means pass away."[21]

When God gives rights, they are forever. The words of Scripture made that perfectly clear. But the signers had also learned at their parents' knees that we live in a fallen world where sin and wickedness prevail. Every new generation has its share of men and women who attempt to steal God-given rights from their neighbors. Because of this threat, civil government was instituted by God to protect people's rights. The Old Testament stories of those first kings of Israel gave our nation's forefathers the basis upon which to institute a more perfect government in this land.

The signers said it this way: "That to secure these rights, Governments are instituted among Men, deriving their just powers from the consent of the governed."

King George must have known the history of God and the nation Israel. Early in His relationship with that slave people, divided into twelve tribes and living under the bondage of the cruel kings of Egypt, God wanted to rule the people directly. He entered into a covenant, or compact, with them. "I will be your God," he promised. "We will be Your people," they replied. And through God-appointed prophets, priests, and elders to be His voice among the people, He was their King and no other. He rescued them from Pharaoh. He led them through the wilderness by a moving cloud in the day and a pillar of fire at night. And He opened up to them the doors of their land of promise.

But after a while, the people became restless with this agreement. They wanted a king they could see and hear and follow into battle like all the other nations. God warned the people through His prophet Samuel that human kings would misuse and abuse them. "And you will cry out in that day," God warned them, "because of your king whom you have chosen. . . ."[22] But the people refused to listen, so God said to Samuel, "Heed their voice, and make them a king."[23]

Still, God loved His people and wanted to protect their rights against the wicked kings they would appoint. To that end, He ordered a set of limits drawn up that would define the relationship of king and people. And He gave orders for the king to keep that book with him and to read it "all the days of his life, that he may learn to fear the LORD his God and be careful to observe all the words of this law and these statutes, that his heart may not be lifted above his brethren, that he may not turn aside from the commandment."[24]

The apostle Paul reaffirmed this godly pattern for all civil government when he wrote, "For there is no authority except from God, and the authorities that exist are appointed by God . . . . For [a ruler] is God's minister to you for good . . . . [and] God's minister, an avenger to execute wrath on him who practices evil."[25]

The covenant between God, the king, and the people was simple. The king would retain his office as long as he obeyed God and protected the unalienable rights of the people. But if he failed and elevated his own good above the people's good, he would be removed from office. The signers of the Declaration said it this way: "That whenever any Form of Government becomes destructive of these ends, it is the Right of the People to alter or to abolish it."[26]

John Calvin, the sixteenth-century theologian, summarized the biblical case for man's right to depose an unjust monarch with these words: "We are subject to men who rule over us, but subject only in the Lord. If they command anything against Him, let us not pay the least heed to it."[27]

On the tragic day of the worst failure of Saul, Israel's first king, the prophet said to him, "When you were little in your own eyes, were you not head of the tribes of Israel? And did not the LORD anoint you king over Israel? . . . But . . . you have rejected the word of the LORD, and the LORD has rejected you from being king."[28]

As the signers' understood civil government, George III was just a man given permission by his people to be their king. He would hold his office only as long as he used it to perform his duty to protect their God-given rights. King George had broken the compact.

God gave life. Wrote the framers, King George III "plundered our seas, ravaged our Coasts, burnt our towns, and destroyed the lives of our people. He is at this time transporting large armies of foreign mercenaries to compleat the works of death, desolation and tyranny already begun."

God gave liberty. King George III was condemned "for taking away our Charters, abolishing our most valuable Laws, and altering fundamentally the Forms of our Governments."

God gave the right to pursue happiness. King George III was guilty of "imposing taxes on us without our Consent"; of "cutting off our Trade with all parts of the world"; of "declaring us out of his Protection and waging War against us."

The failure of King George III led to the final truth as posited in the Declaration of Independence: "We, therefore, the Representatives of the united States of America . . . appealing to the Supreme Judge of the world for the rectitude of our intentions, do, in the Name, and by Authority of the good People of these Colonies, solemnly publish and declare, That these United Colonies are and of Right ought to be Free and Independent States . . . Absolved from all Allegiance to the British Crown."

The people's rights and the ruler's limits were carefully set in the "Laws of Nature and of Nature's God." King George broke God's law, and our ancestors in America rose up, listed their grievances carefully, proclaimed their liberty, declared their separate and equal status, defended their honor, and defeated their king. And in that process we learn our most valuable lesson from the Declaration of Independence.

Man's law is important, but it must reflect God's law to be truly valid. The colonists tried diligently to obey their king. When the king refused to grant them justice, however, they appealed to a higher authority. What a gift our forefathers have given us. By their example we learn that it is our right and duty as citizens to judge the laws and the lawmakers of this nation by the laws of God in the created order and in God's Word, and then to act.

5

THE VIRGINIA DECLARATION OF RELIGIOUS FREEDOM

JANUARY 19, 1786

Rediscovering Our Heritage of Religious Liberty

History gives us only a basic sketch of that day; the rest we have to imagine. It isn't difficult to picture James Madison hurrying down the street on January 19, 1786, en route to the large tobacco warehouse where Virginia's House of Delegates was about to assemble. He glanced up from the single sheet of paper he was studying to acknowledge the cheery greeting of a blacksmith who recognized Richmond's most famous young citizen. Madison waved at the druggist standing outside his apothecary shop, stopped to mark a sentence on the yellow page he was carrying, then turned to his left and hurried into George's Tavern.

The place reeked with the smell of pork pies and mincemeat, dark ale and stale tobacco. Legislators were huddled in small groups discussing Jefferson's Declaration for Religious Freedom. Its fate would be decided that afternoon in the Assembly. The bill had been before them off and on for six years. They had suffered more petitions for and against its passage, more acrimonious debate, and more personal suffering over this bill than almost any other in Virginia's history. One by one the men grew quiet and turned toward Madison as he entered the dark, smoky room.

Madison was a celebrity even among the leading landowners and prosperous merchants of Virginia. In 1771 he had graduated from Princeton at the age of twenty. He had been a special student of the university's president, John Witherspoon, in religion and law. He was a deeply religious man and a fierce fighter for civil liberties. The Anglican legislators saw Madison as an Anglican with "New Right"

73

leanings, a "fundamentalist" in Establishment clothing. His constant appeals on behalf of the Baptists, Quakers, and other dissenters of Virginia had raised legislative ire time and again, yet no one liked to tangle with him. Not since Thomas Jefferson had left for France had there been a man among them who could equal Madison's logic, eloquence, and wit.

Madison blinked and tried to find one particular face in that crowded room of friends and long-time associates. When he spotted his man, he grinned and headed toward him. Madison didn't bother to sit down in the chair that had been politely emptied. He just leaned down and began to speak something quietly into his colleague's ear. The man listened and frowned as Madison lobbied him on behalf of Jefferson's bill. Madison spoke again and put the marked sheet of paper before him. As he read that one particular line, the man blushed and grinned with embarrassment at the other men at the table. Madison patted him on the back, whispered one last comment, then walked quickly from the room.

The delegates grew quiet again as Madison left the tavern. One by one they paid their bills and followed. The last to leave was the delegate Madison had singled out. He was carrying Madison's own copy of the Declaration of Religious Freedom. Jefferson's words had been underlined: ". . . the impious presumption of legislators and rulers, civil as well as ecclesiastical, who being themselves but fallible and uninspired men, have assumed dominion over the faith of others. . . ."[1]

The delegates continued down 14th Street until it reached Pearl (now Cary). There they turned into an alley and walked up a flight of steps into an old warehouse, only slightly remodeled to accommodate the Virginia House of Delegates. Most of them remembered their first meeting in that barn, when they had sat on tobacco bales, surrounded by mountains of pungent leaves stacked halfway to the ceiling.

Threatened in 1780 by British Revolutionary War forces, the state capital had been moved from Williamsburg to Richmond. In those days the city had fewer than three hundred buildings. When traitor Benedict Arnold invaded Richmond with British forces, the warehouse capitol was so humble and unlikely a building to house the greatest political voices in the land that Arnold ordered half the city burned down but didn't touch the warehouse. Hidden beneath piles of dried tobacco, Virginia's most valuable historic documents were preserved, and from those records we get much of the history that led to the introduction of

Jefferson's Declaration of Religious Freedom and to its passage on this historic day.

Four years had gone by. The Revolutionary War had ended. Thomas Jefferson was at his ambassadorial post in France, and James Madison was making one last eloquent plea on behalf of Jefferson's bill. Then the delegates began to vote. When the vote was counted, sixty-seven men had voted aye and twenty had voted no to disestablish the Church of England as the one legal state church, to end all taxation to support that church, and to grant religious freedom to the white settlers of Virginia.

When the vote was counted, Madison moved slowly among his colleagues, receiving their congratulations. Did he walk straight from the House of Delegates to his temporary residence in an inn nearby to write the good news to Jefferson in France? Whatever else happened that day, we know for certain that Jefferson would count the Bill for Establishing Religious Freedom among the three most important accomplishments of his career. And Madison, whom many call the "Father of the Constitution," would include the bill's sentiments in that document and in the First Amendment of the Bill of Rights. Thus he would extend its benefits to the people of our entire nation.

F or the first 163 years of Virginia history, the Church of England was Virginia's only legal church. By law, every plantation or settlement had a house or a room set apart for the worship of God. That worship was legally bound to follow the English Book of Common Prayer, and everyone—man, woman and child—was ordered to attend.

Of course, a person could sleep in on Sunday, but that little act of civil disobedience would cost one precious pound of tobacco, Virginia's primary crop. And missing church four Sundays cost a fifty-pound fine. Gossiping about the clergyman so that another parishioner was alienated from God or the church meant a fine of five hundred pounds of tobacco and asking the minister for forgiveness at a public meeting. When a Virginian refused to have his child baptized as an infant, the parent was ridiculed and forced to pay a fine of two thousand pounds of tobacco, half to be paid to the informer, half to the public.[2]

The clergyman in colonial Virginia had such control over his congregation that before a farmer could even sell his own tobacco at auction, the minister had to be satisfied that his parishioner had paid his tithe and that no fines were outstanding against him.

From 1643, only Anglican ministers ordained by an English bishop could conduct worship services, baptize infants, conduct marriages or funerals, or even teach or preach—in public or in private—in Virginia. And any clergyman or layman who tried to preach or teach his own views about the Christian faith was required to leave Virginia by order of the royal governor and his council. If necessary, the order could be carried out by force.

In 1689, an Act of Toleration was introduced in England that exempted Protestant subjects of William and Mary "from the penalties of certain laws." That Act of Toleration was confirmed in 1699 by the Virginia House of Burgesses, but was only a small step toward religious freedom in Virginia, allowing for token "indulgences" for "tolerated" groups and some liberty of conscience.

Ten years passed after the Act of Toleration was approved in Virginia before one Presbyterian clergyman was allowed to hold services in his home in Pocomoke. By 1725 Virginia had three licensed Presbyterians and two licensed Quakers.

Finally, in 1738, after more than a century of exclusive religious domination by the Church of England and her clergy, Presbyterian settlers were allowed to move into the Great Valley of the Shenandoah, west of the Blue Ridge Mountains. These Presbyterians were loyal members of the Church of Scotland, driven from their country by poverty and intolerance. They weren't admitted to Virginia for the sake of religious freedom, however, but because they were known to be good soldiers. Virginia needed to secure its western border against growing attacks by the Indians and the French. The Presbyterians would provide a reliable first line of defense.

Baptists had migrated to Virginia from England in 1714 and settled in the southeastern part of the colony. These "General Baptists" worked hard and kept to themselves, establishing a small, unrecognized church in Princess Anne County. In 1743 another group of Baptists came from Maryland into the lower Shenandoah Valley, organizing themselves into a church about 1755. These Baptists were called "Regular Baptists," and "though they were from time to time hindered by mobs and reprimanded by magistrates, they were not seriously interfered with."[3]

In the 1740s and 1750s, the Great Awakening was stirring up religious fervor in New England and in the colonies bordering on Virginia.

With the preaching of Jonathan Edwards, John and Charles Wesley, and George Whitefield, the spiritual enthusiasm could not be checked at the border. By 1770 the Baptists seemed to be everywhere, singing their illegal hymns, preaching their illegal sermons, and giving birth to an illegal revival in Anglican Virginia.

The common people of Virginia were ready for revival. The hard frontiers, the lonely and isolated wilderness, the constant threat of death or injury, and the absence of the comforts and consolations of home led people to think of God and recognize their need for His presence in their lives.

Unfortunately, Anglican worship in Virginia was generally routine and uninspiring. The liturgy of the Old World had been transplanted into the New World with no concessions to frontier people with frontier needs. The people were suffering from spiritual hunger, and the established church just wasn't meeting their needs.

At the heart of this dilemma was the poor quality of the Anglican clergy who had migrated to the New World. One historian of the Protestant Episcopal Church of Virginia described the clergy this way: "They could babble in a pulpit, roar in a tavern, exact from their parishioners, and rather by their dissoluteness destroy than feed the flock." An Episcopal bishop wrote: "Many of them had been addicted to the race-field, the card-table, the theatre—nay, more, to drunken revel." The Bishop of London said in 1743 that the Anglican clergymen coming to America "can get no employment at home, and enter into the service more out of necessity than choice . . . go[ing] abroad to retrieve either lost fortune or lost character."[4]

The salary legislated for a clergyman in Virginia was sixteen thousand pounds of tobacco yearly. However, in some areas, the people were poor and could not pay the huge tobacco fees or provide the productive plantation expected by the clergy. So the Anglican clergy avoided these areas, and the Baptists were more than glad to fill the vacuum.

Although only eighteen Baptist churches were in Virginia in 1770, by 1776 the number was ninety.[5] Seeing this wave of "New Light" Baptists invading their territory, the official Anglican clergy appealed to Virginia law to put down the growing threat to their monopoly on religious faith and practice. Baptist clergy and Baptist churches had to be licensed from the House of Burgesses in Williamsburg. Until licenses were obtained, the Baptists were apprehended, fined, and even placed in jails. The established clergy agreed "that the 'New Lights' ought to be taken up and imprisoned, as necessary for the peace and harmony of the old church."[6]

By 1771 the persecution of the Baptists had gotten out of hand. Small gangs invaded Baptist worship and revival services, interrupting the clergy and ridiculing and threatening the assemblies. Vigilantes on horseback would suddenly appear at an outdoor baptism service, riding down into the water and scattering the congregation. Lies were spread about Baptist theology and Baptist religious practices. Any Baptist's improper conduct "was always exaggerated to the utmost extent."[7] Virginia had no tolerance for the Baptists, especially for those who brought the "New Light" enthusiasm for piety and personal faith into the cold and dry spiritual world of Virginia's established church.

Dr. Hawks, an Episcopalian historian of this time, wrote: "No dissenters in Virginia experienced, for a time, harsher treatment than did the Baptists. They were beaten and imprisoned, and cruelty taxed its ingenuity to devise new modes of punishment and annoyance."[8]

When I was a child, my father fascinated me with true stories of my own Virginia ancestors. Although they migrated here as Anglicans during the late seventeenth and eighteenth centuries, they became Baptists. When they began to practice and preach their faith, they were often ridiculed and sometimes even beaten and placed in the cruel jails of that time, but even from their place of confinement they preached through the bars to the crowd outside.

These family stories of Christian courage and commitment helped kindle in me a love for religious freedom that has never diminished and gave me a great respect for my Baptist ancestors who risked their lives to win it.

But the persecution backfired. Another historian wrote: "The zealots for the old order were greatly embarrassed. 'If,' say they, 'we permit them to go on, our church must come to nothing; and yet, if we punish them as far as we can stretch the law, it seems not to deter them; for they preach through prison windows, in spite of our endeavors to prevent it.'"[9]

In 1771 James Madison wrote to a friend describing his feelings about that time: "I . . . have nothing to brag about as to the state and liberty of my country. Poverty and luxury prevail among all sorts; pride, ignorance, and knavery among the priesthood, and vice and wickedness among the laity . . . . That diabolical, hell-conceived principle of persecution rages among some, and, to their eternal infamy, the clergy can furnish their quota of imps for such purposes." Madison went on to describe the plight of "five or six well-meaning men" who were in jail "for publishing their religious sentiments, which, in the main, are very orthodox." Already Madison had begun his fight for the religious freedom of his Baptist and Quaker friends. "I have squabbled and scolded," he admitted, "abused and ridiculed so long about it, to little purpose, that I am without common patience. So I must beg you to pity me and pray for liberty of conscience to all."[10]

As a result of all these conditions, petitions for more religious freedom and for an end to persecution in Virginia were flooding the royal governor, his council, and the House of Burgesses. On February 25, 1772, the Virginia House put forward for consideration a Toleration Bill recommending that the request of "the society of Christians called Baptists, . . . that they may be treated with the same kind indulgence, in religious matters, as Quakers, Presbyterians, and other Protestant dissenters enjoy . . . is reasonable."[11]

The first Toleration Bill was not passed. It was discussed and tabled. The Revolutionary War was brewing. England had levied the Sugar and Stamp acts to raise the money to support her army in the colonies. The people were enraged. Patrick Henry voiced the colonists' rage at England with his words, "Give me liberty or give me death." It was a cry for civil liberty, but echoes of that cry filtered down to the persecuted Baptists, Quakers, Methodists, Lutherans, Presbyterians, and even Catholics, giving them hope for religious liberty as well.

In 1775 Virginia's colonial leaders—Patrick Henry, Thomas Jefferson, my own ancestor Benjamin Harrison, and young James Madison—returned to Philadelphia. On May 10, 1775, the Second Continental Congress appointed George Washington, another Virginian, as commander-in-chief of the Continental Army. In the war years that followed, little time was free for the fight for religious freedom. With citizens from every colony, the people of Virginia, loyal Anglicans and dissenters together, began to enlist in the companies of volunteers who would march against the armies of their homeland.

In 1775 the king's governor of Virginia called the Virginia House of Burgesses into session. But frightened by the angry spirit of rebellion in Williamsburg, he fled with his family to an English warship waiting in Chesapeake Bay and returned to England.

The House of Burgesses declared the governor abdicated and elected a leader from their own body. The first Colonial Convention met in Richmond on July 17, 1775. On August 17 they reviewed the dissenters' petitions and invited a Baptist preacher, Jeremiah Walker, to address them. One year before, Walker had been in jail in Chesterfield for preaching without a license. Now, he stood before that body of Anglican legislators to assure the Assembly that though they and the Baptists were divided by religious differences, they all were united in their loyalty to Virginia. The Baptists had determined that it was lawful to join this war against Great Britain's "unjust invasion, tyrannical oppression, and repeated hostilities." Walker announced that Baptists were free to enlist in the colonial militia without fear of censure, and they asked permission to send chaplains and conduct Baptist worship services for their troops without fear of persecution from the established church.[12]

The petition was well received and immediately granted. The Anglican leaders agreed that "those who fought their battles ought to be indulged with freedom of conscience." But they had also another, more practical reason. By 1775 almost a hundred legal and illegal Baptist churches were in Virginia, with approximately five thousand members and at least thirty-five thousand more Virginians who sympathized with their cause.[13] With a total population of just over five hundred thousand people, more than half of them slaves, the Anglican leaders recognized the Baptists as a powerful new minority in their colony and a growing ally in the colonies' struggle for freedom.

Fifty years later, a leading Virginian recalled Jeremiah Walker's speech and the response it elicited from James Madison: "He [Madison] well knew, as I am told he often declared, that the Baptists had been in all his time the fast and firm friends of liberty." Then Madison summarized the Baptist's speech in these words, "They declared that the tenets of their religion did not forbid their fighting for their country, and that the pastors of their flocks would animate the young of their persuasion to enlist for our battles."[14]

Because of that speech, the first legal action was taken by the Virginia Assembly to place the clergy of all denominations on an equal footing in that colony.

On June 12, 1776, George Mason's Bill of Rights written for the Colony of Virginia was presented to the Assembly. In the first draft, the sixteenth article of that bill began as follows: "That religion, or the duty which we owe to our Creator, and the manner of discharging it, can be directed only by reason and conviction, not by force or violence; and therefore all men are equally entitled to the free exercise of religion."[15]

But the Anglican Church remained the established church in Virginia, favored by the protection of civil authorities and supported by the taxes of all the people. When the Virginia Assembly met again in October 1776, the delegates were faced with a mountain of petitions from across the colony asking for the disestablishment of the Anglican Church and for complete religious freedom.

In 1779 Thomas Jefferson introduced for the first time his Bill for Establishing Religious Freedom in Virginia. But it was defeated, and because Jefferson was elected governor of war-torn Virginia, the bill was not reintroduced for almost a decade.

It was not the time to create division within the colony. The Revolutionary War had come again to Virginia. Like the nation, Virginia was struggling for its life and had no time to settle the matter of religious freedom.

Then, after eight years of bloody conflict, on April 30, 1783, General George Washington proclaimed a cessation of hostilities. The Revolutionary War ended. The final treaty of peace between Great Britain and the United States was signed in Paris on September 3, 1783.

Following the war, on December 3, 1784, the Virginia Assembly proposed a General Assessment Bill to tax everyone for the support of the teaching of Christian religion: "The general diffusion of Christian knowledge hath a natural tendency to correct the morals of men, restrain their vices, and preserve the peace of society," and "learned teachers" were needed to provide such training.[16]

The Episcopalians knew that their days as the one established church were ending. Though monies gathered by this bill would be shared with dissenting churches, Episcopalians were confident of maintaining the advantage of being the majority church, thus controlling the majority of the funds gathered.

The Presbyterians were divided for and against the bill, but generally supported it, knowing that as the second largest denomination in the new state, they, too, would greatly benefit by its passage.

Only the Baptists were 100 percent against compulsory taxation of the people to support religion. Standing against any vestige of union between church and state, they said that Jesus Himself had instructed the church to use voluntary offerings in the support of clergy and church programs. The state had no business taxing the people to raise funds for churches. In fact, the Baptists believed that the state had no business helping or hindering the Christian church in any way. What would the state want in exchange for its support? they asked. What censorship or control would follow?

In 1784, when the Assembly adjourned, Virginia Baptists stood alone as a denomination in opposing the General Assessment Bill, and everything pointed to their defeat. Remember, a majority of the legislators were Episcopal churchmen. But a growing majority of the people were dissenters, so the Baptists appealed to them.

In 1785 the Assembly distributed a copy of the Assessment Bill throughout Virginia and posted the names of the legislators who had voted for it. Dissenting preachers used their pulpits to explain Jesus' words about Christian stewardship and to oppose state taxation to support the churches. Christian laymen lobbied against the bill with their neighbors. The public was convinced. Legislators who had favored it were turned out of office. And men across the state took their stand against all interference by the government in matters of religion.

James Madison took the most eloquent, moving, and persuasive position against the Assessment Bill in his "A Memorial and Remonstrance." In that brief, memorable document, Madison wrote:

> The Religion then of every man must be left to the conviction and conscience of every man; and it is the right of every man to exercise it as these may dictate. This right is in its nature an unalienable right. It is unalienable, because the opinions of men, depending only on the evidence contemplated by their own minds cannot follow the dictates of other men: It is unalienable also, because what is here a right towards men, is a duty towards the Creator.[17]

Madison carefully presented the position that the Baptists had championed. And the Baptists and their allies won the day. The Assessment Bill died in committee and was never presented again.

In 1785 Madison dusted off Jefferson's Bill for Establishing Religious Freedom one more time and presented it to the State Assembly. Two hundred years later, we examine it again to see why it was such a landmark in the history of religious freedom in America. The bill was not limited to a discussion of religious freedom but began with an eloquent appeal that man's mind be free of all restraints. Jefferson wrote:

Well aware . . . that Almighty God hath created the mind free, and manifested his supreme will that free it shall remain by making it altogether insusceptible of restraints; that all attempts to influence it by temporal punishments, or burthens, or by civil incapacitations, tend only to beget habits of hypocrisy and meanness, and are a departure from the plan of the holy author of religion, who being lord both of body and mind, yet chose not to propagate it by coercions on either, as was in his Almighty power to do, but to extend it by its influence on reason alone.[18]

Then, systematically, Jefferson took his stand against those Virginia laws that established one Christian church over all others and compelled citizens "to furnish contributions of money for the propagation of opinions which he disbelieves." That is "sinful and tyrannical," he proclaimed.[19]

Jefferson didn't even believe that government should force a citizen to support a pastor of his own denomination, because that act would deprive him of "giving his contributions to the particular pastor whose morals he would make his pattern, and whose powers he feels most persuasive to righteousness." He added, "Truth is great and will prevail if left to herself."[20]

In conclusion the statute enacted on January 19, 1786, read:

Be it enacted by the General Assembly, that no man shall be compelled to frequent or support any religious worship, place or ministry whatsoever, nor shall be enforced, restrained, molested, or burthened in his body or goods, nor shall otherwise suffer on account of his religious opinions or belief; but that all men shall be free to profess, and by argument to maintain, their opinions in matters of religion, and that the same shall in no wise diminish, enlarge, or affect their civil capacities.

As a footnote, Jefferson added a warning that any future attempt to repeal this freedom or to narrow its operation would be "an infringement of the natural rights of mankind."[21]

Critics of the bill, especially members of the then-disestablished Episcopal Church, accused Jefferson and Madison of using their attack on the Anglican Church as "a blow aimed at Christianity itself."[22]

In fact, the churches of Virginia thrived in their new atmosphere of freedom. The Great Awakening dawned late in that commonwealth, but it dawned nevertheless. A time of spiritual revival and renewal came to

Virginia and all its denominations after religious freedom was declared. By 1790, 202 Baptist churches, 150 ministers, and more than 20,000 Baptist churchmen were in the state.[23] And after a difficult time following the loss of official state support, the Episcopal Church discovered its own new life and has gone on to be a vital Christian force in the state.

We conservative Christians have worked for religious freedom from the beginning of this nation's history. One respected American historian wrote, "Freedom of conscience, unlimited freedom of mind, was from the first a trophy of the Baptists."[24] And John Locke, in his "Essay on Toleration," said, "The Baptists were the first and only propounders of absolute liberty, just and true liberty, equal and impartial liberty."[25]

At the close of the Revolutionary War, George Washington wrote a letter to Baptist leaders. "I recollect with satisfaction," he said, "that the religious society of which you are members have been, throughout America, uniformly and almost unanimously, the firm friends to civil liberty, and the persevering promoters of our glorious revolution."[26]

Anyone who thinks that Baptist ministers or their fundamentalist friends of various denominations are interested in using the state to help support or establish their churches doesn't understand the battle for religious freedom in Virginia. We are and will always be opposed to the establishment of one church over any other by civil authorities. Every American has the right to "the free exercise" of religion, speech, the press, and assembly. The important truths of conscience determined by Virginia's Declaration of Religious Freedom became a part of this nation's Constitution and the core of the First Amendment in the Bill of Rights.

But those who think Jefferson's call for "the separation of Church and State" means that men and women of Christian faith should stay out of politics have forgotten the work and other words of Madison and Jefferson. And they have ignored the courageous acts of the Baptists, Presbyterians, Quakers, dissenting Anglicans, and other "New Light" Christians who fought for religious freedom in Virginia.

Those pioneer Christians were persecuted and imprisoned for exercising their political influence on behalf of a biblical view of separating church and state. By their very acts of civil disobedience, they set a precedent for all of us who follow. The separation of church and state means that civil government has no authority over religious belief or practice. It does not mean that men and women of faith are barred from any influence on civil government.

We are Christians and we are citizens. Why should we be asked to separate our Christian values from the political causes we espouse? It is our responsibility to work within this nation's democratic processes to establish truth, justice, and mercy as we see them in the land. And those who attempt to silence us in the name of "the separation of Church and State" have forgotten Jefferson's Declaration of Religious Freedom: "All men shall be free to profess, and by argument to maintain, their opinion in matters of religion, and that the same shall in no wise diminish, enlarge or affect their civil capacities."

6

CONSTITUTION SIGNED

SEPTEMBER 17, 1787

Rediscovering the Purpose and Plan
of Civil Government

On September 17, 1787, forty-one men filed into the same hall in Philadelphia where the Declaration of Independence had been signed eleven years earlier. The Revolutionary War had ended in 1781 with the surrender of eight thousand British troops under General Cornwallis at Yorktown. Now, after a necessary time of recovery, a constitution was being drafted to form a new government for our young nation.

That Monday was the last day of the Constitutional Convention. Fifty-five men representing every state but Rhode Island had spent a long, hot summer shaping the Constitution of these United States. George Washington, the president of the convention, asked that the final version of the Constitution be read to those assembled.

The framers slumped in their chairs or sat nervously through the reading of a document they knew almost by memory. They were exhausted. For more than four sweltering months they had met in Independence Hall to dialogue and debate for five hours every day, six days a week. In the early morning or late evening hours, they had lobbied each other over breakfast or dinner. Every other spare moment had been filled with writing letters, preparing drafts and speeches, and meeting with state delegations or on their assigned committees. The framers had driven themselves tirelessly because they shared "a sense of mission—for all Americans then living, for generations of Americans unborn, indeed 'for the whole human race.'"[1]

The task of drawing up a constitution to replace the old and ineffectual Articles of Confederation had been difficult and demanding. Each state approached the problem with its own set of fears and prejudices.

Small states mistrusted large states. States' rights advocates feared those in favor of a strong central government. Southern and northern states often disagreed.

That the Constitutional Convention in just over four months succeeded in drawing up a document acceptable to these independent, high-spirited, and strong-willed men, and finally to the people of the various states they represented, was a miracle wrought by the hard work, tireless commitment, and masterful diplomacy of the convention's delegates and their leaders.

The framers must have felt great relief that day. Their endless, stressful summer was almost over. The edited version of the Constitution had been read. Washington opened the floor for one last discussion. Soon the votes would be counted and the issue decided for all time. An aging Benjamin Franklin rose with speech in hand at the close of the final reading of the edited document.

"Sir," he said, addressing George Washington, "I agree to this constitution with all its faults, if they are such; because I think a general government necessary for us . . . ." Franklin joked about his own failures and encouraged the assembled delegates to sign the document unanimously. "Sir," he concluded, "I cannot help expressing a wish that every member of the convention who may still have objections to it, would with me, on this occasion, doubt a little of his own infallibility, and to make manifest our unanimity, put his name to the instrument."[2]

When Governor Randolph of Rhode Island refused to sign, Gouverneur Morris from Pennsylvania replied angrily. "The present plan [is] the best that was to be attained," he said. And since without this plan he feared "general anarchy," he took it "with all its faults."[3]

The convention accepted the final version of the Constitution with just three dissenting votes. And while the delegates lined up to sign the document, Ben Franklin pointed at the sun painted on the back of the president's chair and spoke quietly to those standing about him. He had wondered, he said, "whether it was rising or setting: But now at length I have the happiness to know that it is a rising and not a setting one."[4]

Madison closed his record of the convention with these words: "The Constitution being signed by all the members except Mr. Randolph, Mr. Mason, and Mr. Gerry . . . the Convention dissolved itself by an adjournment sine die." According to Washington's diary, the delegates then adjourned to the nearby City Tavern to take a final congenial meal together.[5]

A fierce state-by-state struggle to ratify the Constitution was launched soon after by the Congress. That struggle was resolved on July 26, 1788, when New York became the seventh state to ratify. The union of those first thirteen states was not totally secured, however, until two years later, May 29, 1790, when Rhode Island finally decided to join the United States of America.

What those men achieved in Independence Hall has stood the test of time. The Constitution of the United States has served us well for almost two hundred years of incredible growth. Where once just thirteen colonies clustered together on the Atlantic coastline, now fifty states are spread from sea to shining sea. Where fewer than 4 million people, more than 600 thousand of them slaves, lived, now live more than 230 million free Americans of every color, race, and creed.

On September 17, 1988, America will celebrate the bicentennial of our Constitution. It should be a celebration second to none, for no document, no person, no date in the history of this nation deserves any greater honor than the Constitution of the United States of America.

The Declaration of Independence was signed on July 4, 1776, by fifty-five members of the Third Continental Congress. That Declaration stated clearly the purpose of the government of this nation, which was to preserve and protect certain God-given rights for every citizen. It took almost a decade to win those rights from the tyranny of King George III.

On September 17, 1787, eleven years later, thirty-nine members of the Constitutional Convention signed the Constitution of the United States. That Constitution stated the plan by which government would carry out its purpose. It was a plan for colonial union, or what our forefathers called "a more perfect union." In this magnificent plan, the people first created a central government to which they granted limited powers. Those powers were designed to assist the various states in doing those things, such as providing a national defense, that they could not accomplish alone.

The Declaration of Independence and the Constitution must be seen as one. Each is incomplete without the other. This nation stands strong and free today, two hundred years later, because one foot stands on the Declaration of Independence; the other, on the Constitution. Remove either document and the nation will not stand at all.

Both documents were signed in Philadelphia's Independence Hall by delegates from the same colonies. And though a decade and the War for Independence had passed, at least six of the signers of the Declaration also signed the Constitution. Both documents were crucial in guiding this nation on her journey to liberty, and both documents are now preserved under glass in our nation's capital.

Now, almost every day hundreds and even thousands of school children pass those carefully guarded, air-tight, temperature-controlled chambers in which the documents are preserved. I have joined the children at the National Archives in Washington, D.C., to stare down at those parchment papers with my own feelings of awe, wonder, and respect. But the Declaration and the Constitution are not like the mummies of the great Egyptian pharaohs—embalmed and preserved but shrunken and lifeless. These documents live. Their carefully chosen words still guard our liberty and guide us in its preservation. The Declaration and the Constitution must not simply be revered. Their history must be known and understood, and their words must be read, studied, and debated.

A New Kind of Government Is Born

Every American should make a pilgrimage at least once in a lifetime to visit Independence Hall in Philadelphia. Take the guided tour or stand alone behind the green velvet rope and stare into that single room where the two greatest documents in this nation's history were created. Two hundred years later, we find it difficult to understand the unprecedented and amazing work accomplished there.

Those two documents signed by our forefathers created a form of government almost entirely new upon the earth. For free people from sovereign states to enter into a compact with each other, granting power to a strong central government over their own recently won sovereignty, was a kind of miracle. This voluntary compact among "free and independent states" would forever bind them to each other, yet guarantee them certain powers of their own. It was a bold and daring idea, totally different from all other governments in the world at that time.

On September 17, 1787, the day our Constitution was signed, the absolute monarch Ch'ien Lung, emperor of the Manchu (or Ch'ing) Dynasty, reigned supreme over the people of China. To guard against revolt, Chinese officials could not hold office in their home provinces, and the emperor constantly shuffled government appointees to keep any one man from gaining power against him. Revolts were put down by ruthless military force. China's armies had penetrated Burma and Nepal; even Korea paid tribute.

In Japan the shogun (warriors) of the corrupt Tokugawa chamberlain Tanuma Okitsugu exercised corrupt and totalitarian authority over the Japanese. Japan had been ruled by the ancestors of Tokugawa Ieyasu since the beginning of the seventeenth century. The Japanese, like their Chinese neighbors, were a great people with a great cultural and religious heritage, but the notion of a voluntary contract among peoples to form a democratic government would not be introduced there for almost two centuries.

In India, Warren Hastings, the British Governor of Bengal, had successfully defeated the influence of the fragmented Mogul dynasties that had ruled India since 1600. He also had effectively nullified France's claims on this huge subcontinent.

Catherine II was the enlightened despot of all the Russias. Joseph II was the emperor of Austria, Bohemia, and Hungary. For almost half a century, Frederick the Great had ruled Prussia. Louis XVI sat uneasily on his throne in France just years away from revolution, a bloody experiment in democracy, and the new tyranny of Napoleon Bonaparte. A kind of constitutional government had been created in the Netherlands in 1579 by the Protestant Union of Utrecht, but that constitution was really a loose federation of the northern provinces for defense against Catholic Spain and not a strong, legal contract upon which a lasting central government could be formed.

What was happening in America had no real precedent, even as far back as the city-states of Greece. The only real precedent was established thousands of years before by the tribes of Israel in their covenant with God and with each other. Yet our forefathers moved swiftly and gracefully toward that goal during the tumultuous Congress of 1776 and that long, hot summer of 1787.

Facing Constitutional Crisis

Throughout our history, the Constitution has faced a variety of crises and survived them all. What the convention delegates signed in Philadelphia guided us safely through the organization of a federal govern-ment and the incredible expansion of thirteen small colonies into a great and powerful nation. The Constitution saw us through a Civil War and the impeachment of a president, through a great financial depression, and through devastating foreign wars outside our borders and nightmar-ish racial wars within them. Fortunately, the Constitution has passed each painful test. And it will continue to serve us well if we remember its history and understand its every word.

Task Number One:
Understanding the Background of the Constitution

What model did the framers use to shape this unprecedented Consti-tution? What historic textbook guided them in its creation? I am con-vinced by the documents and by the testimony of the signers themselves that the Old Testament stories of God at work with His people, Israel, and the New Testament stories of the Christian church were two major influences on the creation of our Constitution. The framers and the great legal minds that influenced their deliberations—including Mon-tesquieu, John Locke, Hugo Grotius, William Blackstone, and Samuel Rutherford—all confessed their debt to the Bible and to the example of the church in the shaping of their views of government.

Samuel Adams, the "Father of the American Revolution" and a signer of the Declaration of Independence, wrote: "The right to free-dom being the gift of God Almighty . . . 'The Rights of the Colonists as Christians' . . . may be best understood by reading and carefully study-ing the institutes of the great Law Giver . . . which are to be found clearly written and promulgated in the New Testament."[6]

Some read the Constitution quickly and, because it contains no direct reference to God, conclude that it has no Christian roots, no biblical precedents. That's why reading the Declaration of Independence along-side the Constitution is instructive.

Remember that in the Declaration of Independence, our forefathers appealed to God's laws as revealed in nature and in the Bible ("the Laws of Nature and of Nature's God") as the foundation upon which everything else was built. But the specific shape of the government they would establish in the Constitution is also foreshadowed in the Declara-tion. For example, consider the framers' three primary references to

God in the Declaration of Independence and the three branches of government as defined by the Constitution of the United States.

First, the framers appealed to God as the source of our liberty: ". . . endowed by their Creator with certain unalienable Rights." God is the Lawgiver, a biblical precedent for the legislative branch of government.

Second, they appealed to God as the nation's ultimate protector: ". . . with a firm reliance on the Protection of Divine Providence." God is the Chief Executive, the Commander-in-Chief, a biblical precedent for the executive branch of government.

Third, they appealed to God as the nation's judge: ". . . appealing to the Supreme Judge of the world for the rectitude of our intentions." God is the Chief Justice of the universe, a biblical precedent for the judicial branch of government.

To understand the Constitution is to understand the framers' commitment to biblical wisdom and to the historic traditions of God's definition of government in the Old and New Testaments.

Each colony originated with a charter into which its leaders had voluntarily entered with the king. All of those charters were framed with direct references to God's purpose and plan for civil government. And the members of each colony's churches shared power voluntarily with ministers or priests, deacons, elders, presbyters, or bishops as had the first-century Christians. The framers grew up in colonies and churches governed on ancient biblical principles, and after the Revolutionary War they used those models to create a Constitution for the United States.

Now, as a result, we are a republic, ruled by representatives chosen in free elections by the people. We are not a theocracy, ruled outright by God. Nor are we a theocracy ruled by godly prophets, priests, or elders in His name. The framers did not intend that we strive to be a theocracy in any form. Our government is made by men and women. To protect our God-given rights, the people have voluntarily entered into a contract creating a general government charged with the power to do for all of us together what we cannot do for ourselves alone.

That Constitution, as our manmade plan for government, is not an appropriate or necessary place to speak of God. The Declaration had said enough. God is the source and protector of our liberty, the judge of our good intentions. In His natural and revealed Law we find the purpose and foreshadowings of the plan of this government. But after that, the people make the decisions. Hopefully, God rules in the hearts of the people. But people—however sensitive or insensitive they may be to God's rule—rule government.

That's why our forefathers said correctly that no religious belief qualifies or disqualifies a person from participating in government. They didn't want one denomination favored above another as was then true in Massachusetts and Connecticut and had been true until 1786 in Virginia. They wanted every man to be given an equal chance at governing. This was not a slap in the face of the Christian faith, but a guarantee that no one expression of that faith would dominate in America's new civil government.

The Constitution Was Intended for a Religious People

In fact, the framers believed that the Constitution could not survive a people who did not believe in God or His laws. Whether Anglican or Pilgrim, Puritan or Baptist, Presbyterian, Catholic, or Quaker, our forefathers knew well those biblical passages that describe the sinful, fallen nature of man. In fact, the balance of power between people and government, between state and federal governments, and between the legislative, executive, and judicial branches of the federal government bears eloquent testimony to the founding fathers' belief in sinful man who should not be entrusted with too much power. "In God We Trust" was their motto, not "In Humanity We Trust."

They had just survived a bloody war with a king who talked of justice while forcing tyranny upon them. In that war they saw what men were made of, good and bad, and they concluded that without a people governed individually by God's laws, the nation would self-destruct.

George Washington said in his presidential farewell address that religion and morality are the two "great pillars of human happiness" and indispensable to "private and public felicity."[7]

John Adams, our second president, said it this way: "We have no government armed with power capable of contending with human passions unbridled by morality and religion. Avarice, ambition, revenge or gallantry would break the strongest cords of our Constitution as a whale goes through a net. Our Constitution was made only for a moral and religious people. It is wholly inadequate to the government of any other."[8]

Thomas Jefferson, the third president, repeated the theme: "Can the liberties of a nation be sure when we remove their only firm basis, a conviction in the minds of the people, that these liberties are the gift of God? that they are not to be violated but with His wrath?"

Do you realize how helpless the police would be to prevent crime or to protect its victims if everybody suddenly decided to break the law? What would happen to the solvency of government if we all chose not to pay our taxes? Our neighborhoods would be transformed into armed camps if we decided that nothing is wrong with stealing our neighbors' goods, raping our neighbors' wives, abusing or kidnapping our neighbors' children. Alone, the laws of this land cannot hold society in check. All the policemen, sheriffs' officers, and highway patrolmen in the nation couldn't stop us if we all decided to disobey them.

Add together all the crimes and all the criminals reported in the past year (and they are many), and you will still find that most people have made it through the year without seriously breaking the law. The people, most of us, have policed ourselves. Why? What keeps most of us in order? What holds us back during those times of lust or anger or disappointment?

Our free society depends on one essential element, the self-restraint of its citizens. And the self-restraint of the citizens in turn depends on one primary belief, that God exists and that one day He will judge us and reward or punish us according to His divine standard. Believing in the just and powerful God of the Old Testament makes a tremendous difference in a society. Believing in the ancient promise of eternal rewards or eternal punishments helps foster self-control.

Jesus introduced a new dimension to the Old Testament law. Christians' desire to live by God's standards is reinforced by the presence of the Holy Spirit and by the comfort and discipline of the church. And though the New Testament presents the good news of God's love and forgiveness in the life, death, and resurrection of Jesus, grace motivates the Christian to want to obey God even more.

Both Old and New Testament standards create a law of the heart. Whether one lives life by the Ten Commandments of the Old Testament or the fruit of God's Spirit in the New, the law of the heart helps regulate your response to the laws of this nation. Imagine how different the world would be without these biblically based constraints. Imagine what might happen to *this nation* without them.

Task Number Two:
Understanding the Words of the Constitution

In an earlier chapter, I suggested you obtain a copy of the Declaration of Independence to read and underline. I hope you take that seriously. This is not just boring history that we are repeating by rote. This is the lifeblood of our country, and unless it flows freely through our political veins, our nation will grow sick and die. Now please find a copy of the Constitution of the United States. Then, let's look at it together.

I spent three years getting my law degree at Yale Law School. From the moment I enrolled, I was assigned huge, leather-bound editions of legal cases to study and discuss. I read what lawyers and judges, professors and historians said about the Constitution. But never once was I assigned the task of reading the Constitution itself. Yet the Constitution is the ultimate authority upon which all the other cases are finally decided.

Over the last decade, however, I have become a student of the Constitution, searching each line for its meaning and intent. Studying the Constitution is like studying the Bible. It is amazing how much more you will learn when you quit studying *about* it and pick it up to read it for yourself.

The Constitution begins with a short, fifty-two-word preamble. That's barely one word for each signer, yet in that collection of words the framers reiterated more fully the goals of government. You learned to say the preamble in grammar school. See if you can remember how it goes without looking:

WE THE PEOPLE of the United States, in Order to form a more perfect Union, establish Justice, insure domestic Tranquility, provide for the common defence, promote the general Welfare, and secure the Blessing of Liberty to ourselves and our Posterity, do ordain and establish this Constitution for the United States of America.[9]

The Declaration of Independence announced that governments were formed by people to preserve and protect the people's unalienable rights, that among these are "Life, Liberty and the pursuit of Happiness." The preamble to the Constitution is a larger, more detailed description of those same rights and the kinds of tasks a government should perform to guarantee them.

Immediately after writing the preamble, George Washington, James Madison, George Mason, Alexander Hamilton, Benjamin Franklin, and the other framers got down to the hard work of establishing a government that would be able to preserve, protect, and defend those rights.

Article I describes the Congress of the United States, the Senate and the House of Representatives.

Article II describes the office of the president.

Article III describes the judicial branch, the Supreme Court and the lesser courts.

The last four articles describe briefly the relationships of the states to each other and to the central government, the issue of debts, treaties, and the effect of laws made by each state upon the other, the process for amending and ratifying the Constitution, and the oath required by national officeholders "to support this Constitution," with the careful qualification that "no religious Test shall ever be required as a Qualification to any Office or public Trust under the United States."

Because Man Is Fallen: Limited Power Is Given to Government

The framers knew the sinfulness of human nature, and they didn't trust it. They had just escaped one tyranny, and they were not about to create another to replace it. They knew they had to give away some power to create a workable general government, but they insisted on keeping the rest of that power in their states, in their counties, and most importantly in themselves.

So our forefathers, working that summer in Philadelphia, decided upon three principles of power.

First: The people would grant powers to a central government, but those powers would be limited.

Second: Three branches of government would balance the distribution of power within the central government.

Third: Various checks by each branch upon the others would keep any one branch from gaining more power than the people intended.

I read a copy of the Constitution just recently in the quaint, antiquated English in which it was written. And by the unique layout of that original document, I began to see something that I had not noticed earlier in my studies. I knew that the three branches of the central government had been created to balance each other and to keep each other in check, but I hadn't realized before how carefully one branch had been assigned more power than the others. Read the first three articles yourself. Study them.

The Power of the Congress

The power reserved for the House and Senate is clearly defined. I have read and reread the Constitution. It doesn't take many readings to see that the responsibilities of Congress are most carefully and specifically stated. They should be. Congress makes the laws. The president executes the laws, and the courts interpret them; but Congress is the branch given responsibility to make them in the first place.

Just to illustrate how much more emphasis the founding fathers gave to Congress, I counted and compared the lines of instructions given—255 to the Congress. Legislators were given power over the nation's purse, to raise money and pay the debts. They could coin money and determine its weight and value. They could declare war and raise and support armies. They could impeach a president and approve or disapprove his programs and his appointments. They could create all the lesser courts for the entire federal judicial system, could determine how many judges sit on the Supreme Court, decide what appellate jurisdiction the Supreme Court would have, and in impeachment proceedings whether the justices had served with good behavior. The Senate alone has the power of advice and consent over certain ambassadors, cabinet officers, all the treaties, and all the federal judges a president might appoint.

The Power of the President

Only 114 lines were written about the president. Though many thought George Washington would make an excellent monarch, they wanted to limit presidential power, and turned to Congress for that task. The president is the commander-in-chief of the armed forces, but he has no armed forces to command unless Congress funds them. He is in charge of conducting foreign relations, yet he cannot make treaties or appoint ambassadors without the advice and consent of the Senate. In a deadlocked election in the electoral college, the Congress has the power to decide who will be president. And it is to the Congress that the president must bring his annual state of the union report, like a chief executive officer to the board of directors of his corporation, to get its approval and support for his programs.

The Power of the Courts

The framers limited their instructions for the judicial branch to just forty-four lines. The Constitution extends judicial power to the Supreme Court and the lesser courts. The various kinds of disputes that arise are carefully enumerated, and the jurisdiction over those disputes is assigned. Trial by jury and the crime of treason are briefly discussed. At this point the Constitution should be carefully studied for what it doesn't say.

The president appoints the judges of the Supreme Court. And Congress has the power to set the appellate jurisdiction of the Supreme Court and to establish whatever lesser courts it desires. Congress even sets the salaries and the numbers of judges on all the federal courts.

Following the ancient traditions of biblical and common law, the framers assumed that judges would know their limits. The judges are asked to judge, no more. They hear all sides in disputes about the law under the Constitution of the United States. They discover and decide the meaning of the laws. They apply the laws. They judge between the parties who disagree about the laws. But they do not *make* laws. Their opinions about a law only affect the parties directly concerned in each case. And those judicial judgments are not laws but only opinions about the law, binding upon the parties in cases and serving as guidelines and precedents.

Read Article III, looking for the line or phrase that gives the Supreme Court power to make laws or to discard laws that the Congress or state and local legislatures have made. You will not find it. The principle of judicial review was recognized by our forefathers and implied in the

Constitution. But the limits of that judicial review are not clearly stated.

Perhaps the framers erred in not making these limits clear. Perhaps they did not believe that modern courts would ever assume a power not granted them by the Constitution. But all along the way, great Americans worried about the possibilities and warned the nation of the consequences.

James Madison wrote this warning in 1788: "In the state constitutions, and, indeed, in the federal one also, no provision is made for the case of a disagreement in expounding them [the laws]; and as the courts are generally the last in making the decision, it results to them by refusing or not refusing to execute a law, to stamp it with its final character. This makes the judiciary department paramount in fact to the legislature, which was never intended and can never be proper."

Thomas Jefferson, in a letter dated September 28, 1820, said it this way: "You seem to consider the judges as the ultimate arbiters of all Constitutional questions: a very dangerous doctrine indeed, and one which would place us under the despotism of an oligarchy. The Constitution has erected no such single tribunal, knowing that to whatever hands confided, with the corruptions of time and party, its members would become despots. It has more wisely made all the departments co-equal and co-sovereign within themselves."

President Andrew Jackson wrote similarly:

> If the opinion of the Supreme Court covered the whole ground of this act, it ought not to control the coordinate authorities of this government. The Congress, the Executive, and the Court must each for itself be guided by its own opinion of the Constitution. Each public officer who takes an oath to support the Constitution swears that he will support it as he understands it, and not as it is understood by others."

The Bill of Rights

With Lord Acton, our forefathers could say, "Power tends to corrupt and absolute power corrupts absolutely." And though the powers granted the federal government were limited, though those powers were balanced among three branches of government, and though checks were on those three branches—primarily in the hands of their directly elected representatives—the citizens of the United States still weren't satisfied.

So the people appealed to James Madison to write a Bill of Rights that would be attached as a rider to the Constitution. Again they placed limits on the Congress. In the first amendment our forefathers required that "Congress shall make no law respecting an establishment of religion, or prohibiting the free exercise thereof." The rights to free speech, a free press, and free assembly to petition the government were also guaranteed. The other amendments further limited the Congress, the president, and the courts in their power over the God-given rights of the people.

And in the tenth amendment, the people took one last step to guarantee their freedoms when they said: "The powers not delegated to the United States by the Constitution, nor prohibited by it to the States, are reserved to the States respectively, or to the people."

Without a Return to Balance, the Constitution Cannot Stand

Throughout our history as a nation, recurring shifts of power among the branches of our federal government have taken place. Powerful presidents, powerful courts, and powerful Congresses struggle among themselves for control. But thanks to the Declaration of Independence and the Constitution, supreme power is left with the people.

What happens, however, when the struggle for power gets out of hand? What happens in a constitutional crisis that threatens to undo us? Once again our forefathers left us guidelines for just such a day.

On June 28, 1786, Benjamin Franklin stood before his colleagues in the Constitutional Convention when the framers were having a constitutional crisis of their own. For days they had been debating a particularly difficult states' rights issue. The delegates were weary and afraid. Franklin, known for his own sometimes cynical views of the church and of churchmen, reminded them of God's presence throughout the nation's history and of their daily need to seek His presence in their deliberations:

> Have we now forgotten that powerful friend? or do we imagine that we no longer need his assistance? I have lived, Sir, [Madison] a long time, and the longer I live, the more convincing proofs I see of this truth—*that God governs in the affairs of men.* And if a sparrow cannot fall to the ground without his notice, is it probable that an empire can rise without his aid? We have been assured, Sir, in the sacred writings, that "except

the Lord build the House they labour in vain that build it." I firmly believe this; and I also believe that without his concurring aid we shall succeed in this political building no better than the Builders of Babel: We shall be divided by our little partial local interests; our projects will be confounded, and we ourselves shall become a reproach and bye word down to future ages. And what is worse, mankind may hereafter from this unfortunate instance, despair of establishing Governments by Human Wisdom and leave it to chance, war and conquest.[11]

Perhaps it is time once again for that old statesman to rise up in our midst and remind us of our spiritual heritage. Maybe somewhere in that historic room in Philadelphia's Independence Hall Ben Franklin's voice still echoes, asking, ". . . have we now forgotten that powerful friend? Or do we imagine that we no longer need his assistance?"

7

GEORGE WASHINGTON INAUGURATED

APRIL 30, 1789

Rediscovering the Role of Personal Faith in Public Policy

A t the dawn of the auspicious day, thirteen cannons were fired from the battery guarding the southern end of New York Island (now known as Manhattan).[1] The city awakened early and began its preparation for the inauguration of the first president of the United States.

In his private quarters near Wall Street, George Washington powdered his hair and dressed himself in a brown broadcloth suit made in Hartford, Connecticut. The general had decided to use this great occasion to promote American-made goods. Each button of his new brown broadcloth suit was etched with a spread eagle to celebrate the nation's freshly won liberty. Washington wore long white silk stockings and black leather shoes with silver buckles.

Just after sunrise the people began to gather in the street and around the house where Washington was staying. By 9:00 the early morning fog had burned away, and the sun warmed and cheered the noisy crowd. Militia arrived to protect the new president and move the crowds away from his front door.

Finally, a great coach—pulled by four matched horses, escorted by three uniformed footmen, and followed by soldiers and dignitaries—entered the crowded street and moved slowly toward Washington's home. Hearing the sounds of cheering and the tramp of marching soldiers, the general calmly folded the text of his inaugural address and placed it in his pocket. He strapped on the steel scabbard of the dress sword of his triumphant Revolutionary army and walked alone into the street to board the waiting coach.

The presidential procession stopped on Broad Street just south of Wall Street, in front of Federal Hall. Washington was escorted into the Senate chamber where both houses of Congress and various officials of the new government were awaiting his arrival.

The lawmakers and their guests stood quickly as Washington walked past them to the raised dais, above which were three windows draped in crimson damask. He bowed to the crowd and to Vice President John Adams, who awaited him. After simple greetings were exchanged, Adams led Washington out onto a balcony overlooking Wall and Broad streets.

Eyewitnesses say that Washington was greeted by a great, booming cheer from a sea of smiling faces that filled the streets in all directions. Washington bowed humbly toward the crowds, then sat down in an armchair to await his inauguration. Secretary of State Samuel Otis lifted the large, leather-covered Bible from its crimson velvet cushion and stood between Chancellor Robert Livingston and Washington.

"Do you solemnly swear," the chancellor began, "that you will faithfully execute the office of President of the United States and will, to the best of your ability, preserve, protect, and defend the Constitution of the United States?"

"I solemnly swear," Washington replied, repeating from memory the oath as prescribed by Article II, Section 1, of the recently ratified Constitution. Then, quite spontaneously, he added, "So help me God." Even as he added that short prayer of commitment, the first president of the United States bent forward to kiss the Bible in Secretary Otis's hands.

"It is done," Livingston said quietly. Then, turning to the jubilant crowd, he added, "Long live George Washington, president of the United States!" One eyewitness said the crowd roared back, "God bless our president."

Washington bowed. Another eyewitness described that moment as "tearful ecstacy . . . succeeded . . . by shouts which seemed to shake the canopy above them." At that moment, the American flag was being raised above the cupola on top of Federal Hall. From the battery came the sounds of cannon firing, and all across the city, church bells began to ring. Even as the crowds cheered, Washington bowed one last time and re-entered the building.[2]

He bowed again to the cheering crowd inside the hall, glanced up at the sun and stars above him on the ceiling, reached into his pocket for his inaugural address, and unfolded it carefully. Still the people cheered; many wept. Each knew something of the price in blood, grief, and suffering paid by the people of this nation to reach that first inauguration day. And no one understood the cost of liberty better than Washington himself.

"Fellow-Citizens of the Senate and of the House of Representatives," Washington said in a deep, low voice, ". . . no event could have filled me with greater anxieties . . . ."[3] He spoke humbly of his feelings of inadequacy for this great office: "Inheriting inferior endowments from Nature," he claimed, "and unpracticed in the duties of civil administration," one ought to be "peculiarly conscious of his own deficiencies." Washington hoped that history would forgive him if he were accepting his high office for any wrong motives.

Then, immediately, he appealed to God for help and wisdom in his task. "It would be peculiarly improper," he said to the assembled members of the government, "to omit in this first official act my fervent supplications to that Almighty Being who rules over the universe, who presides in the councils of nations, and whose providential aids can supply every human defect, that His benediction may consecrate to the liberties and happiness of the people of the United States a Government instituted by themselves for these essential purposes . . . ."

In the remainder of his short address, Washington raised only a few questions related to his new office and asked that the Congress limit his pay "to such actual expenditures as the public good may be thought to require." Then in closing he added:

> I shall take my present leave; but not without resorting once more to the Benign Parent of the Human Race, in humble supplication that, since He has been pleased to favor the American people with opportunities for deliberating in perfect tranquillity, and dispositions for deciding with unparalleled unanimity on a form of government for the security of their union and the advancement of their happiness, so His divine blessing may be equally *conspicuous* in the enlarged views, the temperate consultations and the wise measures on which the success of this Government must depend.

Following his inaugural address, Washington and his guests were immediately escorted from Federal Hall through the crowded streets to St. Paul's Cathedral, where Congress had voted to go in order "to hear divine service, performed by the Chaplain of Congress."[4] Inside the crowded chapel at the beginning of his presidency, George Washington knelt to pray, to sing the *Te Deum,* and to receive God's strength for his journey.

It is time once again to remember George Washington and the spirit of this man who would begin and end his term in office with humility, generosity, and deepest faith. In our first president we have an example for all times of the spirit and shape of the presidency. And in his whole life among us, we have an example of the spirit and shape of the people as well.

Ge|orge Washington awakened on the first full day of his first four-year term as the first president of the United States, the first nation of its kind in history. The only job description he had that morning of May 1, 1789, was the Constitution of the United States, and the only specific directions he had been given in his oath of office the previous day were "to preserve, protect, and defend" that Constitution.

President Washington faced an unenviable and largely unknown task. Remember, before his involvement in Virginia politics he had been a surveyor. I wonder if at the dawn of that first day as president he unfolded one of the primitive maps of the great, undeveloped wilderness over which he presided and studied with awe those 890 thousand square miles with borders stretching from the Atlantic to the Mississippi, from the Great Lakes to just short of the Gulf of Mexico. It was a nation larger than Italy, France, Germany, Spain, Britain, and Ireland combined, and it was the responsibility of his government to unite that land, establish peace and prosperity within its borders, and secure the nation against its enemies.

As a delegate from Virginia to the Constitutional Convention and as commander-in-chief of the Continental Army, Washington had traveled throughout the colonies meeting many of the nation's people. During his first term in office, he would make two more strategic journeys—one into the northern and one into the southern states—to familiarize himself with the people and their problems. So from the beginning Washington was aware of the complex and often confounding mixture of people already living in this new nation.

Imagine his consternation that first day in office as President Washington thought about the diversity of his constituents and the various demands they would place immediately upon him. Under his direct jurisdiction were 2,247,380 white people of European ancestry, and 681,834 black people, those who had been kidnapped from their homes in Africa and sold into slavery in America, as well as their children who had been born into slavery. And uncounted (and certainly unloved) Indian people, hundreds of thousands of them, already were being crowded from their homelands toward the frontiers of this rapidly expanding nation.

George Washington's task would not be an easy one—to lead this heterogeneous mass of men, women, and children, spread across the original thirteen states in cities, towns, villages, settlements, isolated farms, and plantations. But it was Washington's responsibility as the first president of the United States to lead them toward "a more perfect union," and immediately he set about to do it.

Washington organized the office of the president, hired his personal staff, and appointed his first distinguished four-man cabinet: Thomas Jefferson, secretary of state; Alexander Hamilton, secretary of the treasury; Henry Knox, secretary of war; and Edmund Randolph, attorney general. He addressed the Congress and began to determine how he would work in partnership with this group. He appointed the nation's ambassadors, other public ministers and consuls, and the judges of the Supreme Court. He established a sound financial basis for the federal government and created a national bank to handle federal bonds, notes, and deposits. He insisted that the nation remain neutral when France and England went to war. He put down tax rebellions and political insurrections at home, and he negotiated final war settlement and trade treaties with Great Britain. And almost miraculously, President Washington kept two of his own cabinet officers—Jefferson, a Republican, and Hamilton, a Federalist—from destroying each other and threatening the nation as the struggle they personally represented gave stormy birth to the two-party political system in America.

And though Martha Washington longed to retire to Mt. Vernon after their first four-year term in the presidency, George Washington consented to a second term, was elected unanimously by the electoral college, and was inaugurated in Philadelphia. During his eight years as America's first president, Washington set standards of excellence that have inspired and informed all the presidents who followed him. Resolutely he kept his oath of office. And in spite of his immense popularity with the people, he refused to extend his presidential power beyond the limits assigned him by the Constitution.

Washington brought dignity and respect to the office of the presidency. In New York and Philadelphia, he rented great houses, entertained elegantly, and rode in a coach drawn by four to six smart horses with outriders and attendants in rich livery. He attended receptions dressed in a black velvet suit with gold buckles. He wore yellow gloves, powdered hair, a cocked hat with an ostrich plume, and a sword in a white leather scabbard. He returned no calls and shook hands with no one, acknowledging salutations by a formal bow. He was regal in taste and bearing, as he thought his office warranted. And though the people might gladly have appointed him king, Washington refused to exercise any power not granted him by the Constitution.

Scrupulously, he lived within the limits of presidential power. He did not usurp the place of Congress or the courts. He guarded the rights of the individual states and the unalienable rights of the people. And when his eight years in office had ended, Washington gladly surrendered the power of the presidency to those who would succeed him.

Two years after his farewell address to the nation, on December 12, 1799, Washington, again a gentleman farmer, was caught in a snowstorm while riding on his plantation. He contracted a serious throat infection and was bled heavily four times, as well as given gargles of "molasses, vinegar, and butter." A preparation of dried beetles was placed on his throat, too, in an attempt to cure the infection. After those primitive, desperate, and sometimes counterproductive measures to save the father of this nation, Washington grew weak. On his deathbed he said to his physician: "I die hard, but I am not afraid to go . . . . I thank you for your attentions; but I pray you to take no more trouble about me. Let me go off quietly. I cannot last long."[5]

After giving burial instructions to his personal secretary, George Washington died in his home at 10:00 P.M. on December 14, 1799. He was just sixty-seven years old, but already he was the one American almost universally acclaimed as "first in war, first in peace, and first in the hearts of his countrymen."[6]

The Role of Faith in His Life

From childhood I have been fascinated by our first president and inspired by his Christian faith. Not once during his distinguished service to this nation did he minimize or shelve his deeply felt commitment to God, to the Bible, or to his Lord and Savior, Jesus Christ. And during those years of public service as a Virginia legislator, as the commander-in-chief of the Continental Army, as chairman of the Constitutional Convention, and as the nation's first president, he established for all time how Christian people can live by their own convictions and at the same time govern all the people fairly and wisely.

That George Washington was a fair, wise, and able president has been well established by history. But little has been done to illustrate Washington's commitment to the Christian faith or how that commitment helped to shape his presidency. In his speeches, his letters, and his public policy, the first president offers fascinating and informative insights into the effects of his faith on his words and actions.

Long before Washington was noticed by history, he was an Anglican churchman. For twenty years he served as vestryman (trustee) of that church, and at least three different times he served the vestry as churchwarden.[7] He was reported as "consistent, if not always regular" in attendance.[8] As a communicant of the Anglican church, Washington regularly joined with the worldwide communion of Christians who even today repeat the Apostles' Creed, which begins with these words: "I believe in God, the Father Almighty, Maker of heaven and earth, and in Jesus Christ, His only Son, our Lord."

And though he was a loyal, tithing, committed member of his parish, Washington "displayed total disinterest in the doctrinal disputes that preoccupied many ardent churchmen of his time."[9] Remember, Washington was a surveyor. His training was in mathematics and science. From the beginning he seemed gifted with an ability to cut through wordy debate in religious and political circles and get to the essence of an issue.

Sometimes his lack of interest in the theological or philosophical sides of an issue led Washington into making unwise, even sectarian, decisions. He favored the establishment of the Episcopalian church in Virginia and the religious assessment plan in that same state. But he was open to counsel and able to reverse his views when proved wrong. He changed his mind about those two policies, for example, when he realized the anguish they caused, especially for his Baptist friends. When it was clear that under Thomas Jefferson and James Madison's leadership the Anglican church would be disestablished, and that the plan to tax citizens to pay for Christian instruction would be defeated, Washington quickly assented to the will of the majority.

On May 13, 1774, four regiments of British troops under General Thomas Gage had occupied Boston after the colonists dumped British tea into Boston Harbor. In compassionate response, George Washington made this offer to his fellow delegates in the Virginia House of Burgesses: "I will raise one thousand men, subsist them at my own expense, and march myself at their head for the relief of Boston."[10] After the Declaration of Independence was signed in 1776, Washington's first general order as chief of the newly organized Continental Army was to call on "every officer and man . . . to live and act as becomes a Christian soldier, defending the dearest rights and liberties of his country."[11]

Eighteen years earlier, in 1758 when Washington was a colonel in the Virginia militia, he established the post of chaplain to serve in each military regiment. As commander-in-chief of the Continental Army in 1776, Washington authorized a corps of chaplains to serve troops fighting in the Revolutionary War. Ministers would be paid twenty dollars a month and maintain the same pay and privileges as a commissioned captain.

Washington believed that "religion and public worship are essential to morale both in civil and in military life."[12] He required church attendance of his soldiers, and he regularly worshiped with his officers and men. Perhaps the most controversial of all the stories about Washington's Christian faith during the Revolutionary War is the story of his kneeling in prayer during a snowstorm at Valley Forge.

The classic bronze bas-relief sculpture of Washington on his knees at prayer in Valley Forge and the 1847 quotation from the *Family Circle* magazine have become a part of American tradition. An unknown author describes the scene: "In this hour of darkness and of danger, when 'foes were strong and friends were few,' when every human prospect presented to the commander at Valley Forge was disheartening, he retired to a sequestered spot, and there laid the cause of his bleeding country at the throne of Grace. . . . As we honor him, and teach our children to give him honor, may we also love and honor, and teach our children to acknowledge the God of our fathers, who alone giveth the victory."[13]

It is true that George and Martha Washington lived in a borrowed farmhouse during that terrible winter of 1777 and that the commander-in-chief could have done his praying on a braided rug before a blazing fire. It is also true that no eyewitness saw him praying there and no written historical record of the event exists. But why many public school teachers have chosen to minimize the Valley Forge tradition that has risen up around our first president is a mystery to me. He was a man who prayed publicly and privately. He was a man who consistently called the nation to prayer in troubling times. His praying alone in Valley Forge would be consistent with everything we know about George Washington, and we have absolutely "no evidence that he did not pray" alone in that small, cold grove of trees.[14]

In 1779 chiefs of the Delaware Indian tribe visited General Washington in a military encampment. They presented three Indian children to Washington for education in schools like Dartmouth College that were being raised up expressly for the education of Indian youth. Washington assured them that Congress would "look upon them as their own Children" and then made the following suggestion: "You do well to wish to learn our arts and way of life, and above all, the religion of Jesus Christ. These will make you a greater and happier people than you are. Congress will do every thing they can to assist you in this wise intention; and to tie the knot of friendship and union so fast, that nothing shall ever be able to loose it."[15]

From the perspective of these past two centuries and our nation's often treacherous dealing with the Indian peoples, these words of Washington, like the prayer at Valley Forge, have been taken out of context and ridiculed. In fact, they are a part of the lasting public record of Washington's sincere commitment to Christian faith and his desire to share that faith with colonist and Indian alike. It is tragic that the Christian spirit of the man who became our first president was not maintained as public policy throughout the history of our nation's westward expansion.

Yet, to see Washington's rather evangelistic posture toward the Indians turned into a sectarian indictment against him would be to miss the other and equally significant truth about his view of Christian faith. During those pre-war years when Washington was a legislator in Virginia and a practicing member of the established church in that colony, his attitude and action toward my Baptist ancestors, a persecuted minority in Virginia, illustrate how a committed Christian can share his faith and recommend it and still be pluralistic and evenhanded to men and women of every Christian denomination or of no religious commitment at all.

When Washington was elected president, my Baptist brothers and sisters wrote a letter to thank him for his consistent support. Their letter and his reply are part of a two-hundred-year-old tradition in this nation that, if properly understood, should help alleviate the fears of those who criticize Christians who seek to influence public policy or who run for public office.

> Sir—Among the many shouts of congratulation that you receive from cities, societies, States, and the whole world, we wish to take an active part in the universal chorus, in expressing our great satisfaction in your appointment to the first office in the nation . . . .
>
> When the constitution first made its appearance in Virginia, we, as a [Baptist] society, had unusual strugglings of mind, fearing that the liberty of conscience, dearer to us than property or life, was not sufficiently secured. Perhaps our jealousies were heightened by the usage we received in Virginia . . . when mobs, fines, bonds and prisons were our frequent repast.
>
> Convinced, on the one hand, that without an effective national government the States would fall into disunion and all the consequent evils, and on the other hand, fearing that we should be accessory to some religious oppression, should any one society in the Union preponderate over the rest; amidst all these inquietudes of mind our consolation arose from this consideration—the plan must be good, for it has the signature of a tried, trusty friend, and if religious liberty is rather insecure in the Constitution, "the Administration will certainly prevent all oppressions, for a WASHINGTON will preside."[16]

In the Episcopalian president, my eighteenth-century Baptist kin saw a protector of their hard-won liberty of conscience. And in Washington's reply we find guidelines appropriate for any Christian or non-Christian leader who would succeed him.

> Gentlemen—I request that you will accept my best acknowledgments for your congratulations on my appointment to the first office in the nation. . . .
>
> If I could have entertained the slightest apprehension that the Constitution framed by the Convention, where I had the honor to preside, might possibly endanger the religious rights of any ecclesiastical society, cer-

tainly I would never have placed my signature on it; and if I could now conceive that the general government might be so administered as to render the liberty of conscience insecure, I beg you will be persuaded that none would be more zealous than myself to establish effective barriers against the horrors of spiritual tyranny and every species of religious persecution; for you doubtless remember I have often expressed my sentiments, that any man, conducting himself as a good citizen, and being accountable to God alone for his religious opinions, ought to be protected in worshipping the Deity according to the dictates of his own conscience.[17]

Washington continued to display an evenhanded approach to personal Christian belief and public policy throughout his eight years as our president. At his first inauguration in New York City, he actually enlarged the oath of office as we saw earlier, and presidents from that day have followed Washington's example.

During his first year in office, President Washington proclaimed Thursday, November 26, 1789, a day for national thanksgiving. In that historic act he urged all Americans to "unite in most humbly offering our prayers and supplications to the great Lord and Ruler of Nations, and beseech him to pardon our national and other transgressions."[18] Good men opposed such a proclamation, including Thomas Jefferson, but the president carefully established his right to recommend behavior to a nation based on his own deeply felt personal convictions without legislating or enforcing his will. It was his suggestion that the nation take time to give God thanks. And the tradition of presidential proclamation has survived to this day.

On other occasions Washington formally called on the country to pray. On January 1, 1795, the president proclaimed a day of prayer and thanksgiving when America narrowly avoided being dragged into a war that revolutionary France had declared on Great Britain, Spain, and the Netherlands. A year later when the treaty John Jay had negotiated with England was sustained, again the president proclaimed a day of public thanksgiving and prayer. He officially set aside February 19, 1795, for grateful prayer when the Whiskey Insurrection in western Pennsylvania had been put down by a four-state militia of 12,400 men led personally by Alexander Hamilton.

Washington was both principled and practical in exercising his prayerful prerogatives as president of the United States. He was principled in that he truly believed the power of God was necessary to establish this nation. In his first inaugural address he spoke clearly of the "Invisible Hand" and the "providential agency" that guided the people of the United States through those stormy revolutionary years.

But he was also practical, believing that "True religion affords to Government its surest support."[19] Washington believed that the virtues resulting from religious faith were "piety, philanthropy, honesty, industry and economy." These virtues, he claimed, are "particularly necessary for advancing and confirming the happiness of our country." He believed that with the right to religious freedom came the responsibility to demonstrate these virtues in our lives as citizens of the nation: "For no man who is profligate in his morals, or a bad member of the civil community, can possibly be a true Christian, or a credit to his own religious society."[20]

In George Washington we find a president who modeled in his private life and public policies a commitment to his Christian faith that makes life better and safer for everyone.

1. *He was a committed Christian who served his local church and worked faithfully for his own denomination.*

2. *He was equally committed to the greater Protestant Christian community* and as president was pleased "to see Christians of different denominations dwell together in more charity, and conduct themselves, in respect to each other, with a more Christian-like spirit, than ever they have done in any former age or in any other nation."[21]

3. *He stood firmly against every anti-Catholic act or sentiment, guaranteeing equal religious freedom to Protestant and Catholic Christians alike.* He appointed a Catholic officer as his aide-de-camp during the Revolutionary War and appointed qualified men to positions in the federal government regardless of their Protestant or Catholic backgrounds. And when rowdy Protestants hanged and burned the papal effigy, he outlawed Guy Fawkes Day as well as standing against the rabid anti-Catholicism employed by some to stir up Anglican support for the Revolution.

4. *He was equally committed to the rights of religious freedom for the growing Jewish population in America.* The congregation of a major Hebrew synagogue in Newport, Rhode Island, wrote the following words to President Washington in 1790:

Deprived, as we have hitherto been, of invaluable rights of free citizens, we now—with a deep sense of gratitude to the Almighty Disposer

113

of all events—behold a government erected by the majesty of the people, a government which gives no sanction to bigotry and no assistance to persecution, but generously affording to all liberty of conscience and immunities of citizenship, deeming every one, of whatever nation, tongue or language, equal parts of the great governmental machine. This so ample and extensive Federal Union, whose base is philanthropy, mutual confidence and public virtue, we cannot but acknowledge to be the work of the great God, who rules the armies of the heavens and among the inhabitants of the earth, doing whatever deemeth to Him good.[22]

5. *He was committed to the right of free conscience for all people.* And though he believed in God and in the free and responsible exercise of religion, no person would be penalized by him or his government for unbelief or for holding religious beliefs or practices different from those of the majority.

Before withdrawing his support from the Virginia bill that would have taxed all citizens to support religious education in the state, Washington wrote that Jews and Moslems should be exempted from such taxation.[23] And in his moving response to the Hebrew synagogue in Newport, President Washington wrote:

> The citizens of the United States of America have the right to applaud themselves for having given to mankind examples of an enlarged and liberal policy worthy of imitation. All possess alike liberty of conscience and immunities of citizenship. It is now no more that toleration is spoken of as if it were by the indulgence of one class of people that another enjoyed the exercise of their inherent natural rights, for happily the Government of the United States, which gives to bigotry no sanction, to persecution no assistance, requires only that they who live under its protection should demean themselves as good citizens in giving it on all occasions their effectual support.[24]

On Monday, March 4, 1797—the last day of his eight-year tenure as president of the United States—George Washington walked alone to Congress Hall. As he approached the door of the House, the echo of cannons firing their last salute to the first American president was drowned out by a great ovation from the mass of men and women who filled the hall, flowing down the steps and out into the streets. Washington quickly took his place in the crowd.

Vice president-elect Thomas Jefferson preceded president-elect John Adams from his carriage and into the House to a second burst of enthusiastic applause. Adams, a man of simple, plain tastes, had dressed in "a pearl-colored broadcloth suit, a sword and cockade" for his inauguration.[25] After the third burst of applause quieted, Adams addressed the crowd and then was sworn into office by Chief Justice Oliver Ellsworth while Washington looked on nearby.

During that inaugural celebration, the new president must have caught the eye of ex-President Washington. For Adams wrote of his old friend: "[His] countenance was as serene and unclouded as the day. He seemed to me to enjoy a triumph over me. Methought I heard him say, 'Ay! I am fairly out and you fairly in! See which of us will be happiest!' "[26]

At the close of the inaugural ceremonies, Washington made his way to the Francis Hotel to pay tribute to his successor. The biographer Douglas Southall Freeman wrote: "A throng followed him at respectful distance and watched as the General was lost to view within the building. Then suddenly, as if in answer to their unvoiced bidding, the door reopened and Washington turned to acknowledge the homage of the crowd. His eyes were wet with tears as he then slowly closed the door."[27]

Before Washington closed that door, he had written a farewell address the previous fall and given it to a reporter from the *American Daily Advertiser*. On Monday, September 17, 1796, George Washington's final love letter to his country was published.

In what has become Washington's most famous public message, the Christian soldier and statesman took one last opportunity to make known his feelings about the Christian faith and the public good. He warned one last time that no one should believe "that national morality can prevail in exclusion of religious principle."[28]

Today, when a candidate speaks of Christian faith and morality, many in the audience and most in the press will turn away in scorn or speak loudly about the separation of church and state. They forget that the Father of our Country was a Christian whose faith in God and whose respect for God's Word were the central pillars of his public policy. And rather than dividing the nation, he drew the nation together. Rather than threatening the new union, he made it strong.

Washington was our first president. He died almost two hundred years ago. But before he died, he set a course for this nation that we need to follow today. And any person who would lead us would do well to remember Washington's role in our nation's past to get a clear and accurate bearing for our nation's future.

8

LEWIS AND CLARK BEGIN THEIR EXPEDITION

MAY 14, 1804

Rediscovering Respect for the Land and the People

No colorful sunrise heralded that cold, bleak day in May 1804 when William Clark and Meriwether Lewis began their journey across America's newly acquired inland wilderness. Although the trees were in blossom and the fields along the Wood River were knee-deep in corn, a deluge from the dark gray clouds overhead threatened to dampen the spirits of this small band of explorers on the first day of their adventure. Even after sunrise the temperature hovered just above freezing, and the three sergeants and thirty-eight working hands shivered with cold as they prepared to launch the boats and sail down and across the Mississippi for just a few miles before turning west up the thaw-swollen waters of the Missouri.

According to their journals, a gentle breeze was blowing that morning as Captain Clark directed the final loading of the large keelboat and the two long dugout canoes at his command. Captain Lewis was completing business for their Corps of Discovery in St. Louis, a booming frontier town on the fertile crescent of land formed by the merger of those two great American rivers. Final supplies remained to be acquired, route maps to be charted, and one last letter to President Thomas Jefferson to be sent by military courier.[1]

After all, this journey was Thomas Jefferson's idea. Somehow, his fellow Virginian, young James Monroe, had managed to purchase all of Louisiana from Napoleon's sly and shifty foreign minister, Talleyrand. In fact, the United States had just been bargaining to buy New Orleans and acquire trade routes along the inland rivers of the Louisiana Territory. Now the president was trying to discover what he had actually purchased and whether there was a route by river to the Pacific across that wide, uncharted wilderness.

Louisiana was the vast region stretching north from the mouth of the Mississippi River to its source and west to the Rockies, a tract of some 828 thousand square miles. No one knew exactly what the president had purchased with those 15 million American dollars he had wrestled from the Congress. The exact boundaries of the Louisiana Territory were unknown. But Jefferson figured at four cents an acre it had to be a bargain, even if the land was barren and the wilderness beyond claim.

Nevertheless, to find out exactly what the nation now owned, Jefferson called upon Lewis and Clark and the forty-one men they commanded to chart the waterways, map the land, and establish peaceable relationships with Indian tribes along the way.

To Meriwether Lewis, Jefferson wrote, ". . . the object of your mission is to explore the Missouri River & such principal streams of it, as, by it's course & communication with the waters of the Pacific ocean, whether the Columbia, Oregon, Colorado, or any other river, may offer the most direct & practicable watercommunication across this continent for the purposes of commerce."[2]

In his own cramped but tidy handwriting, Jefferson conveyed to his former secretary his orders for their journey in fascinating and exact detail. He wanted the inland waterways charted and maps made of the new territories they explored. He wanted to know about the soil, the vegetation, and the animals observed along the way. He wanted geological data and mineral samples collected. He wanted to know about climate and seasons, about fossils and topography. He even asked for information as divergent as volcanoes and fur trade.

But Jefferson was especially interested in the Indian nations peopling America's new frontier. Lewis and Clark were "to treat [the natives] in the most friendly and conciliatory manner." Lewis was to warn any tribes with whom they wintered about smallpox and leave medicine there for its treatment. And he was to invite a few of their influential chiefs to visit Jefferson in Washington and "to have them conveyed to this place at the public expense."

This exploration by Lewis and Clark of America's first new territory was almost a secret mission for the third president of the United States. Just a handful of farmers and their families gathered at Wood River to see the heavily laden keelboat, fifty-five feet long with one large sail and twenty-two oars, and the two accompanying dugout canoes set sail that day. A single shot was fired.[3] Then, except for the sound of oars dipping into the river and wind whipping at the little canvas sail, all was quiet on the river once again.

Only three thousand people lived in all of Washington, D.C., when our third president, Thomas Jefferson, was inaugurated there in 1800. One eyewitness described that primitive little village as "a place with a few bad houses, extensive swamps, hanging on the skirts of a too thinly peopled, weak and barren country."[4]

The president's official home had only recently received its final coat of whitewash. Pennsylvania Avenue was an empty trail cut through thick forest and infested marsh, with not a single structure standing along its mile-and-one-half axis. And Capitol Hill was barren but for the north wing of the building where the legislature met above the wide Potomac. Washington was a frontier town of dirt streets, wooden shacks and shanties, old and new store fronts, boarding houses, a few new brick homes and churches, and clearings of scarred earth and fallen trees where a young nation was building itself a home.

But Thomas Jefferson had long-term dreams for the expansion of the capital and for the expansion of the nation it served. At the heart of his dream was that great, uncharted wilderness called the Louisiana Territory. The purchase, exploration, and development of that important piece of real estate made it possible for this nation to expand from a cluster of states clinging to the Atlantic coastline to a mighty nation stretching across the continent. Looking back on that great doubling of the land and the president whose foresight and wisdom helped it happen, we see one of the most exciting and instructive lessons from our nation's early history.

Thomas Jefferson ranks among the most brilliant and creative men ever to serve the American public. In an address to a gala White House dinner honoring America's Nobel Prize winners in 1962, John F. Kennedy stood before a crowd of America's great scientists, artists, and diplomats and said, "I think this is the most extraordinary collection of talent, of human knowledge, that has ever been gathered in the White House, with the possible exception of when Thomas Jefferson dined here alone."[5]

Near the end of Jefferson's life, he asked that his three most satisfying accomplishments be carved into his marble memorial: the writing of the Declaration of Independence, the writing of the Virginia Declaration of Religious Freedom, and the founding of the University of Virginia. But the Lewis and Clark expedition into the Louisiana Territory really should be included among his greatest achievements.

In Jefferson's instructions to Lewis and Clark, and in their careful commitment to those instructions, we are reminded of the two most important guidelines for moving a nation gracefully into the future: cherish the land, and cherish the people of the land. In those two instructions, the first based on the Old Testament account of creation and its care, the second based on the life and teachings of Jesus, Jefferson showed us how to be a frontier people, how to explore and develop any new territory that we discover for our good and for the good of all humanity.

He Cherished the Land

In his first inaugural address, Thomas Jefferson, then fifty-seven years old, described the new nation as "kindly separated by nature and a wide ocean from the exterminating havoc of one quarter of the globe; . . . *possessing a chosen country, with room enough for our citizens to the thousandth generation* [italics mine]."[6]

Jefferson was never too busy caring for the present to spend some extra time and energy caring for the future. One can't plan much further ahead than a thousand generations; yet on his inauguration day, Jefferson was already looking that far into the future. He anticipated havoc in Europe that would send immigrants to the New World in ever-increasing waves. He foresaw our constant and rapid population growth and knew that the original limits of the land placed upon the colonies by King George III would not be adequate.

Just thirty-seven years before Jefferson's inauguration day, King George had proclaimed the boundaries of his original colonies as extending from western Florida north into the Canadian plains. The land beginning on the western slope of the Appalachian Mountains and extending to the Mississippi River the king had designated as Indian reserves. The Louisiana Territory, the vast and uncharted lands stretching west beyond the Mississippi, had been claimed by France in the name of Louis XIV in 1682, had been traded to Spain in 1762, and had been transferred back to Napoleon of France about the time of Jefferson's inauguration. Our third president watched and waited with more than casual interest as France and Spain battled for ownership of America's front yard.

Among Jefferson's endless scientific interests was amateur cartography. He had measured and mapped portions of his beloved Virginia, especially around his home at Monticello. He had studied the parchment maps of the original colonial grants and the birch bark maps of the few hardy souls who had ventured into the wilderness. Jefferson knew that the states, recently united, clung to the eastern edge of vast land. Few people had crossed the Appalachian Mountains, let alone seen the wide Missouri or Mississippi rivers. And what plains and mountains, rivers and deserts lay between those boundaries and the distant glimmering Pacific were a mystery. At his inauguration, Jefferson was already making plans to solve that mystery with an expedition into the wilderness led by his own personal secretary, Meriwether Lewis, with William Clark as adjutant, or coleader.

Jefferson's inaugural address claiming enough land for a thousand American generations was a clue to the president's dream for the future of the lands between the Appalachians and the Pacific Ocean. And though they were then owned by Europeans, Jefferson could not resist his urge to navigate the great river systems and explore and chart the mountains and plains waiting there. He was afraid that Napoleon's gunboats would seal up the Mississippi at New Orleans and limit our use of the territory's river systems. So Jefferson instructed our ambassador in France to begin immediate negotiations to buy New Orleans and secure for this nation the privilege of navigating the rivers of the territory.

Jefferson knew the nation would grow westward, and he began immediately to prepare the way to accommodate that growth. While most Americans were putting down roots along the Atlantic coastline, Jefferson was reaching for the Pacific. While Washington was just a frontier town itself, Jefferson was dreaming of cities, territories, and states across the wilderness.

Jefferson was never too preoccupied with the known to be curious about the unknown. Maps of the Louisiana Territory covered with imaginary seas, rivers, mountains, and deserts existed even before the Lewis and Clark expedition. The only honest maps of the area were blank. Jefferson wanted desperately to fill in those blanks.

Jefferson's lifelong calling had been to fill in missing information in various fields from anatomy to zoology. "I have sworn upon the altar of God," he said in a letter to his friend Benjamin Rush, "eternal hostility against every form of tyranny over the mind of men."[7] To Jefferson, blankness was a kind of tyranny. Not knowing what lay out there beyond the limits made it impossible for him to plan. For our third president, the first requisite of good planning was "to possess the country for the mind."[8] He had been trying for two decades to get the Louisiana Territory explored, but without success.

In 1784 when Jefferson was minister to France, he urged John Ledyard of Connecticut, who had been in the Pacific on Captain Cook's famous expedition, to explore the great Northwest and West, via Russia and Siberia. But when Jefferson approached Catherine the Great of Russia for permission for his young protégé to begin the journey, she refused. And when Ledyard traveled to Russia to seek permission, he was arrested, taken to the Polish border, and deported.

Ten years later, while Jefferson was Washington's secretary of state in 1793, he encouraged André Michaux, a French botanist, to make the journey into Louisiana, warning him to watch carefully for any signs of the giant prehistoric mammoths, whose bones had been found in Kentucky. But Michaux turned out to be an agent provocateur of Citizen Genet, ambassador to America from the new French republic, and that expedition went down in a cloud of military muscle-flexing and steamy political rhetoric.

For more than twenty years Jefferson lobbied with private individuals and with the colonial and federal governments to see what lay out there beyond the borders. Though each attempt failed, Jefferson persisted. He placed the exploration at the top of the agenda for his first term as president. He was determined that Lewis and Clark would succeed where everyone else had failed. The nation would expand and the president would prepare the way. And when Congress hesitated at giving Jefferson the $2,500 he needed to start up the Lewis and Clark expedition, he answered them in an eloquent and persuasive secret presidential message: "While other civilized nations have encountered great expense to enlarge the boundaries of knowledge, by undertaking voyages of discovery, and for other literary purposes, in various parts and directions, our nation seems to owe to the same object, as well as to its own interests, to explore this, the only line of easy communication across the continent, and so directly traversing our own part of it."[9]

Jefferson knew it cost money to fill in the blanks, and he wasn't above appealing to self-interest to get the funding needed. To excite the Congress, Jefferson said the expedition was commercial. To get Spain's permission to cross her territory, Jefferson suggested that the mission was purely "literary."[10]

Jefferson wasn't lying. His motivations for exploring the region were both commercial and scientific. He hoped that somewhere in that wilderness the Missouri and Columbia rivers would unite, providing the long-dreamed-of Northwest Passage to the Pacific.

But above all other motivations was Jefferson's life-long love of the land and his all-consuming curiosity about its mysteries. For many years he had been a gardener, planting rare trees, flowers, and grass in the soil at Monticello. He had written a "Garden Book" reporting his discoveries there. He was a farmer as well and walked the fields around his Virginia estate, supervising the cultivation, planting, and harvesting of his crops. He wrote a "Farm Book," again describing what the land had taught him.

Jefferson cherished the earth and envied the men who toiled there. "Those who labor in the earth," he said, "are chosen people of God, if ever he had a chosen people, whose breasts He has made His peculiar deposit for substantial and genuine virtue."

From the beginning of his long and fruitful political career, our third president used the language of the soil. "The tree of liberty must be refreshed," he admonished, "with the blood of patriots and tyrants. It is its natural manure."[11]

Throughout his long and productive lifetime, Jefferson was an impassioned student of natural history and all the natural sciences. His commitment to the earth and all its wonders prepared Jefferson uniquely to launch an expedition into the waiting wilderness.

The Spanish had sent soldiers to the New World in search of fabled cities of gold, and the French had sent seasoned mountain men in search of furs and the Indians who would trade them. But Jefferson had another kind of explorer in mind. Lewis and Clark were, in fact, military men. They had proved themselves tough, courageous, and creative under fire. And they were trained and experienced in wilderness survival. But Jefferson's goals for this expedition into the newly gained Louisiana Territory would demand much more than military expertise or survival on the journey.

Before Lewis and Clark could begin, Jefferson sent them to Philadelphia to be trained in natural history with Benjamin Smith Barton and

Caspar Wistar, in astronomy with Robert Patterson and Andrew Elli-cott, and in medicine with Jefferson's friend Benjamin Rush. They learned to use the sextant for determining latitude and longitude by the sun, the moon, and the stars. They learned to use the theodolite for measuring horizontal and vertical angles. They studied botany, zoology, cartography, geography, and meteorology. Jefferson saw these two men as his eyes and ears in the wilderness, and he trained them as he had trained himself.

His handwritten instructions to them should be mounted in the National Archives next to the Declaration of Independence and the Constitution. Each line reveals Jefferson's love of the earth and his curiosity about all things above and below it. "Your observations are to be taken with great pains and accuracy," he commanded, warning them to copy their extensive notes at the end of every day to protect them "against the accidental losses to which they will be exposed." He even recommended that one of the copies be made on "the cuticular membranes of the paper-birch, as less liable to injury from damp than common paper."

Jefferson wanted information on "the soil and the face of the country, its growth and vegetable productions." He wanted a complete description of each animal they observed along the way, and asked that remains or fossils of animals be collected. He wanted them to look below the earth for minerals, "metals, limestone, pitcoal, & saltpetre; salines and mineral waters." He wanted them to look above the earth to measure "climate . . . the proportion of rainy, cloudy & clear days, by lightening, hail, snow, ice, by the access and recess of frost, by the winds prevailing at different seasons, the dates at which particular plants put forth or lose their flowers, or leaf, times of appearance of particular birds, reptiles or insects."[12] Jefferson also wanted the rivers mapped and the mountains measured.

And Lewis and Clark seized the opportunity with both hands. Their geographical accomplishments are astounding. They achieved Jefferson's goal to chart the Missouri and its principal streams. They failed at finding a river route to the Pacific only because there was none. They were the first to discover the incredible breadth of our land. They learned that instead of one major mountain system separating the Missouri headwaters from the Pacific, there were two, the Rockies and the Cascades. They discovered and named hundreds of important topographical features in the west. As Paul Russell Cutwright observes:

"Today more towns, rivers, creeks, counties, animals, and plants bear the names of Lewis and Clark than any other figures in American history with the possible exception of such illustrious leaders as Washington, Jefferson, Franklin, and Lincoln."[13]

In zoology, Lewis and Clark discovered and reported to their mentor numerous fish, reptiles, birds, and mammals unheard of previously. They collected bird skins, horns, bones, hides, and a treasure trove of other materials and shipped them east for study. Their journals report in thorough and accurate detail their sightings of 122 different species and subspecies of animal life, including the first studies of the American grizzly, the mountain lion, the Oregon bobcat, and the Missouri beaver.

In botany, Lewis and Clark were the first to study plants indigenous to the western plains, mountains, deserts, and river valleys. Their reports included detailed information on 178 different kinds of plant life (117 can be found today in the Lewis and Clark Herbarium at the Academy of Natural Sciences of Philadelphia). They collected and preserved specimens of herbs, shrubs, and trees in the remote areas of our country. They introduced seeds, roots, and cuttings from the West, and with Jefferson's enthusiastic support they soon had them growing in the eastern regions.

In cartography, they mapped the West thoroughly. America made its claim to Oregon and established a beachhead on the Pacific based on the findings of Lewis and Clark. And the journals of their expedition, once published, became one of "the glories of American history." Paul Russell Cutwright paraphrases Elliott Coues thus: "The more closely they are scanned, in light of present knowledge, the more luminous they appear."[14]

"O Lord, our Lord, . . ./When I consider Your heavens, the work of Your fingers . . . ."[15] I believe Jefferson and his colaborers took seriously God's command to cherish the earth. In the years that followed, covered wagons carried families that were guided on their journey by the vision of Thomas Jefferson and the maps of Lewis and Clark.

He Cherished the People of the Land

But in his careful instructions to Lewis and Clark at the beginning of their journey, Jefferson was even more specific about their treatment of the Indian peoples they would meet along the way. He ordered the explorers to acquaint themselves carefully

> with the names of the nations & their numbers; their relations with other tribes or nations; their language, traditions, monuments; their ordinary occupations in agriculture, fishing, hunting, war, arts, & the implements for these; their food, clothing and domestic accommodations; the diseases prevalent among them, & the remedies they use; moral and physical circumstances which distinguish them from the tribes we know; peculiarities in their laws, customs, and dispositions; and articles of commerce they may need or furnish, and . . . what knowledge you can of the state of morality, religion and information among them.[16]

Those orders reflected the curiosity of Jefferson, the scientist. But the words that followed reflected the commitments of Jefferson, the humanitarian and student of Jesus' life and teachings: "In all your intercourse with the natives, treat them in the most friendly and conciliatory manner," he ordered. Then he instructed Lewis and Clark to carry medicine for smallpox and "encourage them [the Indians] in the use of it."[17]

Compare the journey of Lewis and Clark among the great Indian nations in the Louisiana Territory to the adventures of Andrew Jackson in Florida. Compare Father Junipero Serra's journey through California with the Spanish conquistadors in North and South America. The military men left a trail of bloodshed and hatred. Lewis and Clark, Father Serra, and those who followed in their spirit left an open door to peace and understanding.

Jefferson believed that "the care of human life and happiness, and not their destruction, is the first and only legitimate object of good government."[18] Jefferson's sentiments can easily be traced to his respect for the teachings of Jesus, which "if filled up in the true style and spirit of the rich fragments he left us would be the most perfect and sublime that has ever been taught by man."[19]

It would be naive, however, to think that Jefferson was always a tower of virtue in dealing with the Indians. In 1781, while governor of Virginia and still at war with the British and their Shawnee allies, Jefferson is reported to have muttered angrily, "The same world will scarcely do for them and for us." And though Lewis and Clark accomplished an amazingly peaceful journey, their party was once forced to fire upon an attacking group of Indian braves, killing two of them.

Still, by every possible standard, Lewis and Clark opened the West in peace. They did more than simply pass out their medallions inscribed with a picture of Jefferson on one side and two hands clasped in friendship below a peace pipe on the other. They lived with the Indians and studied their ways. They shared medical knowledge and supplies. When they could, they ministered directly to the immediate health and safety problems within and among the tribes. They secured the release of Indian prisoners and saw them returned safely to their homes and families.

Lewis and Clark initiated the first official relations between the United States government and the Indians of the Missouri Valley, the Rocky Mountains, and the Columbia watershed. They actually "discovered" such important tribes as the Shoshone, the Flathead, the Nez Perce, the Yakima, the Walula, and the Wishrams. They defined and described the great Indian cultural areas of the West, namely, plains, plateau, and northwest coast. They instituted the first studies of at least six new Indian language groups. And they recorded the only available information on the Chinook tribes that became extinct just years after their journey.

Everywhere they traveled, Lewis and Clark left a legacy of friendship among the Indian peoples. The Indians remembered these first loving encounters with the white men and preserved them in their own legends and folklore. Tragically those legends would soon be tested by an ugly epoch in American history when the rights and lives of the Indian peoples were not cherished as Jefferson and Lewis and Clark had cherished them.

The history of this nation's relationships with its native Indian peoples is checkered. Sometimes we only remember the bloodshed and betrayals, the broken treaties and piles of fallen bodies. But we must remember, too, that along those same peaceful trails that Lewis and Clark opened into the wilderness marched missionaries like Dr. Marcus Whitman and his wife, Narcissa, who taught the Indians to farm and to pray. Another was the Christian mountain man, Jedediah Smith, who "made the lone wilderness his place of meditation, the mountaintop his altar, and . . . religion an active, practical principle, from the duties of which nothing could seduce him."[20]

It was inevitable that the nation would grow. Explorers, fur traders, mountain men, soldiers and settlers followed the great trails west across the Louisiana Territory. The borders were widened even farther by the addition of Florida in 1819, Texas in 1845, and Oregon in 1846. The continental boundaries were completed in 1848 with the Treaty of Guadalupe Hidalgo and the addition of California and the great Southwest. In 1853 southern Arizona was added with the Gadsden Purchase, and in 1867 we acquired Alaska.

The Closing of the American Frontier

We were a frontier people, but in 1879 the frontiers were closed. We would annex the Hawaiian Islands on July 7, 1898, and establish claims in Puerto Rico, Guam, and the Philippines that same year, but there were to be no more uncharted open spaces. Until 1879 the United States Census Bureau had accepted an arbitrary definition of the "frontier" as an area containing not fewer than two nor more than six inhabitants to the square mile. Lines were drawn on the census maps in each decade to mark the location of those frontiers. Gradually the western lines merged with the lines traveling east, and in 1890 the superintendent of the census posted a historic bulletin that went almost unnoticed. The frontier, he announced, had been closed.

On January 10, 1807, just eighty-three years before those frontiers closed forever, Meriwether Lewis appeared at Thomas Jefferson's home in Monticello after charting that first great wilderness frontier. Captain Meriwether opened his trunks of magnificent treasures: horns of black-tailed deer and mountain ram; buffalo robes and other colorful Indian dress and headwear; carefully preserved animal skeletons and pelts and skins of the red fox, white hare, and antelope; earthen pots filled with seeds, leaves, cuttings, and roots; and cages filled with living squirrels, magpies, prairie hens, mice, and even tiny insects.

Greatest among the treasures stood the smiling king and queen of the Mandan Indian peoples. Jefferson greeted Lewis warmly and welcomed the Indian leaders with the pomp and pageantry reserved for European royalty. It was a moment this nation must remember. Picture it— Jefferson and the king and queen of an American Indian tribe hang a weird but wonderful collection of treasures on the walls of Monticello, stuffed heads and horns of elk, deer, and buffalo, Indian artifacts, and painted Indian robes. Then Jefferson leads the king and queen to his garden, opens a tin of seeds, kneels down in the soil and plants them. Together they tamp down the loose soil and then walk together in the quiet garden, the president and American Indian royalty chatting amiably through their interpreter and mutual friend, Meriwether Lewis.

When Jefferson retired from active political life, he returned to Monticello and spent his remaining years continuing his scientific experiments, writing letters, and tending his precious garden. "I am an old man," he wrote, "but a young gardener."[21] It is time once again to water the seeds he planted deep in this nation's history. As we stand before the new frontiers around us, above us, and below us, we need to remember how much he cherished the land and how much he cherished the people who lived upon it.

9

CHARLES FINNEY'S SERMON AT UTICA (AMERICA'S SECOND GREAT AWAKENING)

FEBRUARY 3, 1825

Rediscovering the Power of Spiritual Renewal for Social Change

On that Sunday morning, a Presbyterian church in Utica, New York, was jammed with parishioners, visitors from churches across the city, and students from nearby Hamilton College. Among the undergraduates present was Theodore Weld, an angry young campus leader who had been tricked into attending by his devout and wily maiden aunt. The church's pastor, Reverend Aiken, had been scheduled to speak, but at the last minute Charles Finney, a visiting evangelist, took his place.

"One sinner destroyeth much good," Finney began, looking down from the pulpit directly into the eyes of Theodore Weld.[1]

The poor, unsuspecting fellow had been squeezed into a front pew between this aunt and her collaborating friends to prevent his escape. Weld, a forceful orator in his own right, had been outspoken in his criticism of Charles Finney and the nightly revival meetings being held in that church.

But his aunt, with whom he boarded, had pestered her nephew to attend the services until he felt forced to oblige. "I began to preach," Finney wrote about that night in his *Memoirs,* "and to show in a great many instances, how one sinner might destroy much good, and how the influence of one man might destroy a great many souls. I suppose that I drew a pretty vivid picture of Weld, and of what his influence was, and what mischief he might do." Finney must have been watching the young student carefully, because the evangelist remembered Weld's awkward and embarrassed response: "Once or twice he made an effort to get out; but his aunt perceiving it, would throw herself forward, and lean on the slip in front, and engage in silent prayer, and he could not get out without arousing and annoying her."[2] Finally the sermon and the service ended. Weld stormed from the revival service, determined to get revenge for the personal attack he had received at the hands of Charles Finney.

That next morning he went looking for the evangelist and found him in a little store on the main street of Utica. "He fell upon me very unceremoniously," Finney remembered, "and talked to me in a most abusive manner . . . . His tongue ran incessantly." Apparently, Weld "was gifted in language" and soon had attracted a large crowd of curious bystanders. "All business ceased," Finney recalled, "and all gave themselves up to listening to his vituperation."[3] Finney waited quietly. He loved a good battle, and he admired the boy's courage. Besides, Weld was right. Finney, the Reverend Aiken, and Weld's aunt had conspired against him. Of course, they sincerely believed it was for his own good, but that certainly was no defense; so Finney answered just a few words. Weld ended his angry tirade and left the room.

Charles Finney was famous for his pointed sermons. He was criticized by clergy and laity alike for his confrontational, almost slanderous approach to preaching; yet God used his direct, even abusive, style to stop people like Weld in their tracks just long enough to get them to listen. And often, as in Weld's case, the results in changed lives were well worth the risk.

That night, Weld returned to his aunt's home to apologize to Finney. But Finney took him by the hand, assured him that there was no need to apologize, and urged the boy "to give his heart to God." Later Weld told Finney that on that evening, "He walked his room by turns, and by turns he lay upon the floor. He continued the whole night in that terrible state of mind, angry, rebellious, and yet so convicted that he could scarcely live."[4]

Finney stood to preach the following evening and was pleased and a bit surprised to see Theodore Weld sitting in the back of the church. Suddenly the student stood up and interrupted the sermon. Finney didn't know what would happen next. But the boy, instead of renewing his angry attack, made a humble public confession of faith.

Weld told the entire congregation about the long previous night when "a pressure came upon him that crushed him down to the floor; and with it came a voice that seemed to command him to repent, to repent now. He said it broke him down to the floor, and there he lay, until, late in the morning, his aunt coming up, found him upon the floor calling himself a thousand fools; and to all human appearance, with his heart all broken to pieces."[5]

Theodore Weld quit Hamilton College that same day and joined Finney as a student and coworker in ministry. Although the abrupt and offensive techniques of Finney and the seemingly hysterical response of Weld would be called pathological by modern standards, the fact is that through Charles Finney the life of young Theodore Weld was revolutionized. And through Weld and his amazing contributions to the abolition of slavery and the cause of women's suffrage, the history of our nation was changed forever.

When Theodore Weld was born in 1803, only 5,305,937 people were living in the thirteen original American states on a fairly narrow strip of land between the Atlantic and the Appalachian Mountains. But by 1860, the nation's population had grown 600 percent to 31,443,322 people, and the land they occupied stretched across the entire continent to the Pacific Ocean. This rapid, unwieldy expansion of our nation's size and the sudden, unsettling explosion of population caught the country unaware and devastated old lifestyles and values.

In the seventeenth and eighteenth centuries, Americans worked the soil and lived on farms and plantations. They grew up in tightly knit family units. They attended the same schools and churches their fathers and grandfathers had attended. And they inherited a shared sense of values and traditions from their colonial ancestors. The old way may have seemed narrow and constricting, but it was safe and certain.

But by 1825 when Charles Finney began his revival meetings in Weld's hometown, the old ways seemed gone forever. People were living in rapidly growing population centers and working in factories and office buildings. With the growth of these great, sprawling cities, it was difficult, if not impossible, to maintain traditions. Church attendance was no longer required by law. Shared moral values were no longer enforced by town marshals and civil magistrates. A new sense of freedom blossomed in the cities, but with that freedom came disorientation. Traditional roots had been pulled up out of the country soil, and people were having trouble replanting them in the city.

A confusing mix of religious and moral options faced Theodore Weld and his fellow students at Hamilton College. Robert Ingersoll and his atheist predecessors were lecturing against the Bible and Jesus' divinity. The deists and the transcendentalists were departing from the core of Christian faith without attacking it directly. The Unitarian and Universalist churches seemed cold and intellectual. And the fervor and excitement of the Great Awakening of the Wesleys, George Whitefield, and Jonathan Edwards had become institutionalized in dry, dull, defensive denominational churches. It is estimated that in 1800 fewer than 7 percent of the people had any formal membership in a local church or denomination.[6] Theodore Weld, like the nation, was ready for another spiritual renewal.

The president of Yale, Timothy Dwight, began to preach and teach revival at the close of the eighteenth century. His students, especially Congregationalist preacher Lyman Beecher and Yale theologian Nathaniel W. Taylor, carried on the revival. But this nation's second Great Awakening really began to flourish under the preaching of Charles G. Finney.

Finney and the Second Great Awakening

Charles Grandison Finney was a sensitive, self-taught lawyer from Oneida County, New York. He was six feet, two inches tall, handsome, erect, alert, full of energy, an athlete, a musician, and a dancer. His father had been a soldier in Washington's Continental Army and reared his family on a farm in primitive pioneer conditions. Finney had almost no religious training as a child, but he was converted without the aid of preacher or evangelist as he studied the Bible on his own.

Finney himself had known the long night of agony that Theodore Weld experienced after hearing Finney preach in Utica. In his *Memoirs,* Finney recalled that winter night alone in his new law office when he felt he "met the Lord Jesus Christ face to face." The experience came as a complete surprise. "I wept aloud like a child," he said, "and made such confessions as I could with my choked utterance. It seemed to me that I bathed his feet with my tears."[7]

After continuing in this emotional state for much of the evening, Finney went into his living quarters and was about to stir up a dying fire in the fireplace when God stirred up another kind of fire within him. "I received a mighty baptism of the Holy Ghost. Without any expectation of it, without ever having thought in my mind that there was any such thing for me, without any recollection that I had ever heard the thing mentioned by any person in the world, the Holy Spirit descended upon me in a manner that seemed to go through me, body and soul. I could feel the impression, like a wave of electricity, going through and through me . . . in waves of liquid love . . . . It seemed like the very breath of God."[8]

Finney quit his law practice immediately and submitted himself to candidacy for the Presbyterian ministry. His pastoral advisor suggested he enroll in Princeton, but Finney was impatient to begin his ministry. In spite of the lack of formal theological training, he was ordained in 1824 and began a series of evangelistic tours God would use to launch the second Great Awakening.

For Charles Finney, the solution to humanity's dilemma was simple. It was found in the Bible. Men and women had been created by God. They had sinned and needed God's forgiveness. God offered that forgiveness through the life, death, and resurrection of His only Son, Jesus. Any man, woman, or child who confessed his or her sins would be forgiven. And Finney believed that in a "second work of God's grace," God's Holy Spirit would move into that forgiven person, providing victory over sin and death forever.

Finney's enthusiasm for the gospel and his commitment to its power to change lives could not be contained. From the pulpit he pleaded with people like Theodore Weld to come to the front of the tent or auditorium, to sit or kneel at a mourners' bench before the congregation, and to pray publicly for God's forgiveness. Finney was direct, naming people in the audience, appealing to their reason, warning them against resisting the call of God in their lives, and kneeling to pray beside them, where they responded to his prayers with tears of repentance and shouts of joy.

The Second Great Awakening and Spiritual Change

The revival swept first through New England among Congregationalists, Presbyterians, Methodists, and especially the Baptists. Then it moved down to the Mid-Atlantic states, into the South and out across the Appalachian Mountains to the frontier farms and settlements. Tens of thousands of lives were changed. The Baptists grew from 100 thousand members across the nation in 1800 to more than 800 thousand members at the mid-century mark.[9] And though critics inside and outside the church warned that Finney's emphasis on personal salvation would have only short-term effect on a handful of people, the second Great Awakening brought massive and permanent spiritual changes to this country and the world.

The spirit of revival in America led to a growing concern on the part of those most affected by it for spiritual renewal in other nations. New Christians longed to share their faith. Across the nation, individual churches began to organize small societies to sponsor mission work at home and abroad. Almost at the same time, these local societies organized to form national organizations for world mission. The Congregational Church created the American Board of Commissioners for Foreign Missions in 1810, and it sent Luther Rice and Adoniram Judson to India. The Baptists formed their General Missionary Convention about the same time; the Presbyterians followed in 1817; the Methodists did likewise in 1818; and the Episcopalians joined the effort in 1820.

Other nondenominational societies were formed to distribute Bibles and tracts, to promote education and the Sunday school, and to organize nationwide charity and reform efforts. The American Education Society was formed in 1815. The American Bible Society was organized in 1816. The American Sunday School Union and the American Tract Society followed in 1817 and 1825.[10]

The Second Great Awakening and Social Change

The second Great Awakening led to social reform as well as spiritual renewal. In 1826, the American Society for the Promotion of Temperance was formed to help slow the alarming growth of alcoholism and drunkenness in the country. The temperance movement, which led to the ill-fated experiment with constitutional prohibition in 1920, traces its origins in America to the Reverend Lyman Beecher's 1813 sermon, preached during one of his New England revival campaigns. The American Peace Society was founded in 1828, and the American Anti-Slavery Society was formed in New England in 1831.

The Christian Abolitionists

Voices had been calling for the abolition of slavery in America for almost two hundred years, from the very first day in August 1619 when Africans were brought to Jamestown on a Dutch trading vessel. Yet 156 years passed before Benjamin Franklin and a handful of Quakers in Pennsylvania formed the first antislavery society on April 14, 1775.

America had 650 thousand slaves by then, 90 percent in southern states, where agricultural economy was thought to be dependent on the slave trade. By the time of the Constitutional Convention in 1787, the debate over the institution of slavery was heating up between North and South. In the northern states, where slavery was of minor economic importance, Massachusetts had already emancipated its slaves, and the process of emancipation was well on its way in New Hampshire, Connecticut, Rhode Island, and Pennsylvania.[11]

Although men and women of good will, North and South, believed that slavery should and eventually would end in the United States, nobody had created a timetable to guarantee the abolishment. Even the Quakers were divided over the issue, and almost without exception abolitionists saw the ending of slavery as a long and gradual process. In 1787, at the time of the Constitutional Convention, little hope was held that slavery could be condemned in the nation's Constitution. Such an act would have ended all hope for its ratification. Picture it: "On one hand, a blow at slavery, however masked and glancing, in the Constitution itself would have invited certain rejection in the southern states. . . . On the other, any additional display of tolerance . . . would have invited rejection in the North."[12]

The framers were searching for a workable compromise, and that compromise still hadn't been found when Thomas Jefferson warned: "the day is not distant when it [the nation] must bear and adopt [emancipation], or worse will follow . . . . If, on the contrary, it is left to force itself on, human nature must shudder at the prospect held up."[13]

The abolition of slavery was seen as a necessarily long, slow process by almost everyone in America *until* the second Great Awakening. To

Finney, to Weld, and to a growing number of those "new way" evangelical Christians at the heart of the nineteenth-century revival, slavery was a sin. And sin of any kind could not be tolerated. Nor was eliminating sin a long, slow process. It was, rather, an immediate and necessary act.

"When I first went to New York," Finney recalled in his *Memoirs,* "I had made up my mind on the question of slavery, and was exceedingly anxious to arouse public attention to the subject. I did not, however, turn aside to make it a hobby, or divert the attention of the people from the work of converting souls. Nevertheless, in my prayers and preaching, I so often alluded to slavery, and denounced it, that a considerable excitement came to exist among the people."[14]

The "considerable excitement" that Finney's preaching stirred up resulted indirectly in Harriet Beecher Stowe's *Uncle Tom's Cabin* and the ground swell of antislavery sentiment that rapidly led to Abraham Lincoln's Emancipation Proclamation and the end of slavery in the nation. How Charles Finney, Theodore Weld, and the second Great Awakening influenced Harriet Beecher Stowe, the writing of *Uncle Tom's Cabin,* and the eventual end of the institution of slavery is a fascinating and little-known story.

Harriet Beecher Stowe

Harriet Beecher Stowe was born on June 14, 1811, to the Reverend Lyman Beecher, the Congregationalist minister whose evangelistic preaching helped launch the second Great Awakening and whose stand against alcoholism and drunkenness led to the founding of the American Temperance Union. Harriet's sister Catharine was the founder of the American Woman's Educational Association, an organization active in establishing schools for girls throughout the Midwest. Her brother, William Ward Beecher, was a controversial, evangelical preacher like his father.

When Lyman Beecher was appointed president of Lane Seminary in Cincinnati, Harriet Beecher moved to Ohio to be with her father. There she fell in love with a recently widowed theology professor, Calvin Stowe, whom she married in 1836. But first, in 1833 Harriet Stowe met Theodore Weld, a first-year theology student at Lane Seminary. After his conversion, Weld had studied and traveled with Finney for several years and then begun his seminary training at Lane. Harriet Beecher had already experienced the radical spiritual renewal so typical of the second Great Awakening. But in Theodore Weld she would experience the radical social commitment of that great revival as well.

Under Finney's tutelage, Weld learned the biblical view of sin and its effects on man's personal life and society. He believed that sin could be forgiven through Christ and that individuals and society could be liberated from its power and from its immediate and long-range consequences. Anything that was destructive or dehumanizing to human life was seen as sin, and sin, whether personal or corporate, must be confronted and overthrown, whatever the price.

Together, Finney and Weld studied the Old Testament stories of the tribes of Israel liberated by God from Egyptian slavery. They studied the life and teachings of Jesus, who gave his life for the emancipation of all humanity. Like Finney, Weld made his decision. Slavery was sin. The slave system was destructive to slave and master alike. And sin in every form must be rooted out. It could not be tolerated, not even temporarily. Therefore, the abolition of slavery could not be a gradual process. Slavery must be attacked and overthrown through the power of God's Holy Spirit in the believer's life.

During Weld's first year at Lane, he began the Lane Anti-Slavery Society. He and other Lane students opened a night school for freed slaves on the campus. They taught black adults and children to read and write. They held picnics on the campus lawn for ex-slaves, men and women alike, and were seen walking through the town, black and white together. It was just 1833. Kentucky was only a few miles away. Needless to say, the "radical" behavior of Weld and the other evangelical students scandalized certain powerful citizens of Cincinnati and members of the Lane Seminary Board of Trustees.

Lyman Beecher was an evangelical and an abolitionist. He had even enrolled an ex-slave as an official student at Lane, a courageous act far before its socially accepted time in America. But Beecher believed in gradual abolition, and Weld's tactics weren't gradual by anybody's standards. In fact, Weld's campus antislavery group had become a station on the underground railroad. Slaves "liberated" from their masters were being housed, trained, and equipped by Lane students. The seminary, its staff and students, its patrons, and the citizens of Cincinnati entered into a debate about slavery that introduced Harriet Beecher Stowe to the issue and motivated her to begin a study of slavery on her own.

When Weld was not satisfied that Lane Seminary was moving quickly enough toward immediate and total abolition, he led an exodus of students, especially the members of the Lane Seminary Anti-Slavery Society, to newly formed Oberlin College. That act led to great trauma in the Beecher household and to the eventual demise of Lane Seminary. Whatever Harriet Beecher Stowe felt about Weld's antislavery tactics, however, she was convinced he was right about the institution of slavery.

"The slave system," she wrote, "as a *system* perhaps concentrates more wrong than any other now existing . . . ." And later, in an eloquent warning to the country, she added, "No nation can remain free with whom freedom is privilege and not a principle."[15]

Later in her life when she commented on the tactical disagreement between her father and Weld, she wrote to praise "the vigorous, radical young men" of Lane Seminary, "headed by that brilliant, eccentric genius, Theodore D. Weld," who transformed Lane Seminary into "an antislavery fort." As one biographer points out, "she ignores the fact that they failed to carry Lyman Beecher with them and consequently 'blew up the fort.' "[16]

Cincinnati's proximity to Kentucky gave Harriet Beecher Stowe almost instant access to firsthand knowledge of the slave system. She spent time observing slaves and their owners on a nearby plantation that she later called Colonel Shelby's place in *Uncle Tom's Cabin*.

Stowe was a Connecticut-born Yankee who never lived in the South, but she met and talked at length to many southern men and women as she prepared her novel. She interviewed slaves and slave owners, abolitionists and antiabolitionists alike. She collected hundreds of case histories of slaves, their mistreatment, their escapes, their recaptures, and their returns. She carefully verified each story and filed them in her memory. Gradually she was transformed by what her one-woman investigation was uncovering.

In 1850, by then the busy mother of six young children, Harriet Stowe moved with her husband to Brunswick, Maine, where she felt a divine call to begin writing down the stories about slavery she had uncovered in her seventeen-year investigation. In the evenings she read those stories to Calvin and their children. Eventually a weekly abolitionist journal published them, and on March 20, 1852, it issued them as a two-part novel titled *Uncle Tom's Cabin*.

Mrs. Stowe decided to attack slavery as a system in her novel and not to attack the men and women of the South, whom she felt were as victimized by that system as were the black men and women they owned.

"The great error of controversy," she affirmed, "is that it is ever ready to assail *persons* rather than *principles*." Mrs. Stowe had been transformed into an avid Christian abolitionist by her research, but not into an avid anti-Southerner. In fact, she was convinced that the white Southerners she had met, at least most of them, were "enlightened, generous, and amenable to reason." She was convinced that enemies of slavery were wrong to attack Southerners and wanted the attack to be focused directly on the system itself. "If the system alone is attacked," she said, those same white Southerners "will be the first to perceive its evils, and to turn against it; but if the system be attacked through individuals, self-love, wounded pride, and a thousand natural feelings, will be at once enlisted for its preservation."[17]

Though Mrs. Stowe struggled to keep the debate about slavery from deteriorating into an ugly, painful confrontation between people of equally good will, she failed. Upon the publication of *Uncle Tom's Cabin*, she herself became a target for men and women representing almost every side of the slavery issue. Each day at least one full bag of mail was delivered to her home in Maine. Most of the letters were written by angry readers convinced she had gone too far or convinced she hadn't gone far enough.

Uncle Tom's Cabin sold more copies in those next few years than almost any other book up to that time in the history of American publishing.[18] And the waves of antislavery sentiment that her book helped create led directly to the Civil War, Lincoln's Emancipation Proclamation, and the end of the institution of slavery in America.

The evangelical abolitionist Theodore Weld went on to become an agent for the American Anti-Slavery Society, preaching against slavery and organizing chapters throughout Ohio and the western portions of New York and Pennsylvania. His success led to the training of agents like himself. The facts that Weld chose seventy, as Jesus chose seventy "and sent them . . . into every city and place,"[19] and that "their method was the evangelism of the Great Revival, that their doctrine was a doctrine of sin and their program was to convert congregations" once again illustrated the influence of Finney and the second Great Awakening on the life of our nation.[20]

In 1835 just 225 Auxiliaries of the American Anti-Slavery Society operated in the northern states; by 1838, thanks to Weld and his friends, 1,346 local antislavery groups; and by 1840, 1,650 chapters with a total of 130,000 to 170,000 members. In 1837 and 1838 alone, this group, founded and staffed primarily by Congregationalists, Methodists, Presbyterians, and Baptists, worked within evangelical Christian congregations to present antislavery petitions from more than 400 thousand Americans to Congress.[21]

Nearly two-thirds of the leaders in the abolitionist movement were pastors, deacons, and elders of evangelical churches. Even the black abolitionist movement that began in New England during the first half of the nineteenth century was founded and led by black Christian preachers, laymen, and lay women who were motivated by Christ's call to set men free in His name and for His kingdom's sake.

The evangelical view of sin brought slavery to its knees. That view came from preachers committed to the biblical world view of right and wrong, justice and injustice, sin and righteousness. To the men and women of that second Great Awakening, God was the Creator of this world and all its people. Those people had sinned and needed to be forgiven. With forgiveness came the power and the call to fight sin wherever it held people enslaved. And that view led to the overthrow of slavery and the emancipation of millions of black men, women, and children who were its innocent victims.

The Great Awakening and Women's Suffrage

At the same time, those Christian abolitionists committed to the overthrow of racial slavery began to realize the extent of sexual slavery in the nation. Women, too, were victims of discrimination. To Finney, Weld, and their associates in this second Great Awakening, discrimination of every kind needed to be overthrown. And though the Old and New Testament teachings assigned differing roles to the sexes, Finney and Weld found no real biblical support for the injustice and inequality that women faced in the early nineteenth century.

Many, some say most, of the volunteers in the antislavery, pro-women's rights movement between 1830 and 1850 were Christian women. In a recent study of the fifty-one major women founders of the early abolition-feminist movement, twenty-seven grew up in orthodox or evangelical homes; fifteen, in Quaker homes; and six, Unitarian or Universalist.[22]

As these Christian women stood to speak on behalf of the human rights of Negro slaves, they discovered to their shock and surprise that men—even Christian men who agreed with their stand against slavery— were opposed to women's speaking or acting in public on behalf of *any* cause. Other Christian women criticized the female abolitionists for taking on "a man's work" and insisted that the Scriptures limited a woman's role to marriage and the family.

Finney, Weld, and the other New Awakening evangelicals didn't support this limited view of women's roles in society. To them, the Bible was clear: A good marriage and a strong family were responsibilities shared equally by husband and wife. And to attack sin and stand against injustice is the responsibility of everyone, male and female.

Finney believed that Jesus' encounter with Mary and Martha stood squarely against those who would use the Bible to keep women powerless, uninformed, and in the kitchen. But Finney and the others were in the minority on this point. Lucretia Mott, an evangelical Quaker used to speaking publicly in Quaker meetings, was a mobilizing and directing force for the men assembled for the first convention of the American Anti-Slavery Society in 1833. But neither she nor the other women present were asked or expected to be asked to sign the antislavery document produced.

Even when the women abolitionists organized themselves that same year in Philadelphia, they asked a male black to preside over their meetings, not daring to allow a woman to act as "chairman," even of a women's group. Lucretia Mott later explained, "At that time . . . Negroes, idiots and women were in legal documents classed together; so that we were very glad to get one of our own class to come and aid in forming that Society."[23]

In 1838, Angelina Grimké presented female antislavery petitions to the Massachusetts legislature and proclaimed at the same time women's equal rights as citizens. "We Abolition Women are turning the world upside down!" she said. And when she was criticized more for taking a stand for women's rights than for taking a stand against slavery, she replied, "I was a woman before I was an abolitionist."[24]

Angelina Grimké was a courageous and outspoken enemy of slavery and an effective and powerful champion of women's suffrage. In 1836 she wrote a prophetic "Appeal to the Christian Women of the South." By 1837 she was addressing small women's groups across the country and had published her second major work, "Appeal to the Women of the Nominally Free States." And in 1838 she and her equally courageous sister, Sarah, published "Letters on the Equality of the Sexes and the Condition of Women." That same year, Angelina Grimké married Theodore Weld, her teacher and coworker in the abolition movement.

Theodore and Angelina Weld, both children of the second Great Awakening, made a deep and lasting impression on those around them. Lucy Stone, whom Elizabeth Cady Stanton called "the first person by whom the heart of the American public was deeply stirred on the woman question,"[25] was just one of many social reformers influenced by the Welds.

Lucy Stone was typical of her friends in the antislavery movement "in her religious fervor, her romantic optimism, and her humorless and almost obsessive Calvinist sense of duty." When Oberlin became the first college in the nation to admit women, Miss Stone enrolled to learn Greek and Hebrew in order to read the Bible in its original form, so she could prove "that inspired truth shows God loves his daughters as well as He loves his sons."[26] And yet Oberlin offered women a separate female curriculum featuring housekeeping and entertaining skills, and women students' studies were interrupted on Wednesdays so they could do the laundry for all the men.

Lucy Stone was the first woman to insist on taking all the courses at Oberlin. But when she completed those courses successfully and was asked to write an essay for the graduation exercises, she refused because she would not be allowed to read her own words at that event. A man would have read them for her.

When Stone decided to become a public speaker on behalf of the rights of slaves and women, her mother protested. Stone answered that conscience and duty demanded she seek the difficult way: "I should have no right to think myself a Christian and I should forever despise Lucy Stone."[27]

Most of these women, including Lucy Stone, suffered mistreatment at the hands of the organized church. Stone remembered "raising her hand to vote on an antislavery issue in their Congregational church and hearing the minister give instructions not to count her." Women in the mainline churches, she said later, were seen "as hewers of wood and drawers of water." It is no wonder that women like Lucy Stone no longer felt welcome in their churches. In fact, Stone, like many others, was expelled from her church because of her radical antislavery views.[28]

It is tragic that so many of the women and men who stood against sin in the form of slavery and discrimination were discriminated against by the very churches that introduced them to the life and teachings of Jesus. And it is even more tragic that so many of them ended their lives outside the church, feeling angry and disappointed that the church did not live by the standards it taught. Still, these same men and women grew up in Christian homes and churches and were permanently and positively affected by the spirit of that second Great Awakening.

Women like Harriet Beecher Stowe and Lucy Stone who fought for justice in the nineteenth century had heard the Old Testament stories of Queen Esther and of Deborah, the prophetess who rescued Israel. They had heard the New Testament stories of Martha and Lydia and Mary. They had been shaped in their childhood by the life and teachings of Jesus. In their youth, many of them had accepted Him as their Lord and Savior in the revival meetings conducted by Finney and the other second Great Awakening preachers. And as adults working against slavery and for the rights of women, they quoted Jesus and lived as best they could by His example.

Overtly and covertly, these courageous women were shaped by the biblical view of sin and righteousness. Their fight for justice and equality was motivated and directed by a Christian world view. And when people asked them why they had risked their honor and their lives to take up the tasks of abolition or women's suffrage, they often pointed to the example of Jesus, who lived and died to bring salvation to the world. "Without the shedding of blood," Lucy Stone wrote to her mother, "there is not remission for sin."[29]

In 1865 Harriet Beecher Stowe and Theodore Weld witnessed that moment when slavery was abolished from the land forever. Their fight was over. Their battle had been won. The thirteenth amendment added these simple words to the Constitution of the United States: "Neither slavery nor involuntary servitude, except as a punishment for crime whereof the party shall have been duly convicted, shall exist within the United States, or any place subject to their jurisdiction."[30]

Lucy Stone, the Grimké sisters, Lucretia Mott, Susan B. Anthony, and most of their allies died without realizing their dream for women's suffrage. However, it is fortunate for all of us that others took up their cause when they were forced to lay it down. Finally, in 1920, after more than a hundred years of struggle, the nineteenth amendment was added to the Constitution: "The right of citizens of the United States to vote shall not be denied or abridged by the United States or by any States on account of sex."

Harriet Beecher Stowe, Lucy Stone, Theodore Weld, and their co-workers were all children of the second Great Awakening. God used the preaching of Charles Finney and others like him to transform their lives and through them to transform the life of the nation. The following words of Finney have as much significance to us in this century as they had to those who heard him preach them more than 150 years ago: "The time has come that Christians must vote for honest men and take consistent ground in politics or the Lord will curse them. God cannot sustain this free and blessed country which we love and pray for unless the church will take right ground. Politics are a part of religion in such a country as this, and Christians must do their duty to the country as a part of their duty to God."[31]

10

THE CIVIL WAR AND LINCOLN'S GETTYSBURG ADDRESS

NOVEMBER 19, 1863

Rediscovering the Source of Our Nation's Unity

At exactly 10:00 A.M., President Abraham Lincoln left the Wills residence in Gettysburg, Pennsylvania, and mounted a young, beautiful chestnut horse for his short ride to the military cemetery nearby. Lincoln wore "a black suit, high silk hat, and white gloves."[1] A crowd had gathered to see the president, and Lincoln, still on horseback, chatted with them until almost 11:00 A.M.

The president had been cheered by two telegrams he received during the night. Secretary of War Edwin Stanton assured Lincoln that no real war news to worry about was evident, and Mrs. Lincoln informed him that their son Tad was much improved from a troubling illness.

Government officials, military officers, state governors, mayors, at least one regiment of soldiers, other dignitaries, and members of the nation's press paraded in carriages and on horseback through the countryside to the nearby site of the new military cemetery that was to be dedicated that day to the men, known and unknown, who were buried there.

A crowd estimated by eyewitnesses at somewhere between fifteen thousand and fifty thousand people lined the parade route and massed before the speaker's stand. As the parade began, witnesses report that Lincoln sat tall and erect in the saddle, riding "easily, bowing occasionally to right or left."[2] But the sights along the way and the memories they must have inspired caused a change in the president's demeanor. He saw many wounded men who remained in Gettysburg, as well as the still-fresh graves of thousands who would never leave that place. The

145

American flags posted at Gettysburg flew at half-mast, recalling the terrible carnage that had happened on the fields and hillsides of that small Pennsylvania village. The bloated corpses of dead horses, the deep scars of artillery shells, the bent and broken forests all gave grim, silent testimony to the intensity of the battle fought on this tragic landscape just four months earlier.

On July 2, 1863, Union forces including the Second, Third, and Fifth Army Corps under the command of General George G. Meade were attacked at Cemetery Ridge by the forces of General George E. Pickett's division of the First Confederate Army. On that bloody day the Confederate Army lost twenty thousand men to death or serious injury, and the Union Army counted twenty-three thousand men dead or dying on the field. Already, Gettysburg had become the symbol of our nation's growing horror and inconsolable grief. As Lincoln rode through that battlefield remembering the men and boys who died there, eyewitnesses saw his body gradually slump into a melancholy posture.

The presidential parade lasted just fifteen minutes. The military band played a forty-five-minute concert as eight state governors, six Union generals, foreign ministers, congressmen, and members of Lincoln's war cabinet assembled on the platform.

Finally, the Reverend Thomas H. Stockton, chaplain of the United States House of Representatives, began his opening prayer. Reporters present from the *Philadelphia Press* and the *Cincinnati Daily Gazette* reported that President Lincoln's eyes were filled with tears at the close of Chaplain Stockton's prayer.

Then, one of the great orators of that Civil War era, the Honorable Edward Everett, rose to speak, bowed low to Lincoln, and began his eloquent though now almost forgotten address. He spoke for nearly two hours and held the audience in rapt attention. Then the Baltimore Glee Club sang a hymn to Gettysburg written by the sometime poet Benjamin B. French, an officer in charge of buildings in Washington, D.C.

When the music ended, Ward Hill Lamon, a colonel in the Union Army, announced simply, "the president of the United States." A reporter from the *Cincinnati Commercial* observed that "the President rises slowly, draws from his pocket a paper, and, when commotion subsides, in a sharp, unmusical treble voice, reads the brief and pithy remarks."[3]

Fourscore and seven years ago, our fathers brought forth upon this continent a new nation, conceived in liberty and dedicated to the proposition that all men are created equal.

Now we are engaged in a great civil war, testing whether that nation— or any nation, so conceived and so dedicated—can long endure.

We are met on a great battle-field of that war. We are met to dedicate a portion of it as the final resting place of those who have given their lives that that nation might live.

It is altogether fitting and proper that we should do this.

But, in a larger sense, we cannot dedicate, we cannot consecrate, we cannot hallow, this ground. The brave men, living and dead, who struggled here, have consecrated it, far above our [poor] power to add or to detract.

The world will very little note nor long remember what we say here; but it can never forget what they did here.

It is for us, the living, rather, to be dedicated, here, to the unfinished work that they have thus far so nobly carried on. It is rather for us to be here dedicated to the great task remaining before us; that from these honored dead we take increased devotion to that cause for which they here gave the last full measure of devotion; that we here highly resolve that these dead shall not have died in vain; that the nation shall, under God, have a new birth of freedom, and that government of the people, by the people, for the people, shall not perish from the earth.[4]

Lincoln had bad feelings about his speech that day. "It is a flat failure," he told Lamon later, "and the people are disappointed."[5]

Reporters agreed. "The President acted without sense and without constraint," the *Harrisburg Patriot and Union* reported. "The silly remarks of the President . . . they shall no more be repeated or thought of." The *Chicago Times* wrote: "The cheek of every American must tingle with shame as he reads the silly, flat, and dish-watery utterances of the man who has to be pointed out to intelligent foreigners as the President of the United States." An editor of the *Richmond Examiner* said, "Lincoln acted the clown."[6]

When the speech was finished, polite applause for the president sounded and the dedication was adjourned. Lincoln dined at the Wills residence in Gettysburg and boarded a night train for Washington. They say he sat alone in a drawing room car with a damp towel over his eyes during that midnight journey to the capital. He was the commander-in-chief of a nation at war with itself. It must have been a terrible burden, but President Lincoln knew well his task and ours. It was never more simply and eloquently stated than on that day in Gettysburg.

Abraham Lincoln was not a popular president. In fact, he won the office narrowly. On November 6, 1860, 4,682,069 American men went to the polls to elect the nation's sixteenth president. Only 1,866,452 of those men voted for Abraham Lincoln, but in the Electoral College Lincoln received 180 of the 303 votes cast and was elected to the presidency. Six weeks later South Carolina seceded from the union. By February 4, 1861, six more states (Mississippi on January 9; Florida on January 10; Georgia on January 19; Louisiana on January 26; and Texas on February 1) joined with South Carolina to form a provisional government for the Confederate States of America. On February 9, a provisional Confederate Congress selected Jefferson Davis as the first president of the Confederacy.[7]

Three weeks later, on March 4, Lincoln was inaugurated president of the United States on the steps of the still-unfinished capitol building in Washington. Moments after Chief Justice Taney administered the oath of office, Lincoln read his first inaugural address to a crowd of more than ten thousand people standing beneath the ominous gray sky. The nation faced the greatest crisis in its history. Though the union was shattering, Lincoln refused to acknowledge or accommodate any talk of separation or war.

"The Union is unbroken," he said bravely, promising against the odds to fulfill his constitutional obligation, ". . . that the laws of the Union be faithfully executed in all the States." And though he assured his skeptical and fearful listeners that he would use his presidential power "to hold, occupy, and possess the property and places belonging to the Government," Lincoln also promised both North and South that ". . . there needs to be no bloodshed or violence . . . unless it be forced upon the national authority."

Lincoln expressed his own hope that "intelligence, patriotism, Christianity, and a firm reliance on Him who has never yet forsaken this favored land, are still competent to adjust in the best way all our present difficulty." Then he concluded his address with these stirring and oft-repeated words: "We are not enemies, but friends. We must not be enemies."[8]

The Civil War

Just four weeks after Lincoln's moving inaugural appeal, on April 12, 1861, at exactly 4:30 A.M., a Confederate howitzer was fired at Fort Sumter, the United States military base in Charleston Harbor. After three hours of cannon bombardment, Major Robert Anderson surrendered the fortress to the Confederacy.

Three days later, President Lincoln issued a proclamation calling up seventy-five thousand militia from the states that had not seceded. Kentucky, North Carolina, Missouri, and Tennessee joined the seceding states in their refusal to comply. On April 19, Lincoln announced that all southern ports would be closed and blockaded by the Navy, and two weeks later he called for sixty thousand volunteers to join the Union forces.

The Civil War had begun. After the defeat at Fort Sumter, President Lincoln asked Congress to give the President "the legal means for making this contest a short and decisive one." He estimated that 400 thousand men and $400 million would be needed to restore the union. In fact, the "contest" was long and drenched in blood.

The Real Issue Behind the Civil War

Though Lincoln could not prevent the temporary destruction of the union and the nearly fatal war, we can learn priceless lessons from the tragedy and from the man who lived and died at its center.

In his first inaugural address, Lincoln acknowledged the possibility of a civil war and added prophetically, "You cannot fight always; and when, after much loss on both sides, and no gain on either, you cease fighting, the identical old questions as to terms of intercourse are again upon you."

Now 121 years have passed since the Union was saved and North and South were reunited. The wounds of that war have healed enough that we can look more objectively at the "old questions" that caused it. It is easy to understand why our forefathers joined together to fight the British and bring liberty to the land. But it is harder to understand why just eighty-nine years later the grandchildren of those same Revolutionary soldiers went to war against each other in the uniforms of blue and gray. This time again both sides fought for liberty, not to gain it but to define it. What does freedom mean to states voluntarily drawn together? What are the limits of liberty in the land?[9]

The Issue of Slavery

Most people believe that the Civil War was fought because the North wanted to abolish slavery and the South felt dependent on the slaves to maintain an agricultural economy. The loud speeches and bold headlines of those pre-war years constantly drew the attention of both sides to the issue of slavery. But to Lincoln, slavery was only the primary illustration of a much broader issue—what liberty means and who should have it.

In fact, Lincoln was never an abolitionist. Although it was widely known that he hated slavery and opposed its spread to other states and territories, he promised from the beginning not to interfere with slavery in the southern states. During his first inaugural address, Lincoln quoted from the Constitution the guarantee of the return of fugitive slaves, and he promised to keep all his constitutional obligations, even that one.

In that inaugural address, Lincoln also quoted from one of his campaign speeches illustrating his position on slavery from the beginning: "I have no purpose, directly or indirectly, to interfere with the institution of slavery in the States where it exists. I believe I have no lawful right to do so, and I have no inclination to do so."

In 1862, with the nation deep in war, Lincoln read a moving editorial by Horace Greeley entitled "A Prayer of Twenty Millions" urging emancipation of the slaves. Two days later Lincoln answered Greeley in a letter: "My paramount object in this stuggle is to save the Union, and is not either to save or to destroy slavery. If I could save the Union without freeing any slave, I would do it; and if I could save it by freeing all the slaves, I would do it; and if I could do it by freeing some and leaving others alone, I would also do that."[10]

In these, and others of Lincoln's words and actions, is plenty of evidence that behind the war was an issue extending beyond slavery as an institution or the freeing of the slaves.

The Issue of States' Rights

Others say the tension underlying the war was the issue of states' rights. The southern states felt dominated by the antislavery sentiments of Northern abolitionists. They wanted to be able to decide on this issue as they could on every other issue not overtly granted to the federal government. But Lincoln believed as strongly in states' rights as any president before or after him. In his first inaugural address, he made his pro-states' rights position perfectly clear when he said:

> The right of each State to order and control its own domestic institutions according to its own judgment exclusively, is essential to that balance of power on which the perfection and endurance of our political fabric depend, and we denounce the lawless invasion by armed force of the soil of any State or Territory, no matter under what pretext, as among the gravest of crimes.

The Declaration of Independence and the Civil War

To Lincoln, a much larger issue was behind the war than slavery or states' rights. It was related directly to those two issues but larger and more important than either or both of them. On that temporary wooden platform in the new military cemetery in Gettysburg, Lincoln outlined the real issue that he saw behind the Civil War: "Fourscore and seven years ago, our fathers brought forth on this continent a new nation, conceived in liberty and dedicated to the proposition that *all men are created equal*."

It was the first line of his now-immortal Gettysburg Address, and it went directly to the heart of the conflict. Subtract eighty-seven years from that date in 1863 when Lincoln stood in the blood-stained fields of Gettysburg and spoke those simple words. He was recalling the year 1776, when the nation was born. He was quoting from the document that signaled the nation's birth. And the phrase he quoted from the Declaration of Independence captured the primary reason that our forefathers were bold enough to declare their liberty and brave enough to go to war to win it. "We hold these truths to be self-evident, that *all men*

151

are created equal, [italics mine] that they are endowed by their Creator with certain unalienable Rights, that among these are Life, Liberty and the pursuit of Happiness."

Lincoln's reference to the Declaration of Independence at the site of the bloodiest battle in this nation's Civil War was no accident. Nor was it a cheap political trick. The war had stretched on for two years. Both sides were facing terrible losses in life, property, and resources. Both sides were asking why this terrible war was being fought. And in that short phrase—"all men are created equal"—the nation's president was pointing to the answer.

At the beginning of this nation's history, our forefathers built their claim to independence on this simple fact: "All men are created equal [and] they are endowed by their Creator with certain unalienable Rights." Then they added that "to secure these rights, Governments were instituted among Men."

Lincoln had one task made clear by the Declaration and implemented in detail by the Constitution: "to secure these rights" for all the people.

In a debate with Stephen A. Douglas (June 26, 1857, in Springfield) just three years before his election to the presidency, Lincoln made clear his interpretation of those basic rights and how he would carry them out if elected president. He said:

> I think the authors of that notable instrument intended to include all men, but they did not intend to declare all men equal in all respects. They did not mean to say all were equal in color, size, intellect, moral developments, or social capacity. They defined with tolerable distinctness in what respects they did consider all men created equal—equal in "certain unalienable rights, among which are life, liberty, and the pursuit of happiness." This they said, and this they meant.
>
> They did not mean to assert the obvious untruth, that all men were enjoying that equality, nor yet, that they were about to confer it immediately upon them. In fact, they had no power to confer such a boon. They meant simply to declare the right, so that the enforcement of it might follow as fast as circumstances should permit. They meant to set up a standard maxim for a free society, which would be familiar to all, and revered by all; constantly looked to, constantly labored for, and even though never perfectly attained, constantly approximated, and therefore constantly spreading and deepening its influence, and augmenting the happiness and value of life to all people of all colors everywhere.[11]

Douglas, the man who would beat Lincoln for the Senate seat from Illinois, had been stumping up and down the state with a very different idea about those basic rights and about government's responsibilities to secure them. Those two new "maxims about liberty" that Douglas was advocating can be summarized in two phrases that he repeated over and over in his famous debates with Lincoln.

First, Lincoln quoted Douglas as saying he "'don't care whether slavery is voted up or voted down.'" Why did that statement make Lincoln so angry? Didn't Douglas have the right to have an opinion about slavery? We are, after all, a democracy, a government, as Lincoln said in the Gettysburg Address, "of the people, by the people, for the people." Isn't a democracy a place that respects all opinions about all ideas?

Lincoln's answer was no. He referred to the Declaration of Independence to show limits on people's rights, even within this democracy. Those limits on our liberty are carefully spelled out in the Declaration. They are few, but they are basic. Humanity's equal, unalienable rights to life, liberty, and the pursuit of happiness were not ideas that were up for grabs. They were not rights given by one person to another but rights, again quoting the Declaration, that were granted to all "by their Creator."

Therefore, what Douglas or anyone else thought about those basic rights was not important. "The Laws of Nature and of Nature's God" had made clear to our forefathers that those rights are a gift of God, and thus they stand—whatever people think about them.

Douglas was saying before vast, enthusiastic crowds, "I don't care what you do about slavery."[12] For Lincoln, slavery was the withholding of certain God-given rights from more than 4 million black people living in America. Whether Douglas cared about those rights or not, God cared. Douglas was elevating his own values above God's values, and that, to Lincoln, was going beyond the limits of liberty. What God cared about had been carefully written into the Declaration of Independence. And as the sixteenth president of the United States, Lincoln had inherited the task of "securing those rights" for all men.

Second, Lincoln accused Douglas of claiming that "whatever community wants slaves has a right to have them." Both Douglas and Lincoln were strong States' rights advocates. But Douglas had sponsored the 1854 Kansas-Nebraska Act, which stated that the people of the Kansas and Nebraska territories could decide for themselves whether to enter the Union as slave or free states.

Again, Lincoln objected. What God had endowed to all men was not an issue that could be settled by an election, even by a democratic majority vote. The states were free to decide about most important issues, but not about a person's basic equality or his right to life, liberty, and the pursuit of happiness. Once again, Lincoln was trying to explain that democracy had its limits. Those rights originated with the Creator and had been written into national public policy through the Declaration of Independence. They were rights that no city, county, state, or national government could vote away.

But Lincoln knew that at various times and for various reasons people's God-given rights had in fact been withheld by one group from another. He also knew that sometimes the act of granting those natural rights needed to be delayed until a more appropriate time to avoid an even larger catastrophe.

Lincoln was willing to make such a compromise on behalf of the southern states who had inherited the system of slavery from their grandfathers 150 years before Jefferson wrote the Declaration of Independence. In fact, Lincoln admitted he would have protected slavery in the southern states forever "if that would preserve the union."[13] Just two days after South Carolina seceded, Lincoln wrote to his friend Alexander H. Stephens, a Georgian who would soon be appointed Vice President of the Confederacy, to say: "Do the people of the South really entertain fears that a Republican administration would, directly or indirectly, interfere with their slaves or with them, about their slaves? If they do, I wish to assure you, as once a friend, and still, I hope, not an enemy, that there is no cause for such fears."[14]

But Lincoln was unalterably opposed to expanding the institution of slavery into any new states or territories where it was not already a long-standing tradition. He believed that it was his constitutional obligation to move all people in this country at least one step closer to equality and to include within the sphere of life, liberty, and the pursuit of happiness anyone he could who had been previously left out of it.

In another debate with Douglas (July 10, 1858), Lincoln explained his views in the language of the New Testament:

> It is said in one of the admonitions of the Lord, "As your Father in Heaven is perfect, be ye also perfect." The Savior, I suppose, did not

expect that any human creature could be as perfect as the Father in Heaven; but he said, "As your Father in Heaven is perfect, be ye also perfect." He set that up as a standard, and he who did most towards reaching that standard, attained the highest degree of moral perfection.

So I say in relation to the principle that *all men are created equal,* let it be as nearly reached as we can. If we cannot give freedom to every creature, let us do nothing that will impose slavery upon any other creature.[15]

Testing the Issue

Lincoln's second sentence in the Gettysburg Address said specifically what the Civil War would test: "Now we are engaged in a great civil war testing whether that nation, or any nation so conceived and so dedicated, can long endure."

Picture Lincoln standing there in that field that was still red with the blood of forty-three thousand Americans from the Union and the Confederacy. Testing the permanence of a government based on the idea that "all men are created equal" was costing thousands of lives and billions of dollars. But he was determined that the nation should pass the test.

This was not just a test of slavery or of states' rights, but a test of the nation's commitment to the wider definition of liberty best expressed in the Declaration of Independence and held up as a vision and a hope that one day they would be enjoyed by people everywhere, in this land and around the world.

Throughout his lifetime, the Declaration of Independence and its definition of liberty was one of Lincoln's favorite themes. There has never been a president who spoke so beautifully or so clearly about liberty. As I reviewed his written and spoken words for this chapter, I was deeply moved by his eloquence. In the next few pages, I've let Lincoln himself make his case. As you read Lincoln's words about liberty,[16] think about his times and about our own:

August 24, 1855
From a Letter to Joshua F. Speed

As a nation we began by declaring that "all men are created equal." We now practically read it "all men are created equal, except Negroes." When the Know-Nothings get control, it will read "all men are created equal, except Negroes and foreigners and Catholics." When it comes to this, I shall prefer emigrating to some country where they make no pretense of loving liberty—to Russia, for instance, where despotism can be taken pure, and without the base alloy of hypocrisy.

September 11, 1858
From a Speech at Edwardsville, Illinois

When you have succeeded in dehumanizing the Negro; when you have put him down and made it impossible for him to be but as the beasts of the field; when you have extinguished his soul in this world and placed him where the ray of hope is blown out as in the darkness of the damned, are you quite sure that the demon you have roused will not turn and rend you?

What constitutes the bulwark of our own liberty and independence? It is not our frowning battlements, our bristling sea coasts, our army and our navy. These are not our reliance against tyranny. All of those may be turned against us without making us weaker for the struggle.

Our reliance is in the love of liberty which God has planted in us. Our defense is in the spirit which prized liberty as the heritage of all men, in all lands everywhere. Destroy this spirit and you have planted the seeds of despotism at your own doors. Familiarize yourselves with the chains of bondage and you prepare your own limbs to wear them. Accustomed to trample on the rights of others, you have lost the genius of your own independence and become the fit subjects of the first cunning tyrant who rises among you.

April 6, 1859
From a letter to H. L. Pierce and others

Those who deny freedom to others deserve it not for themselves, and, under a just God, cannot long retain it.

February 22, 1861
From a Speech at Independence Hall, Philadelphia

I have never had a feeling, politically, that did not spring from the sentiments embodied in the Declaration of Independence . . . . I have often inquired of myself what great principle or idea it was that kept this

Confederacy so long together. It was not the mere matter of separation of the colonies from the motherland, but that sentiment in the Declaration of Independence which gave liberty not alone to the people of this country, but hope to all the world, for all future time. It was that which gave promise that in due time the weights would be lifted from the shoulders of all men, and that all should have an equal chance. This is the sentiment embodied in the Declaration of Independence. . . . I would rather be assassinated on this spot than surrender it.

July 4, 1861
From a Message to Congress in Special Session

This is essentially a people's contest. . . . It is a struggle for maintaining in the world that form and substance of government whose leading object is to elevate the condition of men—to lift artificial weights from all shoulders—to clear the paths of laudable pursuit for all—to afford all an unfettered start, and a fair chance, in the race of life.

December 1, 1862
From Second Annual Message to Congress

The fiery trial through which we pass will light us down in honor or dishonor to the last generation. We say we are for the Union. The world will not forget that we say this. We know how to save the Union. The world knows we do know how to save it. We, even we here, hold the power and bear the responsibility. In giving freedom to the slave, we assure freedom to the free—honorable alike in what we give and what we preserve. We shall nobly save or meanly lose the last, best hope of earth. Other means may succeed; this could not fail. The way is plain, peaceful, generous, just—a way which if followed the world will forever applaud and God must forever bless.

March 4, 1865
From Second Inaugural Address

With malice toward none, with charity for all, with firmness in the right as God gives us to see the right, let us strive on to finish the work we are in.

March 17, 1865
Address to an Indiana Regiment

I have always thought that all men should be free; but if any should be slaves, it should be first those who desire it for themselves, and secondly those who desire it for others. Whenever I hear anyone arguing for slavery, I feel a strong impulse to see it tried on him personally.

The Civil War ended on April 9, 1865, when Confederate General Robert E. Lee surrendered to Union General Ulysses S. Grant in a two-story brick house in the little village of Appomattox Court House in Virginia. In those four terrible years the nation had undergone a nearly fatal struggle. Cities, farms, factories, communication and transportation systems, schools, homes, and churches from Pennsylvania to Louisiana lay in ruin. The South had spent more than $1.5 billion conducting the war, while the North figured direct costs at more than $3.25 billion. That total estimate of $4.75 billion grew to more than $10 billion after pensions, interest on the federal debt, and property losses had been added.[17]

But the real price, the price in broken, bloodied bodies that littered the battlefields, was inestimable. The Union lost 359 thousand soldiers and sailors, while the Confederacy lost 258 thousand. Hundreds of thousands of men and women from North and South had been wounded or made invalids for the rest of their lives. Millions of American families were damaged or destroyed by the war. We are still suffering the human consequences of that great and tragic conflict.

Lincoln ended his speech at Gettysburg with a moving tribute to those young men who gave their lives for liberty: "We cannot dedicate, we cannot consecrate, we cannot hallow, this ground. The brave men, living and dead, who struggled here, have consecrated it, far above our [poor] power to add or to detract. The world will very little note nor long remember what we say here; but it can never forget what they did here."

On the evening of April 14, 1865, just five days after the war had ended, Lincoln joined the ranks of those who died in that terrible conflict. John Wilkes Booth shot our sixteenth president as he sat in Ford's

Theater in Washington. The next morning, on Good Friday, Lincoln died.

The Gettysburg Address will stand for all time as the most eloquent statement of the nation's most eloquent president. At the close of that speech on the bloodiest battlefield of the Civil War, Lincoln added this challenge to our great-grandparents who lived through the war and to each of us who succeeded them:

> It is for us the living, rather, to be dedicated here, to the unfinished work that they have thus far so nobly carried on. It is rather for us to be here dedicated to the great task remaining before us; that from these honored dead we take increased devotion to that cause for which they here gave the last full measure of devotion; that we here highly resolve that these dead shall not have died in vain; that this nation shall, under God, have a new birth of freedom, and that government of the people, by the people, for the people, shall not perish from the earth.

11

STATUE OF LIBERTY DEDICATED

OCTOBER 28, 1886

Rediscovering the Diversity of Our Heritage

One hundred years ago, the Statue of Liberty's original dedication day dawned gray and damp in New York City. A gentle rain began to fall about the time the parade marched down Fifth Avenue toward the Battery and the waiting Lady on Bedloe Island. Soaked confetti fell from office and apartment buildings, mingled with the rain, and clogged the open drains and gutters. Still, hundreds of thousands of cheering Americans lined the route of march. Nothing seemed to dampen the jubilant, hopeful spirit of that day.

Twenty thousand soldiers, sailors, and veterans of the Civil War followed marching bands, baton twirlers, floats, and fire engines across Fifty-seventh Street, down Broadway, and to the Battery at the very end of Manhattan Island. All along the route, French flags flew alongside the Stars and Stripes, and French and American representatives stood together proudly in the reviewing stand at Madison Square Park. President Grover Cleveland was this nation's host to Frédéric Auguste Bartholdi, the man who designed and created the Statue of Liberty, and to the great Ferdinand de Lesseps, the engineer-dreamer behind the Suez Canal and, later, the Panama Canal.

"You are the greatest man in America today," President Cleveland shouted to Bartholdi over the final majestic chords of the Marine Corps band led by John Philip Sousa.

"Through your courtesy," the sculptor replied diplomatically.[1]

At 1:00 P.M., the land-bound parade ended and the nautical parade began. Great ocean liners shadowed tugboats, private yachts, tall-masted schooners, fire boats, fishing boats, and dinghies as they began their journey to Bedloe Island. Not one woman had been invited to participate in the ceremony. So a group of enterprising women, ignoring the snub, hired a sleek, fast vessel and darted among the other boats, waving flags and shouting friendly protests to the male dignitaries.

The entire flotilla moved slowly down the Hudson River to form a half-circle between Manhattan and the statue. As President Cleveland and his guests sailed by French and American war vessels in the harbor, a twenty-one-cannon salute thundered across the water. For those watching from Manhattan, the view of Bartholdi's great iron and copper statue was almost obliterated by the haze, the sulfurous smoke, and the damp, low-lying fog that surrounded her.

President Cleveland and his party were transferred from the *USS Dispatch* first to a launch, then to a float, and from there up a rather unstable ladder to the pier beneath the statue. Assisting the president, a man of considerable girth, up that long and narrow ladder was not an easy matter. One eyewitness was afraid the celebration would be marred by an unceremonious dunking of the president of the United States into the chilly waters of New York Harbor.[2]

As President Cleveland and de Lesseps mounted the speakers' platform, which was colorfully decorated in red, white, and blue, Bartholdi walked to the base of the statue and began to climb the stairway within. At the climax of the dedication, Bartholdi would pull in through the open crown a great flag of France that covered the statue's face.

Massed bands played. Three thousand invited and uninvited guests crowded onto the small (only eleven acres) island. A prayer was offered. De Lesseps spoke eloquently of the long and significant friendship of the French and American people. Senator William Evarts was the last speaker on the program, and when he paused momentarily to catch his breath, the signal was given for Bartholdi to pull in the flag. With that a spectator cried, "Hail Liberty!" and chaos broke loose on the island, across the waters, and among the masses cheering from the shores of distant Manhattan.

Cannons were fired. Ship bells clanged. Sirens, horns, and claxtons sounded. And for at least fifteen minutes the noise echoed out across the water as the people cheered "The Statue of Liberty Enlightening the World."

I have wondered if Emma Lazarus was somewhere unnoticed in the cheering crowd that day. Emma was the thirty-four-year-old Jewish poet who wrote the words most often associated with Lady Liberty. She submitted her sonnet "The New Colossus" in 1883 to the committee trying to raise money to build the statue's base. They printed it in a souvenir booklet and then promptly forgot all about her masterpiece.

Finally, in 1903 another artist, Georgiana Schuyler, a sculptor, found a faded, yellow copy in a used bookstore and had the sonnet inscribed on a small bronze tablet. After the usual bureaucratic runaround, Miss Schuyler got permission to mount the sonnet on the second-floor landing inside the Statue of Liberty. Immigrants and tourists visiting the statue began to read, copy, and even memorize the last five lines of Miss Lazarus's tribute to our nation and to the statue that stood before our nation's open door. And just before President Reagan relit the torch of Liberty on July 3, 1986, massed choirs sang those same words written one hundred years before.

Emma Lazarus never saw her poem in its place of honor. She died of cancer in 1887 at the age of thirty-eight. For sixteen years after her death, the poem disappeared. No one, especially Miss Lazarus, ever dreamed that one day it would stand as large a monument to liberty as the statue itself.

> Not like the brazen giant of Greek fame,
> With conquering limbs astride from land to land;
> Here at our sea-washed, sunset gates shall stand
> A mighty woman with a torch, whose flame
> Is the imprisoned lightning, and her name
> Mother of Exiles. From her beacon-hand
> Glows world-wide welcome; her mild eyes command
> The air-bridged harbor that twin cities frame.
> "Keep, ancient lands, your storied pomp!" cries she
> With silent lips. "Give me your tired, your poor,
> Your huddled masses yearning to breathe free,
> The wretched refuse of your teeming shore.
> Send these, the homeless, tempest-tost to me,
> I lift my lamp beside the golden door!"

At the close of that rain-drenched official dedication celebration of the Statue of Liberty in 1886, the spectators set off a near-stampede into the waiting boats. The day was too dark and the weather too ominous for the fireworks and the lighting of the statue that had been planned. Guests and stowaways rushed to board the departing vessels, hoping not to be abandoned on this island in the middle of a harbor darkened by an approaching storm.

Lady Liberty seemed unperturbed by all the excitement at her base.

And for these one hundred years she has stood serenely in the midst of the growing chaos around her, holding up the hope of liberty to this nation and to the world beyond.

A fter the Civil War ended in 1865, thoughtful people wondered if true liberty would ever really be established in the land. Its spirit had been deeply wounded by the war. Some thought the wounds were fatal. Hatred and bitterness prevailed. War-tired Northerners were faced with broken families, ruined marriages, emotionally and physically damaged lives, and a huge national war debt. Southerners stumbled through the shattered ruins of their once-proud-and-prosperous states.

Southern cities, towns, and countrysides had been the scene of fierce battles for four disastrous years. Plantations and farms had been destroyed. Houses, barns, farm buildings, rail stations, schools, and even churches had been burned. Fences had been torn down. Livestock had been killed or driven away. The tools of farm production had been destroyed. The railroad tracks had been pulled up and engines and rolling stock lost or rusted and in ruin. Confederate money was worthless. The slaves were free, but the economy and morale of the southern states had been devastated, and federal troops would occupy the region for twelve more bitter years of reconstruction.

To make matters worse, Abraham Lincoln was dead. The president who had a dream of a time of reconstruction "with malice toward none, with charity for all" was replaced by angry congressional leaders seeking revenge. Lincoln's successor, Andrew Johnson, made feeble attempts to carry out the president's dream, but Congress overrode the chief executive and adopted a bitter, arbitrary plan for reconstruction. Eventually, the spirit of our forefathers prevailed. The Union was restored. And North and South set to the task of rebuilding a broken nation.

Restoring the Spirit of Liberty

During those last decades of the nineteenth century, the northern states and eventually even the South began to experience a time of growth and prosperity. The nation moved from an agricultural to an industrial economy. Two years before the beginning of the Civil War, in

1859, oil had been discovered in Pennsylvania. The war itself had demanded factories and office buildings for the mass production and distribution of war supplies. At the close of the war, the inventors and manufacturers turned their creativity and expertise toward the production of peacetime consumer goods.

It didn't take long after the Civil War to restore and even improve transportation and communication systems throughout the nation. In 1868 C. L. Sholes's first "type writer" was in production. Alexander Graham Bell spoke the first words through his "telephone" in 1876, and Thomas Alva Edison recorded and reproduced sounds on his "phonograph" in 1877. George Selden patented the first "gasoline carriage" in 1879. In 1882 Edison's first electric power plant began operation in New York City. In 1896 Langley's airplane made its first experimental flight, and by 1901 Orville and Wilbur Wright were gliding in their fragile wood and fabric creation above the sand dunes of Kitty Hawk, North Carolina.

With the Union re-established, people of North and South found themselves looking west with awe and ambition. The nation had grown to cover a vast and bountiful land of 3,738,000 square miles. And the population of that expanded nation had boomed. At the beginning of the nineteenth century, approximately 4 million people lived within our borders. By the end of that same century, we counted 76 million people in the continental United States and 9 million more living beneath the American flag in territories from Alaska in the north to Hawaii and the Philippines in the west and Puerto Rico in the east.[3]

Of those 76 million inhabitants, about 66.8 million were descended from white Europeans. About 22 million of those were recent immigrants, either foreign-born or of foreign parentage, while the remaining 44 million were descended from the immigrants of earlier generations. An estimated 9 million Americans were descended from African ancestors, and just over 100 thousand were of Oriental ancestry. The native American Indians, living on their scattered reservations, made up approximately 237 thousand people.[4]

"We Are All Immigrants."

At the July 3, 1986, rededication of the Statue of Liberty, ABC news anchorman Peter Jennings looked out across the water at the statue bathed in light and said, "Tonight, we are all immigrants." And except for the native Indian peoples (who also migrated to this continent), Jennings was absolutely right. Each of us is a product of an Old-World heritage. Most of us, if we had the time and inclination, could trace our roots back to those other worlds from which our grandparents came. Every time we see the statue, we should remember the price our ancestors paid to establish our families here. Most were poor. They saved a lifetime for the journey. They sold everything they had to buy passage on those primitive sailing ships. And when they said good-bye to their old worlds, they left behind their families and lifetimes of friendships and acquaintances.

They walked for weeks from their hometowns and villages, pushing their remaining possessions in trundle carts. The more fortunate rode in creaky, horse-drawn wagons or in second-class train compartments on their journeys to the great, crowded port cities on the sea. There, they lived in cheap rooming houses or camped in vacant lots, sometimes for months, as they bargained with ship captains for passage on sailing ships or steamers.

The Atlantic journey took four months; the trip from Asia, even longer. Most immigrants were given narrow quarters in steerage beneath the decks. They had limited water rations and ate the food they had prepared and stored for the long and dangerous journey. The summer days at sea were stifling. The winter crossings were perilous and icy cold. Seasickness prevailed. Many people, especially the old and the very young, died and were buried at sea. Most arrived exhausted, ill, frightened, and penniless.

When I am in New York City and have an extra moment, I like to stand on the docks at Battery Park on the southern tip of Manhattan Island and look out across the waters at the Statue of Liberty. For twenty-five cents you can take the Staten Island Ferry and sail right past the statue. It is easy to imagine how grateful and excited our ancestors felt as they sailed past Lady Liberty on their way to Ellis Island and their entry into this New World.

Why Did They Come?

During the 1986 rededication, I was reminded that the statue is not a symbol belonging just to this nation, but a symbol of the entire world.

That Lady standing in New York Harbor has her back to this country and her face to the Atlantic Ocean and the old countries beyond. She is holding up the hope of liberty, not just to these fifty states, but to the entire world.

That great throng of people who came to honor her in 1986 were not just Americans. They came from more than one hundred nations. The great nautical parade of ships that sailed past the statue was not just made up of American ships. They sailed to New York to celebrate Miss Liberty from their port cities on seas and oceans around the globe. That same evening the largest fireworks display in history lit up the sky, not with American pyrotechnics alone, but with colorful exploding shells from twenty-one Asian and European nations as well. And though the great massed bands played "The Stars and Stripes Forever" and "The Battle Hymn of the Republic," they also played "Hail, Britannia," *"La Marseillaise,"* "When Irish Eyes Are Smiling," and the national anthems, ballads, and marching songs of at least a dozen other countries from which our ancestors came.

What has made the Statue of Liberty such a universal symbol? What inspires the people of the world to look to this nation when they think of liberty, even though they also know that our own record of civil liberties is uneven at best? They know how long our nation tolerated slavery, and they realize that even after we paid such a terrible price to eliminate it, racial prejudice and inequality still exist in the land. They know how long women had to fight for the right to vote in America and that their struggle for equality is still not fully realized. They know, too, that various minorities still struggle here for liberty and justice. Yet, with all our faults, the people of the world also know that in these United States, more liberty has been realized for more people than in any other nation or at any other time in history.

Look back again to the beginning of the nation, to 1776 and the Declaration of Independence. For the first time in world history a group of people, our forefathers, made this claim: "We hold these truths to be self-evident, that all men are created equal, that they are endowed by their Creator with certain unalienable Rights, that among these are Life, Liberty and the pursuit of Happiness. That to secure these rights, Governments are instituted among Men . . . ."

Don't ever get tired of reading or hearing these words. They are the foundation upon which the nation was built. And they are the bricks and mortar that patched a broken, bitter country back together again. These words point to God, our Creator, as the one and only source of liberty, and they exclaim to all the world that God's gifts were meant for everyone. That's why our grandparents came to these shores. And that's why millions more are seeking to enter this land, legally and illegally, every year. We have built a nation on the claim that life, liberty, and the pursuit of happiness are God-given rights of all people everywhere. It is no wonder that they came in the past and are still coming today.

Even before the Statue of Liberty held up her lamp of welcome to the oppressed and liberty-starved people around the world, this nation seemed to offer the world's best hope for freedom. And so believing what our forefathers had declared, that those basic rights were God-given and unalienable from anyone, millions of people came seeking that independence for themselves and their posterity.

From the beginning, our forefathers believed that the freedom to leave one country and take up residence in another was a God-given right. In the Declaration of Independence, one of the primary complaints our forefathers registered against the tyranny of George III was that he had placed limits on those wishing to migrate to the New World. In the Declaration of Independence we read: "He [the king] has endeavoured to prevent the population of these States; for that purpose obstructing the Laws for Naturalization of Foreigners; refusing to pass others to encourage their migration hither."

Our forefathers believed that the nation was ennobled and enriched by those who migrated here. During the Constitutional Convention in 1787, James Madison encouraged immigration when he noted how much the nation gained with each new wave of immigrants: "That part of America which has encouraged them [the immigrants] has advanced most rapidly in population, agriculture and the arts."[5]

From the beginning, our leaders saw America as a place of refuge to which the world's oppressed could flee. President Washington recommended in his Thanksgiving Proclamation of 1795, ". . . humbly and fervently to beseech the kind Author of these blessings . . . to render this country more and more a safe and propitious asylum for the unfortunate of other countries."[6]

And when the first settlers and their children began to complain about the numbers of new arrivals who also came seeking liberty, President Jefferson asked, "Shall we refuse to the unhappy fugitives from distress that hospitality which the savages of the wilderness extended to our fathers arriving in this land? Shall oppressed humanity find no asylum on this globe?"[7]

"Give Me Your Tired, Your Poor . . . ."

At the beginning of the nineteenth century, immigration to the United States had almost completely stopped. In 1807 the Congress prohibited any further importation of Africans for the purpose of slavery. And the War of 1812 with Great Britain temporarily closed down the migration of Europeans to these shores.

But with the Treaty of Ghent, the first nineteenth-century wave of immigration to North America began. It started with just a trickle of 152 thousand immigrants, primarily from England and Ireland, coming to the United States between 1820 and 1830. Between 1830 and 1840, more than 599 thousand people migrated here, primarily from England, Ireland, Germany, and Scandinavia. During the next decade, the rate of immigration increased 300 percent. In that time, 1,713,000 people made the journey to the New World, with a large increase in numbers from northern and central Europe. Then for the next thirty years, more than 2.5 million people immigrated every decade from England, northern and southern Europe, and Scandinavia. Between 1880 and 1890, more than 5 million immigrants came to the United States, with the largest number from southern Europe. And though the numbers decreased during the last troubled decade of the nineteenth century, during the first decade of the twentieth century almost 9 million immigrants arrived. All told, between 1820 and 1984, 51,950,000 people immigrated legally to America.[8]

From the beginning of our nation's history, more than 5 million Protestants came from England. They were Pilgrims, Puritans, Anglicans, Quakers, Presbyterians, and Methodists determined to worship freely. An almost equal number of Catholics came from Ireland also seeking religious freedom, and in the 1840s and '50s to escape the suffering produced by the disastrous Irish potato famine.

Approximately 7 million Germans migrated here to escape the tyranny of kings and chancellors and eventually of Adolph Hitler's Third Reich. And 3.5 million Russians joined them, fleeing the despotism of the czars and of the Communist elite who succeeded them. Almost a million French immigrants came out of their own bloody revolution and to escape plagues, poverty, and religious persecution in Europe. Half a million men and women immigrated from the turmoil and poverty of Poland.

More than 4 million people fled the tyranny of the Austria-Hungary Empire. From Rumania another 200 thousand people came, sometimes whole villages traveling to the New World together. To date approximately 5 million Italians have migrated to cities on the east and west coasts of America, while almost the same number of people have come from the Scandinavian countries to settle in the Midwest and California.

Approximately half a million Chinese and half a million Japanese migrated to the West Coast. Some came as slaves to mine gold from western streams or to build our intercontinental railroad. Others migrated freely, bringing their "gentle dreams" to this new western world.[9]

More than 60 million immigrants have come to America fleeing oppression and revolution. They came seeking religious and political freedom. They came to plant farms and build houses, to raise families, and to seek a new life in a new world. They came seeking life, liberty, and the pursuit of happiness, and most of them have found it here.

In turn these immigrants have enriched our nation with their presence. They have helped provide the skilled and unskilled labor needed to maintain our economy. They have fought and died for America in two world wars, in Korea, and in Vietnam. They have brought new richness to the culture, language, and folklore of America. The immigrants have proved to be industrious, loyal, and hardworking. From their ranks have come great scientists, doctors, politicians, clergy, artists, and inventors. Through our nation's open doors have come the best and the brightest in our midst.

Wave after wave of immigrants traveled to these shores believing that everything was possible in America. The Statue of Liberty became a symbol to all the world of this nation and her commitment to freedom. And around the world where there was tyranny or injustice, famine or plague, hopelessness or despair, the story would be told by one victim to another of the Lady in the Harbor and the land of new beginnings. Old and young alike would lie down amidst the ruins of their old worlds and make their exciting plans for traveling to the new. For generations people dreamed about one day going to America, and that dream alone was enough to get them through the night. The freedom and hope that fuel that dream must never be allowed to die.

PART TWO

LOSING
OUR
WAY

12

WOODROW WILSON CALLS FOR WAR ON GERMANY

APRIL 2, 1917

The Loss of Old World Dreams and Values

The floor of the United States House of Representatives was packed with noisy senators and congressmen. The president's cabinet was assembled with the chiefs of staff and other high-ranking military officers. The Supreme Court was seated in a half-circle just in front of the Speaker of the House. Ambassadors, government officials, the public, and the press mobbed the galleries, cloakrooms, and hallways of the Capitol. The mood was almost jubilant. Suddenly, the approaching hoofbeats of a full squadron of cavalry horses could be heard, and the loud sound of marching men echoed through the marble chamber.

Seconds later, Woodrow Wilson was escorted into the packed chambers, and the entire audience stood to roar its welcome.

"The president of the United States," announced the Speaker, rapping his gavel loudly for attention. The crowd grew quiet. For a moment President Wilson stood in silence, his head bowed and his eyes closed. His face was pale. His mood was less than jubilant. "I have called the Congress into extraordinary session," he began, "because there are serious, very serious, choices of policy to be made, and made immediately."[1]

The president was ready to ask Congress to declare war on Germany. For almost three years he had struggled to avoid this moment. Late in June 1914, a Serbian revolutionary had assassinated Archduke Franz Ferdinand, the heir to the throne of the dual monarchy of Austria-Hungary. Austria declared war on Serbia in July 1914. Russia, the great Slavic power and "protector" of tiny Serbia, mobilized its armies against Austria. Germany, fearful of its enemies on both borders, declared war on Russia on August 1 and marched on France through neutral Belgium on August 3.

America looked on in shocked surprise as the European powers plunged the world into global conflict. Turkey and Bulgaria joined the Central Powers: Germany and Austria-Hungary. Italy and eventually Greece, Portugal, Rumania, and Japan joined the Triple Entente: Great Britain, France, and Russia. Now, Wilson was asking Congress to join the Allies in an all-out world war against the central powers.

"The world must be made safe for democracy!" Wilson declared. Painfully, he reviewed the bloody, belligerent acts of the Central Powers. Few in the audience needed to be reminded of the sinking of the British liner *Lusitania* in the Irish Sea on May 7, 1915, causing the deaths of 1,198 people including 124 Americans. German submarines, in their attempts to blockade England, had not discriminated between military and civilian shipping. And the Central Powers were waging a bloody land war against civilians and soldiers alike. Wilson said, "Property can be paid for; the lives of peaceful and innocent people cannot be . . . . The wrongs against which we now array ourselves are no common wrongs; they cut to the very roots of human life."

The audience interrupted Wilson's speech regularly with bursts of enthusiastic applause and loud cheering. They had no question about the general consensus that the Central Powers threatened all of civilization. The free world was fighting for its life, and the United States would join that just cause. Wilson continued:

> It is a fearful thing to lead this great peaceful people into war, into the most terrible and disastrous of all wars, civilization itself seeming to be in the balance. But the right is more precious than peace, and we shall fight for the things which we have always carried nearest our hearts. . . . To such a task we can dedicate our lives and our fortunes . . . with the pride of those who know that the day has come when America is privileged to spend her blood and her might for the principles that gave her birth and happiness and the peace which she has treasured.

Then, with a prayer borrowed from Martin Luther, Wilson concluded his moving call to war, "God helping her, she can do no other!"

The next day, Wilson's private secretary reported that the president was stunned by the people's enthusiastic response to his call to arms. They had cheered him at every stage of the evening's tragic proceedings. "My message was a message of death to our young men," Wilson said incredulously. "How strange to applaud that!" The secretary remembered that Wilson slumped into a chair in his White House office and talked briefly of the evening's events: "After dwelling upon the tragedies inseparable from war, President Wilson let his head fall on the cabinet table and sobbed as if he had been a child."[2]

President Wilson had more than one reason to weep that day. In those next years of warfare, 116,516 young American soldiers, sailors, airmen, and Marines would die in battle, and 234,428 more would be seriously injured on European battlefields including Cantigny, the Marne, and in the great Meuse-Argonne offensive, the final push of the war involving 1,200,000 American men.

But the launching of a world war signaled another kind of death to President Wilson. To understand his tears is to understand the dream that died for him and was dying for all the world that day.

The Era of "Progress"

During those amazing years at the end of the nineteenth century and the beginning of the twentieth, the world had witnessed an era of technological progress unmatched in human history. Electricity lit up towns and cities. Combustible engines powered automobiles, trucks, tractors, ships, and planes. The oceans, mountains, and great distances between the nations had been bridged. Alfred Nobel's dynamite blasted open vast deposits of natural resources. The electrical and chemical industries were born. Pig iron was converted into steel, and steel revolutionized the new industrial world. Telephones and telegraphs connected once-isolated peoples in a network of instant communication. The radio, the phonograph, and moving pictures all helped to inform and entertain the people of America and to bridge the distances between people in every nation. In less than one hundred years, the world had witnessed an unprecedented era of progress. Optimism reigned. "Mankind has no limits," or so it seemed during those heady days of progress and discovery.

Mankind at the Center of the Universe

During that same century of progress, humanity began to discover vast new resources within itself. People were creating a brand-new world, and with each new invention they were more amazed and more impressed by their own achievements. Contemporary thinkers with roots in the eighteenth-century Enlightenment began to advance new ideas about humanity and its place in the universe. With all their wisdom, the use and misuse of these new ideas tended to undermine the spiritual foundations laid so carefully by our forefathers.

Charles Darwin

In 1859, at the very beginning of this era of progress, Charles Darwin published in England his *On the Origin of Species by Means of Natural Selection*. Darwin maintained that life had evolved from lower to higher forms and that even mankind was a product of this evolutionary process. In so doing, he allowed for a view of creation that had no real need for God. Rather, as philosopher J. Wesley Robb noted: "The story of creation no longer need be considered as the result of God's creative act of love, but as the result of fortuitous circumstances and the ability of the species to survive."[3]

The Genesis account portrays a loving Creator walking with a man and a woman on the day of their creation in a peaceful garden rich with the various plant and animal species. Adam and Eve, like their modern counterparts, were superior to and different from the plants and other animals from the beginning. Darwin, on the other hand, saw all creation, including people, evolving up from a single source after millions of years of biological struggle. And that evolutionary struggle was determined by natural laws that could be discovered and observed.

Most people forget that Darwin received his training in natural history while preparing for the Anglican ministry at Christ's College, Cambridge. He did not mean his observations about "variation," "over-population and the struggle for survival," and "natural selection" to eliminate God as Creator but were instead to be seen as "the means adopted by the creator to populate the earth."[4]

Nevertheless, in that decade of rapid change, theology and science drew further and further apart. Whereas our nation's forefathers looked to "the Laws of Nature and of Nature's God" to explain the creation of the universe and the origins of mankind, the scientific community turned to their microscopes and test tubes for the answers. If those various evolutionary stages through which creation passed were governed by fixed natural laws as Darwin explained, there seemed to be no real need for God's supervising presence. And if only the fit survived the long, bloody biological battle, there seemed to be no real evidence of a loving Father's constant, unfailing love.

Karl Marx

In 1867 Karl Marx published *Das Kapital*. Marx, a German exile living in London, and his collaborator, Friedrich Engels, were attempting to apply Darwin's evolutionary view of animal life to the history of government and society. Marx wanted to dedicate his first volume of *Das Kapital* to Darwin, but Darwin declined the honor. Like Darwin, Marx believed life was governed by natural laws that determine the future and thus that laws, nations, and classes evolve like plants and animals.

As the feudal system of the old nobility had been replaced by the entrepreneuring capitalists, so capitalism would one day be overthrown by socialist workers. Marx warned that to limit the transformation of institutions by the democratic standards of "ballots for bullets" would prove ineffectual. To reform an old system was simply to delay its inevitable death. Violent conflict was the key to change.

Marx would use the history of our own nation to illustrate his evolutionary premise. England had settled North America as a loyal colony. But the settlers were oppressed by King George III. When they complained of his mistreatment and asked for justice, the king refused to listen. Peaceful negotiations failed. So, the settlers took possession of the land, the tools of production, and the weapons of war. And through a bloody revolution, the oppressed were freed and a new nation was born.

But the agricultural economy of those newly united states was based on slavery. And slavery, said Marx, could not be reformed any better than could the reign of George III. So once again the nation had to go to war. Marx used the Civil War to illustrate the necessity of violent conflict for the emancipation of one class from the domination of another.

In the history of human conflict, Marx saw no evidence of God's powerful, loving presence in the struggle between nations and classes. Religion had been used by the rich and powerful as "the opiate of the masses." Marx believed the old morality that "enslaved people" would one day be swept away, and humanity would at last be free to control its own destiny.

Friedrich Nietzsche

In 1882 Friedrich Nietzsche, a man who ranks with Darwin and Marx in their impact on the thinking of the age that led to two world wars, published *Thus Spoke Zarathustra,* an enigmatic and confusing work. In it, Nietzsche, until 1879 a professor of philosophy at the Swiss University of Basel, developed his idea that all human behavior could be reduced to a single basic drive, "the will to power." In his chapter "On Self-Overcoming," Nietzsche described the "over man" (superman) who triumphs over his mediocrity and recreates himself. He insisted, however, that the evolution of most men leads simply to failure and death.

For Nietzsche, life was an endless cycle. The world was not governed by purpose. God was dead, and Christianity was "born of weakness, failure and resentment and is the enemy of reason and honesty, of the body and of sex in particular, and of power, joy and freedom."[5]

Darwin, Marx, and Nietzsche in their very different ways contributed to the underlying mood of the late nineteenth and early twentieth centuries. God was dead or distant. Humanity lived in a universe governed by scientific laws. No longer did we need religion or the Bible to explain the past or give direction to the future. In fact, religion and its malpractice had inhibited mankind's potential. If we could free ourselves from the negative effects of those old religious restraints, our power would know no limits. The truly "liberated" person would find within himself all the resources necessary to create and manage a beautiful new world.

Sigmund Freud

At the beginning of the twentieth century, humanity had placed itself squarely in the center of the universe. Thinkers like Marx and Nietzsche longed to "free" mankind from all of its emotional limitations so that it might live up to its full potential. At that moment, Sigmund Freud, the father of modern psychology, appeared on the scene. An Austrian neurologist and professor at the University of Vienna, Freud was a pioneer researcher into the mysterious world of the emotions. He began his formal contribution to humanity's emotional healing with the publication in 1900 of his first major work, *The Interpretation of Dreams*.

Freud believed that human emotions, like the human body, needed at least occasional healing. When an arm or leg is broken, Freud noted, a doctor is called to reset the damaged bone and place the fracture in a cast. But when a person's emotions are damaged, the emotional injury is usually ignored. No formal healing process is begun. And if the psychological damage is severe enough, the victim is labeled insane and placed in an asylum.

Freud was one of the first modern writers to attempt to explain the complex emotional functions of the brain, let alone present a process that might lead to emotional healing. That primitive dimension of personality where the need for self-preservation and self-procreation are found, Freud labeled the "id." Moral laws, which have their origin in society and govern the basic impulses of the "id," are found in the "super-ego." That world between human impulse and moral law Freud called the "ego." The "ego" is the reasonable self, the part of a person that decides whether to obey the "super-ego" or the "id."

Humanity could be liberated from its limitations by freeing the "super-ego" from its unreasonable constraints, Freud taught. And thus liberated, mankind could find within itself all the necessary guidelines to protect and advance society, with no need for external, immutable laws. The Bible was interesting and helpful but not to be taken too seriously. The notions of sin and salvation were outdated at best, crippling at worst. The church and religion had caused far too much emotional damage. Once delivered from that psychological damage through hypnotism, dream therapy, and other techniques of modern psychoanalysis, the newly "healed" person could trust himself for guidance.

John Dewey

At the same time that Freud was publishing his first work in psychology, John Dewey, sometimes called the father of modern American education, published his small book *School and Society*. In the midst of the industrial revolution, Dewey believed that schools must cease being "a place set apart in which to learn lessons" and become a laboratory where all ideas and all opinions were tested equally. The purpose of education was not "to transmit fixed beliefs, but to teach the necessity, in a changing environment, of subjecting ideas and values to continual testing and verification."[6]

The center of the classroom and of the curriculum shifted under Dewey from the teacher and a time-honored set of absolute values and priorities to the child and his or her interests and needs. Education's new goal was to help a child face practical problems, not to learn basic truth. In fact, no truths were to be considered eternal. All ethical norms were relative.

The Bible and Form Criticism

To the liberal churchmen associated with the historic denominations, Darwin's evolution became "God's way of doing things." The notion of mankind's evolution led to the liberal Protestant reading of history "as the gradual redemption and sanctification of the race," a corrupted view of the orthodox idea of Providence.

Biblical revelation was also seen as "evolutionary" or "progressive." The higher critics, especially Martin Dibelius and Hermann Gunkel, applied new criteria to understanding Scripture. They analyzed texts by literary type, by author, and by historical setting. Adherents of this method announced that Moses didn't really write the Pentateuch and that the book of Isaiah had at least two authors. The Old Testament seemed to lose its authority in the battle, and the life and teachings of Jesus were "demythologized" in an attempt to discover what was "true" and what was "added" to the text.

Clergy and laity alike were confused by the discussion and either retreated into a defensive posture, missing whatever good might come from a careful literary analysis of Scripture, or quit reading the Bible altogether. "If I can't just read it and trust it all, how can I read and trust any of it?" was the common feeling.

Albert Einstein

The growing public acceptance of the relativity of truth and the death of absolutes was accelerated by the scientific works of Albert Einstein. World War I interrupted the experiments of this thirty-eight-year-old German Jew who in 1905 had published a paper called, "On the Electrodynamics of Moving Bodies." That virtuoso scientific work introduced the world to Einstein's theory of relativity. With photographs of a solar eclipse taken on the island of Principe off West Africa and in Sobral, Brazil, in 1919, the long-accepted scientific explanations of Isaac Newton were undermined by a far more complex and frightening view of reality. Paul Johnson described the panic that followed: "At the beginning of the 1920s, the belief began to circulate, for the first time at a popular level, that there were no longer any absolutes: of time and space, of good and evil, of knowledge, and above all of value. Mistakenly but perhaps inevitably, relativity became confused with relativism."[7]

Historian Johnson reminds us that though Einstein was not a practicing Jew, he acknowledged God and found the extension of his scientific views into the realms of philosophy and theology to be abhorrent.

The "Social Gospel"

As Darwin's evolutionary theory and the popular panic over Einstein's theory of relativity took their toll on the view of Scripture as God's absolute truth, so the teachings of Marx on class struggle and the eventual triumph of socialism began to influence local pastors, especially in urban churches. The "social gospel" was introduced officially by the Reverend Walter Rauschenbusch, the pastor of a small German Baptist church in the heart of the "Hell's Kitchen" slums of New York City. Confronted by poverty and injustice in the ghetto, Rauschenbusch decided that the church must become the agent to change society. In 1907 Rauschenbusch published his critique of Christian responsibility in *Christianity and the Social Crisis*.

Unfortunately, along with the needed emphasis on social concern, Rauschenbusch decided that "the other-worldliness of the evangelicals had to be abandoned." No longer could a minister like himself preach only "Christ, and Him crucified."[8] Of course, fundamentalist Christians struck back with a defense of the "fundamentals." Unhappily the church was divided for more than half a century into two warring camps. That tragic and needless division between the gospel and "social action" further weakened an already ineffectual Christian presence at a moment in history when people desperately needed the gospel preached with confidence and clarity.

The Humanist Manifesto

Gradually, the emphasis on the human side of the gospel at the cost of the divine led to the elimination of the gospel altogether. The Humanist

Society was born simultaneously in New York City and Hollywood in 1929. The New York chapter included on its advisory board Julian Huxley, Albert Einstein, and Thomas Mann. In 1933 the first *Humanist Manifesto* was signed by thirty-four such American notables as John Dewey, novelist Robert Lovett, and Charles Potter, liberal clergyman and author.

The first *Humanist Manifesto* affirmed that the universe was "self-existing and not created," that "the traditional dualism of mind and body must be rejected," that "the time has passed for theism or deism," and that "worship and prayer" would be replaced "in a heightened sense of personal life and in a corporate effort to promote social well-being."

"It follows," declared Item Ten in the *Humanist Manifesto One,* "that there will be no uniquely religious emotions and attitudes of the kind hitherto associated with belief in the supernatural."

The *Humanist Manifesto One* also declared that free enterprise ("existing acquisiting and profit motivated society") had "shown itself to be inadequate" and "a socialized and cooperative economic order must be established to the end that the equitable distribution of the means of life be possible."

In conclusion, the humanists denied the spiritual foundations upon which the nation was built. "We consider the religious forms and ideas of our fathers no longer adequate." And the manifesto claimed in conclusion that "man is at last becoming aware that he alone is responsible for the realization of the world of his dreams, that he has within himself the power for its achievement. He must set intelligence and will to the task."[9]

The foundations for the *Humanist Manifesto One* were laid during those years of prosperity between the Civil War and World War I. Optimism reigned supreme. America was caught up in the European notion that God was dead, that mankind was powerful enough to make it on its own, that the world was evolving toward eventual universal peace and prosperity.

The *Humanist Manifesto One* documents the pulling up of the nation's spiritual roots, the disregard of its Judeo-Christian heritage. As we review the half-century that followed in this second section of *America's Dates with Destiny*, we will see the consequences of that tragic disregard.

A President's Broken Dream

In 1914 Woodrow Wilson was surprised by the sudden announcement of war between Germany, Austria-Hungary, Russia, England, and France. The entire world was stunned by the prospects of global conflict. But like many of his countrymen, President Wilson refused to believe that even America would one day be drawn into the war. He was convinced that the conflict would not boil over into world war and that the inherent goodness of mankind would prevail.

In his second annual message to Congress on December 14, 1914, President Wilson announced, "We are at peace with the world . . . there is no reason to fear."[10] For two years and four months, the president refused to believe the growing evidence that in this great era of progress, when mankind was evolving to a new and higher state, barbarity, cruelty, and despotism still stalked the earth. On April 3, 1917, after calling our nation to war, Wilson wept for those who would die as the nation entered the conflict.

Already Wilson's desk was covered with secret field reports detailing the development of powerful new weapons systems. For the first time in the history of warfare, poisonous gases would be used, and they would cause 91,198 deaths and 1,205,655 injuries to fighting men and civilians alike. For the first time, huge dirigibles and sleek, propeller-powered aircraft would rain down terror from the skies on military installations and on great cities and their innocent civilian populations. And for the first time, submarines would launch powerful torpedoes against warships, freighters, and passenger liners alike.[11]

In this first World War, the Central and Allied Powers would mobilize 65,038,810 men for battle. Of those, 21,228,813 would be seriously wounded, and 8,020,780 more would die. And though no one bothered to keep accurate records of the civilian casualties, at least 6,642,633 civilians would be caught and murdered in the crossfire, and tens of millions more would be maimed and wounded.[12]

With the end of World War I came even further cause for weeping. Wilson's hard-fought gains in Europe and his dreams for a League of Nations would be defeated. In 1924 the president himself would die.

At approximately 3:00 A.M. one sleepless night during President

Wilson's final illness, he said to his personal physician: "Doctor, the devil is a busy man."

Later that morning he had Dr. Greyson read Saint Paul's consoling words from Second Corinthians: "We are perplexed, but not in despair; persecuted, but not forsaken; struck down, but not destroyed."[13]

Turning to Greyson, he said, "Doctor, if I were not a Christian, I think I should go mad, but my faith in God holds me to the belief that He is in some way working out His own plans through human perversities and mistakes."[14]

That is a fitting epitaph for an age of "progress" that in fact led to global economic depression, an even bloodier world war, and the rise of militant Communism that still threatens the future of the globe.

13

AMERICAN CIVIL LIBERTIES UNION FOUNDED

JANUARY 20, 1920

The Loss of the Rights of the Majority

Roger Baldwin, the founder of the American Civil Liberties Union (ACLU), walked quickly down West 13th Street in New York City. A light snow had fallen on that day the ACLU was born, January 20, 1920. The streets were wet with slush. And though he wore a thick woolen overcoat, Baldwin shivered from the cold.

To understand how the ACLU has become a primary force in the destruction of this nation's spiritual heritage is to understand Roger Baldwin, its founder and for sixty-one years its titular head. In 1918, just two years earlier, he had spent three winter weeks waiting for his hearing on draft evasion charges before federal Judge Julius M. Mayer in a dark, dingy prison cell in the old Tombs. When the marshal arrived at Baldwin's cell to escort him those five long blocks to the Federal Building at 15 Park Row, Baldwin was embarrassed at being handcuffed in the city streets. "So," said Baldwin, "I contrived to make him appear the prisoner and I the marshall by the simple device of keeping two paces ahead of him—he was short and fat—and dragging him along."[1]

Roger Baldwin was no ordinary criminal. He was being charged as a deliberate violator of the World War I draft act. He had refused to serve in warfare in any capacity, telling the judge, "I regard the principle of conscription of life as a flat contradiction of all our cherished ideals of individual freedom, democratic liberty and Christian teaching."[2]

Judge Mayer, after hearing Baldwin's long, eloquent testimony against military service, replied: "He who disobeys the law, knowing that he does so, with the intelligence that you possess, must, as you are prepared to—take the consequences."[3]

With that Roger Baldwin was sentenced to one year in the Essex County Jail in Newark, New Jersey. Accompanied by two federal marshals, Baldwin walked along lower Broadway en route to the subway, but his journey was slowed by cheering crowds and falling confetti. On the day Baldwin began his one-year term for avoiding the draft, November 11, 1918, World War I ended.

"They delivered me to a door in a high wall," Baldwin recalled later. "Behind was the old stone prison. I had been in many prisons as an officer of the juvenile and adult courts in St. Louis. I saw at once that this was the better sort of jail. I knew I would feel at home."[4]

But Roger Baldwin was not suited for prison life. Son of a wealthy and influential Boston leather merchant, Baldwin could trace his ancestry to William the Conqueror. His American roots were planted in 1620 when the Pilgrim fathers anchored the Mayflower in Massachusetts Bay. Born January 21, 1884, Baldwin attended public schools and a Unitarian Sunday school in Wellesley, Massachusetts. "I got to revere Jesus," Baldwin said of those childhood days, "not as a divine figure but for what he said. And I still think it's a good doctrine—impossible doctrine, but I think it's great stuff."[5]

Roger Baldwin graduated from Harvard with a master's degree in anthropology in 1904. His grandfather, William H. Baldwin, was the liberal organizing force behind Boston's Young Men's Christian Union, formed as an alternative to the Young Men's Christian Association, which refused membership to Unitarians. Baldwin's uncle, William Baldwin, Jr., though the capitalist president of the Long Island Railroad, was a reformer like his father, a director of the Child Labor Committee, chairman of the New York Committee of Fourteen, which dealt with prostitution, and a trustee of the Negro Tuskegee College.[6] Roger Baldwin grew up surrounded by reformers: "Around me it was an accepted assumption," he said, "that you had to help the underdog—that you had a moral obligation to help the people on the bottom."[7]

After graduation from Harvard and a summer in Italy, Baldwin moved to St. Louis to begin his first job as director of a neighborhood settlement house and to teach ethics at Washington University. In St. Louis, Baldwin's volunteer work with children was noted by the courts, which appointed him a probation officer. Soon city leaders noticed his interest in reform and appointed him director of the St. Louis Civic League.

Also in St. Louis, Baldwin assisted such reformers as Margaret

Sanger, the celebrated advocate of birth control, and Emma Goldman, the "Red Queen of Anarchy." He worked closely with a variety of reform organizations including the Quakers, the Unitarians, the International Workers of the World (IWW), socialists, and Communists. And though Baldwin was opposed to capitalism and disappointed by the Christian churches' apparent lack of commitment to social change, he never officially became a socialist, or a Communist. In fact, he later quoted Jawaharlal Nehru, the Indian prime minister, in condemning their teachings: "They're great ideas, but when they're attached to the machinery of a political state, man must be against them."[8]

On April 2, 1917, the day Woodrow Wilson asked Congress to declare war on Germany, Baldwin returned to New York City to donate his skills to the American Union against Militarism. The AUAM had been founded by social workers in 1914 "to counter President Wilson's demands for a larger army and for more active war preparedness."[9] On May 18, 1917, the Congress passed the Selective Service Act and Baldwin was appointed by the AUAM to direct its Bureau for Conscientious Objectors. In July that bureau's name was changed to the Civil Liberties Bureau. Baldwin lobbied on behalf of conscientious objectors as director of the CLB until he himself was sent to prison. "It is a prison," Baldwin wrote from the county penitentiary where he finished his term, "and as such is part of a wholly ineffective system of treating crime, doing society, in my judgment, more harm than good."[10]

Soon after his release from prison, Baldwin returned to New York and married Madeleine Doty, a well-known writer, lawyer, pacifist, "mild socialist," and committed feminist. He also founded from the ruins of the Civil Liberties Bureau the American Civil Liberties Union.

The ACLU's first offices were in an old, two-story stone residence on West Thirteenth Street in Manhattan. And on that cold, wet day in January 1920, one day before his thirty-fourth birthday, Roger Baldwin hurried across the icy street and into the first-floor office he would share with the other volunteer staff of the ACLU.

He had "dusty hair," one colleague remembers, and he looked "a bit bedraggled." He was "clean and careless" of appearance. His manner was described as "tumblingly hurried." In a 1940 biography, Baldwin was eulogized as "generous, self-disciplined, aristocratic, Galahadian, full of fervor and violent integrity, emotional, ethical, tirelessly seeking the Grail. A genuine article."[11]

When I think of the ACLU, I think of Roger Baldwin. I picture him on January 20, 1920, in that cold, donated office filled with borrowed typewriters and battered desks, wooden chairs, a small conference table, an improvised library piled high with old law books and newspaper clippings, and telephones ringing off their stands.

"The cause we now serve is labor," Baldwin said to the circle of friends and colleagues who surrounded him that day. For Baldwin, "labor" was the worker, the poor person dependent on an employer to survive. "Labor" was one who could not afford a lawyer to defend basic constitutional rights.

During World War I, it was necessary to mobilize the nation for war. Strict laws were passed against "disloyal, profane, scurrilous or abrasive language" about the government, the Constitution, the armed forces, the uniform, or the flag. Federal courts handed out severe sentences to individuals who violated these laws: 15 years in prison for speaking out against the draft; 10 years in prison and a $1,000 fine for opposing the Liberty Bonds; 20 years and a $10,000 fine for calling the government a liar, predicting a German victory, or applauding the sinking of the *Lusitania*.

And the penalties were strictly enforced. Socialist leader Eugene V. Debs was sentenced to ten years in jail for telling an audience in an antiwar speech, "You need to know that you are fit for something better than slavery and cannon fodder."[12]

Rose Pastor Stokes received a ten-year jail sentence for writing a letter to a St. Louis newspaper saying, "I am for the people and the government is for the profiteers."

Baldwin and his colleagues organized to protect the Bill of Rights in a nation that, in their opinion, was so bent on "saving the world for democracy that it was endangering its own democratic traditions."[13]

The Rights of the "Little Man"

By 1920 World War I had ended. The dissenter, the war protestor, the pacifist, and the conscientious objector no longer needed defending. But "labor" was in deep trouble. The economy began to deteriorate at the close of the booming war years. Working hours were stretched to twelve to fourteen hours a day, and "stretch-out" work days of twenty-four hours were demanded every two weeks in the steel industry. An attempt to protect children in the work force was ruled unconstitutional by the Supreme Court. Wages were being cut in every industry. Twenty thousand businesses would fail in 1921 alone. And unions found themselves powerless to cope with the growing panic.[14]

Eight hundred thousand new immigrants would arrive that year, and farm families, many of them immigrants of recent years, left the rural areas and joined the new arrivals in the rush to find jobs in the cities. Consequently, growing, even violent prejudice was directed against foreigners in the work place.

The fledgling American Civil Liberties Union found its legal hands full in the growing chaos. Roger Baldwin organized the defense of Sacco and Vanzetti, two Italian workers who were blamed for an April 15, 1920, murder and holdup of a Massachusetts shoe factory payroll. Both men had convincing alibis; yet, against the xenophobia of witnesses only able to describe the defendants as "Italian-looking," the men were found guilty. Believing their rights violated, Baldwin and his ACLU volunteers worked six long years for their release. But Sacco and Vanzetti, referred to by their trial judge as "dagos" and "sons of bitches," were executed. The nation was bitterly divided. And the ACLU was launched on a crusade to protect "the little man" that has lasted sixty-six years.[15]

Baldwin described the role of the ACLU in these words: "I suppose I pretty much accepted the Christian underdog doctrine that in order to make democracy work you had to have due process and fair trials to protect the rights of the humblest citizens."[16]

It is difficult to fault Baldwin's basic premise. The Declaration of Independence is clear. "All men are created equal." And the Constitution's Bill of Rights guarantees those basic freedoms for every man, woman, and child in America. For every person Baldwin and the ACLU have helped secure justice and equal protection under the law, we should be grateful. There is no doubt that Baldwin himself was sincere and deeply committed to his beliefs. But something has gone terribly wrong with Baldwin's dream, and sickness was lurking behind all those well-intentioned deeds from the very beginning.

From its inception, the ACLU has been a controversial organization. But its critics often oversimplified the problem. For years Baldwin was called a Communist and his organization a "Communist front" (as though that inaccurate label explained the ACLU's long-term negative effects upon the nation).

Almost forty years later, when Baldwin was ninety-two years old, his biographer asked it again: "So then you still say it's impossible to believe in civil liberties and be a Communist?"

"Yes," said Baldwin.

"Flat statement?" pressed the interviewer.

"Flat statement!" Baldwin replied, nodding vigorously.[17]

Baldwin or his ACLU can't be discredited simply on the grounds of their political associations. A deeper tragedy lies here. Roger Baldwin was ninety-six years old when he died on August 26, 1981, still the titular head of the movement he founded. About the time of Baldwin's death, the American Civil Liberties Union had just one hundred staff members, an annual budget of less than $17 million, and only four thousand part-time lawyer volunteers. And yet in the past sixty-six years of instigating, supporting, and defending thousands of cases in every jurisdiction up to and including the Supreme Court, Baldwin and his handful of ACLU lawyers, despite their good intentions, have had a devastating influence on the values and priorities of the nation.

Roger Baldwin and the Majority

The key to understanding how and why the American Civil Liberties Union has done such harm lies in a better understanding of Baldwin's view of the majority. During his years as a youthful reformer in St. Louis, Baldwin convinced the city fathers to adopt a new city charter that allowed 5 percent of the voters to petition any issue for a public vote. That same year, the voters used Baldwin's own charter to legalize segregated neighborhoods. Baldwin, active in the cause of integration, was furious: "In cases where minority rights are concerned," he said, *"you can't trust the majority"*[18](italics mine).

Throughout his lifetime, Baldwin held a deep and growing contempt for the opinions of the majority. He had seen too many "little people" trampled underfoot. He was determined to protect the rights of the minority whatever it cost him. And it cost him plenty. Baldwin defended Communists, anarchists, socialists, and neo-Nazis. In 1978, ACLU attorneys defended the rights of the American Nazi Party to stage a march in Skokie, Illinois, which has a large Jewish population, and fifty thousand dues-paying ACLU members quit the organization in protest. Baldwin, the spiritual leader of the ACLU, would not compromise.

Some people still admire Baldwin's uncompromising stand. They defend the ACLU's belligerent, dogmatic, often intolerant, and even oppressive tactics as necessary to guarantee the "little man's" freedom of expression. Other people, including tens of thousands of former ACLU supporters, have realized the dangerous long-term consequences of consistently putting minority views above the values and priorities of the majority.

Study the history of the ACLU cases during this past half-century and you will find a consistent abuse of majority rights and opinions in the name of civil liberties. And worse, you will find that in the process the ACLU has consistently attacked the foundations upon which this nation was founded. In these past decades, through court decisions in cases instigated or supported by the ACLU, our country's spiritual heritage has been tragically undermined if not replaced altogether.

One Example of the Loss of Majority Rights

As one example of the effects of Baldwin's elevation of minority rights, it is the right of the majority to believe that God created the heavens and the earth as described in the Old Testament book of Genesis. But to Baldwin, John T. Scopes's right to teach Darwinian evolution in his high school biology class in Dayton, Tennessee, superseded the rights of the majority. When school officials asked Scopes to teach the majority position, he refused. When parents, educators, and public officials went to court to stop Scopes in 1925, Baldwin and the ACLU retained Clarence Darrow and Arthur Garfield Hays on Scopes's behalf.

Anyone who has seen a production of *Inherit the Wind* or read H. L. Mencken's on-scene reports of that famous "Monkey Trial" has been moved by those dramatic confrontations between Darrow and William Jennings Bryan. Thanks to the ACLU, John T. Scopes had his day in court. Roger Baldwin was right. Scopes was guaranteed by the Bill of Rights a chance to defend himself, but he lost. The rights of the majority prevailed. Still, Baldwin and the ACLU were not satisfied by the majority's decision.

For the next fifty years, Baldwin and his lawyer volunteers challenged the rights of the majority to teach the Genesis view of creation.

Most schools across the nation had included Darwin's views alongside the views of Scripture. But even a balanced presentation of the options was not enough for Roger Baldwin and the ACLU.

In December 1981, a new "monkey trial" was conducted in Little Rock, Arkansas. In that state the "Balanced Treatment for Creation-Science and Evolution-Science Act"[19] had passed easily through both houses of the legislature and was signed into law by Governor Frank White. The law required public schools to teach scientific creationism alongside evolutionary theory. ACLU attorneys Philip Kaplan and Bob Crealy filed a suit against the act. They claimed that the law violated separation of church and state because it "necessarily encompassed the concept of a supernatural creator . . . . Creation science cannot be taught without reference to that religious belief in a Creator."[20]

The ACLU also maintained that the law abridged academic freedom. After a brief trial, Federal Judge William Overton struck down the Balanced Treatment Act and by so doing prejudiced similar balanced legislation pending in other states.

It was perfectly appropriate for Baldwin and the ACLU to guarantee the rights of "little man" John T. Scopes to have his day in court. And few would criticize the ACLU for insisting that Darwin's views be included in a full-scale presentation of the origins of man. (After all, Darwin himself had claimed that the "laws" behind evolution were God's laws and that evolution was "God's way" of crating the universe.) But it was inappropriate and unfair to the rights of the majority and disastrous to the future of this nation to eliminate the teaching of creation altogether from the classroom. For if there is no Creator, how then can there be "unalienable rights" granted to every citizen by Him as our Declaration of Independence declares?

The Loss of Majority Rights

What happened to the rights of the majority in the issue of creation? In 1982 the results of a nationwide Gallup poll on the origins of humanity were reported in *The New York Times*. Forty-four percent of all Americans polled believed in the account of creation as found in the Old Testament Book of Genesis. Another 38 percent believed that God was involved in the process of evolution, while 9 percent were undecided.

Only the 9 percent remaining believed in a theory of evolution having no place for God.[21]

In case after case instigated, supported, and defended by Baldwin and the ACLU, however, the opinions of the majority have been set aside and a minority opinion has taken their place. The Bill of Rights of the United States Constitution guarantees the right to freedom of speech, freedom of the press, peaceable assembly, petitioning the government, bearing arms, security against unreasonable search and seizure, and speedy and public trial by jury. But nowhere in the Constitution is the minority given a right to silence the majority or to replace majority views with its minority opinions. As the *New Republic* stated, "the battle for minority rights goes on, of course, but does the final victory require the eradication of the majority culture?"[22]

The Loss of Our Spiritual Foundations

As the rights of the majority have been replaced by the rights of the minority, so the spiritual foundations of the nation have been replaced by an entirely secular view of man. Now, for example, in many schools across the nation, the Genesis story of creation has been replaced by a secular view of evolution that eliminates not just the biblical view of humanity's origins, but even Darwin's own view that God used evolution in the creation of mankind. Carl Sagan's television series "Cosmos" is required viewing in many high school biology classes across the nation.[23] Yet Sagan's dogmatic presentation goes beyond science in stating: "The cosmos is all that is or ever was or ever will be . . . . It is the universe that made us."[24]

The Undermining of the Nation's Spiritual Heritage

The Supreme Court case that perhaps best exemplifies the role of the ACLU in the destruction of this nation's spiritual heritage is the case of *Engel v. Vitale*, which was decided on June 25, 1962. Five parents from Nassau County, New York, had protested a twenty-two-word classroom prayer written by the New York State Board of Regents: "Almighty God, we acknowledge our dependence upon Thee, and we beg Thy blessings upon us, our parents, our teachers and our country."

The board recommended the prayer for use at the beginning of each day's classes throughout the state. It was not mandatory nor meant to teach religion. Rather, by "teaching our children, as set forth in the Declaration of Independence, that the Almighty God is their creator," the children might derive security in the turbulent days following World War II.[25]

After the New York State courts supported the school board in requiring this inoffensive and nonmandatory prayer, the New York affiliate of the ACLU appealed the case to the Supreme Court. An ACLU statement said that "since the opinion noted that the Regents' Prayer, even though denominationally neutral and not compulsory, still offends the first amendment principle of separation of church and state, we are confident that when more sectarian religious practices are brought to the Court's attention, they likewise will be declared unconstitutional. Among these are Christmas and Chanukah observances, Bible reading, recitation of the Lord's Prayer, and baccalaureate services."[26]

The Supreme Court was convinced by the ACLU and declared against the regents. In that ruling the tradition of opening the nation's public classes with prayer was forbidden. American leaders were stunned. Former President Eisenhower replied, "I always thought this nation was essentially a religious one."[27] Cardinal McIntyre of Los Angeles declared, "The decision is positively shocking and scandalizing to one of American blood and principles."[28] And Dr. Billy Graham echoed their surprise and disappointment with these words, "Followed to its logical conclusion, prayers cannot be said in Congress, chaplains will be taken from the armed forces, and the President will not place his hand on the Bible when he takes the oath of office."[29]

Perhaps the ultimate irony of that Supreme Court decision is that the Court itself began the session outlawing prayer with its own traditional prayer of invocation.

The ACLU Against the Rest of Us

For the past six decades, Roger Baldwin and the ACLU have been advocates in cases hostile to all forms of public expression of personal faith. They have effectively eliminated the rights of the majority to pray (or to maintain a moment of silence) in the classroom. And though the Bible is the greatest collection of English prose and poetry in the history of our language and the book of wisdom upon which this nation was built, the ACLU has managed to get it taken out of the classroom and has silenced its public reading almost altogether.

In 1986 the ACLU chapter in Los Angeles was able by court action to prevent all prayers or public mentions of God in the high school baccalaureate services in that great city. It has become apparent that the ACLU has determined to strip all signs of faith from the culture of this nation by attacking or threatening to attack in the courts such American traditions as Christmas manger scenes, Easter sunrise services, public invocations and benedictions, and even the spiritual songs and stories of our children.

And what happens when we forget the foundations upon which the nation was built? Remember George Washington's advice to the nation in his farewell address that "religion and morality" are the two "great pillars of human happiness" and indispensable to "private and public felicity."

Remember John Adams's warning: "We have no government armed with power capable of contending with human passions unbridled by morality and religion . . . . Our Constitution was made only for a moral and religious people. It is wholly inadequate to the government of any other."

Remember Thomas Jefferson's prophetic words: "Can the liberties of a nation be sure when we remove their only firm basis, a conviction in the minds of the people, that these liberties are the gift of God? that they are not to be violated but with His wrath?"

The majority of this nation would agree with our forefathers' words of wisdom and warning. But the majority has surrendered its right to act upon those historic traditions. The American Civil Liberties Union and the courts protect the rights of criminals and prison inmates, drunk and drugged drivers, anarchists, Communists and neo-Nazis, atheists and agnostics. At the same time, they undermine the very spiritual foundations upon which those rights were guaranteed. Already we are reaping the consequences foreseen by our forefathers.

When Roger Baldwin was ninety-two, he said: "No fight for civil liberties ever stays won. So I always had to stick with it. I could never quit."[30] This statement is good advice to those of us who oppose the long-range effects of Roger Baldwin and his ACLU upon our nation. We must work as long and as hard to *re-establish* our spiritual foundations and the rights of the majority to believe and proclaim them, and we must never let them become so weakened again.

14

THE CRASH AND THE GREAT DEPRESSION

OCTOBER 24, 1929

The Loss of Fiscal Responsibility

On Black Thursday, October 24, 1929, at 10:00 A.M. the superintendent of the New York Stock Exchange, William B. Crawford, hit the large gong above the exchange floor to signal the opening of another trading day. Eleven hundred brokers and a thousand assistants thronged the twelve horseshoe-shaped trading posts in the main room and six counters in the annex. Approximately seventy-five different stocks were traded at each post by brokers who motioned bids and scribbled orders in a kind of growing frenzy.[1]

From the visitors' gallery extending along the east wall, guests, including Winston Churchill, and members of the world's press looked down on a giant room, almost two-thirds the size of a football field. Around the felt-padded trading floor were unenclosed phone booths, ten phones per cluster with each phone connecting the Exchange with brokerage houses across the nation and around the world.

By 11:00 A.M. the Exchange was in full panic. Bedlam had developed on the floor. Stock values were plummeting. The few buyers present were being mobbed by desperate sellers. In the hysteria that followed, at least one broker went mad and was led babbling from the floor. Other brokers fainted, lost shoes and dentures, or had their shirts torn off and their collars ripped away.[2]

During that first fateful hour, more shares were traded than in an average trading day. The ticker recording stock transactions had fallen far behind. Prices were beginning to collapse, but no one could tell exactly how bad the news was. Great corporations were nearing bankruptcy. Personal fortunes were being lost. And 4 million Americans who had borrowed, mortgaged, risked life savings, or embezzled company or family funds to gamble on the stock market were facing financial ruin.

News about the impending crash spread through New York City. A human wave of businessmen, secretaries, housewives, workers, widowed matrons, and even students who had invested in the market flowed down Broadway toward the corner of Wall and Broad streets and the fortresslike Exchange. Fifty uniformed policemen had been stationed on "the Corner" to control the frenzied crowd. By noon, angry, frightened people filled Wall Street from Trinity Church to the docks along the East River. Police Commissioner Grover Whalen dispatched an extra four hundred patrolmen, one hundred detectives, and a detail of mounted police to keep the mob from rioting.

At exactly 12:00 noon, Charles Mitchell, chairman of the National City Bank; Albert Wiggin, chairman of the Chase National; and William Potter, president of the Guaranty Trust Company met in emergency session with the senior partner of J. P. Morgan's private bank in their offices at 23 Wall, directly across the street from the Exchange. In just twenty minutes they agreed to create a $240 million pool to buy huge blocks of stock in a last-ditch stand to save the market.

At 12:30 the visitors' gallery was closed. By 1:00 P.M. stock values had dwindled by approximately $11 billion. At 1:30 P.M., Richard Whitney, the vice president of the Exchange, walked onto the floor representing that determined pool of bankers and ordered 25 thousand shares of United States Steel at ten points above the asking price. Brokers gasped. For a moment they began to hope again. Whitney moved on to another trading post and then another ordering stocks in ten-thousand and twenty-thousand-share blocks. The brokers began to cheer. That cheer reached the huge crowds outside the Exchange, and the roar of their voices joined in celebration.

By 3:00 P.M., when Crawford finally banged the gong to close the Exchange for the day, 12,894,650 shares had been traded. Though billions of dollars were lost, the slide had been stopped and in some cases even turned around. The *New York Times* rushed out an extra edition reporting "Worse Stock Crash Stemmed By Banks. Leaders Confer, Find Conditions Sound."[3]

It was the last false hope to prop up the spirits of an industrial nation on the way to bankruptcy. Five days later, on Black Tuesday, October 29, 1929, the bottom dropped out. More than 16 million shares were traded at a loss of personal and corporate wealth estimated at between $24 and $75 billion dollars. During that long, erratic slide between September and November of 1929, and especially during those two "black" frantic days of trading in October, the 4 million stockholding families of this nation lost "three times as many dollars as the United States spent in fighting World War I."[4]

The Problem of Greed and Easy Credit

President Herbert Hoover blamed the European economic collapse for America's great depression. Russian economist Nikolai Kondratiev identified a fifty-year "super" business wave and predicted similar fifty-year and less radical nine-year cycles in the future. Milton Friedman cites the "mild decline in the money stock from 1929 to 1930" and claims that "prosperity is dependent upon the size of the money supply." Others quote the Old Testament story of Joseph in Egypt as a biblical model for years of plenty followed necessarily by years of want.[5]

W. W. Kiplinger wrote, "The amazing lesson from this depression is that no one knows much about the real causes of anything!"[6]

We can know for certain at least two general causes of the crash of 1929 and of the massive economic depression of the early 1930s. They are, quite simply, greed and easy credit. During President Coolidge's era of plenty, greed became a national passion, and easy credit fueled the growing greed. Benjamin Franklin, in *Poor Richard's Almanac,* prophetically described the 1920s: "The poor have little, beggars none, the rich too much, enough not one."[7]

At the close of World War I, the United States had to change from a wartime to a peacetime economy. The industrialists and manufacturers turned their energies from war machines to consumer goods—automobiles, radios, and refrigerators. And the farmers who had managed to produce enough grain to meet the nation's wartime domestic needs continued to feed this country as well as export foodstuffs to Europe and beyond. Even though wartime demands had ended, the domestic and foreign markets for America's peacetime farms and factories had great potential.

But domestic and foreign consumers were short of cash. The reason for the European shortfall was obvious. America's allies owed this nation billions of dollars in war loans, and the defeated Central Powers owed billions more in reparations. The war had practically bankrupted the European nations. Yet, our economy was dependent at least in part on getting the loans repaid and on developing a strong European market for our cars, radios, and refrigerators.

The Problem of Foreign Credit

The only solution seemed to be massive infusions of credit. So under the Dawes Plan of 1924 America lent money to Germany. Germany used our money to pay its debts to France and Great Britain. And France and Great Britain used our money to repay their American debts.

American foreign lending grew to $900 million in 1924 and $1.25 billion in each of the years 1927 and 1928. With such large doses of credit in circulation, prosperity was temporarily guaranteed. But real money wasn't circulating among the nations; it was credit. One day there would be principal and interest to pay. Few people in government or in private banking seemed concerned about what might happen if the debtor nations defaulted on the payments of those massive loans. Americans assumed that peace would bring prosperity to everyone, that European nations would rebuild their economies and pay their debts.

Even as the nation was making that risky assumption, Congress began to create trade barriers that would help keep it from happening. Instead of giving free enterprise a chance on both sides of the Atlantic, the president and the Congress gave way to the pressures of the American Federation of Labor and the Association of Manufacturers. The Fordney-MacCumber Tariff Act of 1922 and the Hawley-Smoot Act of 1930 were passed to protect American manufacturers and workers by taxing imports that threatened American goods. Again, restraining free international trade guaranteed temporary prosperity while destroying the world's long-range chance of recovery.

When the European nations complained about our interference in free trade, we simply lent them more money at cheaper interest rates. Those massive doses of easy credit and the resulting inflationary spiral gave nations on both sides of the Atlantic a euphoric but false sense of prosperity.

The Problem of Domestic Credit

The American consumer, like his European counterpart, also became a victim of easy credit and inflation. During that era of progress between the Civil War and the Great Depression, huge fortunes were made by a handful of enterprising Americans. The decade of the 1920s was a time of massive accumulation of wealth. And though the monies trickled down to Americans at every level of society, most of the wealth was shared among just 0.1 percent of the total population. Twenty-four thousand families enjoyed annual incomes of $100 thousand or more in 1929. Of them, 513 reported income at more that $1 million.

This elite minority received more income in 1929 than the total monies earned by 11.5 million poor and lower-middle-class families in America. Those same rich families controlled 34 percent of all the nation's savings, while almost 80 percent of the nation's families—some 21.5 million households—had no savings whatsoever. Imagine it. Just 0.5 percent of the American population controlled 32.4 percent of the nation's wealth.

The 1920s were the most prosperous decade in the nation's history, but the prosperity was not equally shared. And though the standard of living seemed to be rising for all 120 million Americans during President Coolidge's tenure in the White House, the per capita income of the rich increased by 75 percent while all other Americans realized an average 9 percent per capita increase.

To maintain this "prosperity" required a large and active consumer population. And the average person just didn't have enough income to buy his share. Americans were working harder (the average worker's productivity increased by an incredible 43 percent in 1929 alone), but they were not being paid fairly for their productivity. Between 1923 and 1929, output per worker hour increased by 32 percent while wages increased by just 8 percent. In that same period, corporate profits and dividends rose more than 60 percent. The rich were getting richer, but they weren't sharing it. And though during the "roaring twenties" the rich turned conspicuous consumption into an art form, they alone couldn't consume the necessary cars, radios, houses, and refrigerators to keep the economy climbing. So the poor were asked to carry the load.

However, the poor and the growing middle class were using up most of their monthly salaries on necessary goods like food and clothing. Little was left for extra buying, let alone purchasing luxuries. Obviously, once again the solution was credit. Old American values were set aside. Nobody remembered what Ben Franklin had advised during the nation's formative years in *Poor Richard's Almanac*: "For Age and Want save while you may. No Morning Sun lasts a whole day."[8]

The nation had lost touch with its roots. The people flung caution to the wind. Every dime the workers earned, they spent. Advertising stimulated sales. And in 1929, corporate profits soared upward by 62 percent. Still it wasn't enough. The rich wanted more sales, more profits, and more dividends. They turned again to Madison Avenue. Advertising on radio, print, and billboard during the 1920s reached a feverish pitch. Again, the nation ignored Poor Richard's advice: "The borrower is a slave to the lender."[9]

Once persuaded to spend, the nation was easily convinced to spend on credit. By 1929, three of every five cars and 80 percent of all radios were purchased with installment credit. Outstanding credit in the United States doubled from $1.38 billion to $3 billion in 1929 alone. Because payments on the principal and interest of those credit purchases consumed a growing percentage of the debtor's monthly paycheck, little money was left for new buying. So the promotional hype increased. The credit rates were lowered, and the cycle of easy credit and inflation escalated even further. Again, the rich got richer. Stock dividends, paid almost entirely to the wealthy, increased in 1929 by 65 percent.

This amazing amount of credit made available to the debtor nations and the debtor public presents a mystery. The actual currency in circulation in the United States at the beginning of the 1920s was $3.68 billion. In 1929, nine years later, the amount remained almost the same—actually a little less, $3.64 billion. Yet, "the expansion of total money supply, in money substitutes or credit, was enormous: from $45.3 billion on June 30, 1921 to over $73 billion in July 1929, an increase of 61.8 percent in just eight years."[10] That huge amount of credit propped up the economy for a decade and gave the entire world an illusion of prosperity. Then the bubble burst. From where did this disastrous wave of credit flow?

In its 1923 annual report, the Federal Reserve answers that all-important question: "The Federal Reserve banks are . . . the source to which the member banks turn when the demands of the business community have outrun their own unaided resources. The Federal Reserve supplies the needed additions to credit in times of business expansion and takes up the slack in times of business recession."[11]

The Loss of Fiscal Responsibility

To understand the dangerous power held by the Federal Reserve system and its contribution to the crash and Great Depression requires looking back at the Constitution and a brief history of money, banks, and bankers in America. The problem of money was simple enough in the beginning. In Article I of the Constitution, our forefathers gave Congress the power "to coin Money [and] regulate the Value thereof."

The system would be simple. Coins of set value would be minted to exchange for goods. The United States federal government began to mint gold and silver coins just after the Constitution was adopted through the Coinage Act of 1792. For use in wartime emergencies, there were temporary issues of paper money during the wars of 1812 and 1846 (the Mexican War) and during the Civil War. When the federal government continued to print paper money for convenience, a de facto gold standard was established to guarantee that each greenback was backed by solid gold. In 1900 the Gold Standard Act made it official. Paper money represented gold on deposit, and greenbacks could be traded at any time for that precious metal.

During the Depression, however, gold reserves were drained to the point that in 1934 the Gold Reserve Act effectively ended the gold standard. And though various presidents have considered returning the nation to a gold standard, the paper standard has prevailed.

Understanding how paper and promises create a trustworthy financial system is even more complex. When Lincoln first called for Congress to print paper money to assist in the Civil War effort, the nation's bankers were upset. No wonder! Up to that time, banks had enjoyed a practical monopoly on the money supply.

In the Constitution, Congress is also granted the power "to borrow Money on the credit of the United States." If the government needed money, the banks would gladly lend it. The nation borrowed money from a bank exactly as an individual or corporation borrowed it. But banks preferred lending money to the government because the loan was secure; after all, a government can tax people, but individuals and corporations have no such option. And in the meantime, the interest was compounding.

American bankers learned that trick from their European counterparts. After the Napoleonic wars, the bankers of Europe had turned that principle into a gold mine. They offered loans to European royalty to finance their regimes. They knew that kings and queens could eventually get the money from taxation, and they were glad to wait as long as the interest was compounding. Baron Rothschild, a banker, called compounding interest "the eighth wonder of the world."

If a government could bypass the banks and supply money directly, however, the bankers would lose all those loans, the compounding interest, and much of their power. Three times federal banking systems and regulatory agencies were tried in the United States. Each time political pressure by private banking interests overturned the national banking system, and private banking interests regained control.

But after a financial panic in 1907 and the failure of the nation's second (The Trust Company of America) and third (Knickerbocker Trust Company) largest banks, the government intervened. The people wanted to control their financial institutions. They did not want to be victims of powerful, unregulated bankers. A commission was appointed in 1908 to investigate banking and suggest reform. Again, a federal bank was recommended.

To avoid losing their monopoly on the nation's money supply, New York's most influential bankers met secretly in a private railroad car on Jekyll Island, off the coast of Georgia. In just two days a plan was drawn up by the bankers for a central bank with six members appointed by the president and forty members appointed by private banking interests. When the plan was presented in the Congress, the nation grew suspicious. The Aldrich Plan benefited the bankers and not the people. It was soundly rejected.

But the bankers continued to lobby in public and private. On December 23, 1913, the Glass-Owens Bill was signed by President Wilson. That Federal Reserve Act created a central bank for the United States government and a system for regulating private banking in the nation. And though the chairman of the Federal Reserve was appointed by the president, he would act independently of any presidential or congressional controls. In fact, all seven members of the Federal Reserve Board (known as the Fed) appointed by the president would serve independently of him. The remaining members of the Federal Reserve Board represented the private member banks.

Ultimately, the bankers prevailed. The new Federal Reserve system was in reality owned by the twelve individual Federal Reserve banks, which were in turn owned by private investors. The bankers won their struggle to maintain power. There would be a federal bank, but they would own it. And there would be an agency to regulate private banking, but they would control that agency.

The results have been disastrous. The Federal Reserve Board had more power than Congress in creating or regulating money, and more power than free trade over the flow of money in the land. It controlled the supply of money that moved in and out of our nation's economy by controlling the member banks' capacity to lend and the rate at which they could do so.

Those private bankers together with the presidential appointees worked independently of the president, the Congress, or the people. They exercised far too much power and consistently used their power to profit private banks and bankers.

The history of the Federal Reserve Board during the 1920s and the 1930s illustrates its misuse and overuse of power. It was the Fed that poured credit into the European nations at the beginning of the decade. Paul Johnson described the consequences of that unfortunate decision:

> America's ruler, in effect, rejected the rational laissez-faire choice of free trade and hard money and took the soft political option of protective tariffs and inflation. The domestic industries protected by the tariff, the export industries subsidized by the uneconomic loans and of course the investment bankers who floated the bonds all benefited. The losers were the population as a whole, who were denied the competitive prices produced by cheap imports, suffered from the resulting inflation and were the universal victims.[12]

And it was the Fed that helped to fuel the credit buying and frantic, half-crazed speculation of those years before the crash.

People in the 1920s were caught up in "single-minded pursuit of riches."[13] The "roaring twenties" had one primary theme: "Get rich quick, and do it without working." In the mid-twenties, one popular way to do that was with Florida real estate. People bought Florida land without ever seeing it, let alone developing it for homes or businesses.

The availability of unsecured credit and long-term installment payments made the risk seem safe and simple. Victims of their own greed and of the banks' easy credit bought alligator-infested swampland and held it until other victims even more desperate for instant, easy wealth bought the worthless deeds. In 1926 the boom ended in a disastrous crash. Coming just three years before the stock market crash, the land speculation disaster in Florida should have served the nation as a warning. But it didn't.

From that moment until Black Thursday, the stock market succeeded the swamps of Florida as the next big gamblers' paradise. People didn't investigate companies before they purchased stocks. They didn't invest in companies for their dividend or growth potential. They bet on stocks like race horses. And they borrowed and embezzled or risked their savings to buy on margin. Again the Fed fueled the process with easy credit. Paul Johnson described the process: "Domestically and internationally they constantly pumped more credit into the system, and whenever the economy showed signs of flagging they increased the dose."[14]

In July 1927, at a secret meeting of bankers at the Long Island estates of Ogden Mills, the United States Treasury under-secretary, and Mrs. Ruth Pratt, the Standard Oil heiress, Benjamin Strong, governor of the New York Federal Reserve Bank, pushed the Fed "to give a little coup de whiskey to the stock market."[15] As a result, Johnson wrote, the Fed "set in motion the last culminating wave of speculation." That act, as described by a member of the Fed, Adolph Miller, before a Senate investigating committee, "resulted in one of the most costly errors committed by it or any other banking system in the last seventy-five years."[16]

Already we have discussed how the Fed pushed the nation toward inflation with its massive supply of credit during the 1920s. But in the Depression of the 1930s, it made matters even worse. Instead of using its power to expand credit that would have helped American industry rebuild and the American worker find employment, it decreased the money flow by 5 percent in 1930, by 6.4 percent in 1931, by 14.9 percent in 1932, and by 6.6 percent in 1933.

By 1933, when banks were collapsing and the economy was at the bottom, only 71.2 cents was available for every dollar that was in circulation in 1929. The Fed cut lending capabilities and limited the money supply to protect its member banks. The Fed's decision was stupid and irresponsible for the nation, for the world, and even for the bankers. Through its almost unlimited power and self-serving incompetence, the Fed helped push the nation and the world into the most disastrous depression in modern history.

The Great Depression

Between 1929 and 1933, more than 5 thousand American banks and at least 20 thousand American businesses failed.[17] Unemployment rose from 1.5 million in 1929 to an estimated 17 million in 1933. Forty-five million Americans were living "in dire poverty."[18] Hundreds of thousands of families were being evicted from their houses, apartments, and trailers. One New York City judge tried to handle 450 family eviction cases in a single day.[19] In 1932 alone, more than 273 thousand Americans lost their homes to foreclosure. Millions were fed at charity soup kitchens and emergency food lines. The stability and historic structure and values of the American family were shattered and reshaped forever.

Suspicion, hatred, and violence between the races increased a hundredfold. The governor of Mississippi suggested that 12 million black Americans be shipped to Africa. The United Spanish War Veterans urged the deportation of 10 million aliens (nearly 6 million more than the actual number of aliens in the United States at that time). And in 1932 more than three times as many persons left this country as entered it. Author Edward Robb Ellis concludes, "No longer was America the promised land."[20]

The rest of the world, still staggering from the losses of World War I, plunged into almost simultaneous depression with us. Europe suffered its own economic and social nightmare. Meanwhile, in Bavaria, a youthful Adolf Hitler began to dream of a final solution for the worldwide economic chaos. The decade that began in prosperity and hopefulness ended in poverty and despair. During the next decade the world would face a devastating economic depression, and in just ten years the entire world would be at war again.

Given the reality of long wave economic cycles, with overproduction, debt accumulation, and the resultant deflation in commodity prices, merely to say that greed coupled with easy credit caused the crash and the Great Depression would be too simplistic. But both are important factors to remember as we face our choices in the future. At the close of

World War I, the American peace negotiating team was greedy when it demanded excessive reparation payments from the Central Powers in the Treaty of Versailles. In 1922 and 1930 the United States Congress was greedy when it placed restrictive tariffs on foreign trade just as Europe was trying to rebuild its economy. The banks were greedy when they fueled the period of frantic speculation and inflation that led to the crash. And the banks were greedy again when they withheld money from the economy during the depression at the very time the country needed money most. The rich owners and bosses were greedy when they didn't share the profits with the people. And the people were greedy when they overspeculated, using credit in their attempts to get rich quick.

Benjamin Franklin warned about greed and easy credit in those early days of American history when he wrote in *Poor Richard's Almanac,* "Money and Man a mutual Friendship show: Man makes false Money, and Money makes Man so."[21]

Since those devastating days of the crash and the Great Depression, Americans have asked, "Why did it happen, and when could it happen again?" "What is necessary for a new disaster," answers John Kenneth Galbraith, "is only for memories of the last one to fade, and no one knows how long that takes."[22]

15

FRANKLIN ROOSEVELT BEGINS HIS "IMPERIAL PRESIDENCY"

MARCH 4, 1933

The Loss of Power by the People

At 10:00 A.M. the rain stopped. The 500 thousand people who were crowded along the inaugural parade route smiled at that sudden change of fortune. Perhaps the storm had ended. Perhaps the song being played at that moment by the Marine Corps Marching Band was true: "Happy Days Are Here Again." It had been Franklin Roosevelt's campaign song. He had promised a fair, new deal for everyone. The people had believed him, and now he was riding down Pennsylvania Avenue en route to his inauguration as America's thirty-second president.

Retiring President Herbert Hoover, in a silk top hat and scarf, sat beside the president-elect in the open limousine looking sullen and exhausted. No wonder. His term in office began in 1929, the year of "Black Thursday" and the great crash, and ended in 1933, the worst year in more than three ugly years of depression. During Hoover's presidency 5,060 banks had failed, 750 thousand farmers and at least a million businesses had gone bankrupt, and between 15 million and 17 million Americans had lost their jobs. By that time, nobody was keeping track. A Roosevelt historian described the mood in Washington and across the country that day: "The machinery of government was impotent. The banking system was paralyzed. Panic, misery, rebellion and despair were convulsing the people and destroying confidence not merely in business enterprise but in the promise of American life. No man could say into what we would have drifted had we drifted another twelve months."[1]

So, in its moment of despair, willing to sacrifice almost anything to stop "the disastrous drift," the people turned to Franklin Delano Roosevelt to save them. And on his inaugural day, they greeted FDR's ascendency to the presidency with an almost hysterical outpouring of love and trust. As his open car approached the Capitol, the roar of welcome along the parade route was echoed by an equal roar of welcome from the throng of invited guests jammed into the west portico of the Capitol Building.

Hoover left the president-elect and walked alone to his seat in the front row of celebrants. FDR, escorted on the arm of his son, James, approached the platform. The new president placed his hand upon his old Dutch family Bible as Chief Justice Charles Evans Hughes administered the oath of office. President Roosevelt greeted the distinguished guests from around the world and then turned to the microphones that would carry his voice to the frightened, weary millions waiting almost breathlessly for some word of hope from their new president. He began:

> This is a day of national consecration, and I am certain that my fellow-Americans expect that on my induction into the Presidency I will address them with a candor and a decision which the present situation of our nation impels.
>
> This is pre-eminently the time to speak the truth, . . . frankly and boldly. Nor need we shrink from honestly facing conditions in our country today. This great nation will endure as it has endured, will revive and will prosper.
>
> So, first of all, let me assert my firm belief that the only thing we have to fear is fear itself—nameless, unreasoning, unjustified terror which paralyzes needed efforts to convert retreat into advance.[2]

As we look back on that moment, it is easy to understand why the people felt relief as those first words from Roosevelt crackled out over the still primitive, static-laden radio network. His almost regal presence and his calm, fatherly tone of voice gave them confidence. Roosevelt was a tall, attractive man with patrician bearing, a gift for charismatic speech, and a reputation for courage and bravery gained from his triumphant personal struggle with polio. Fear ruled the land, but Roosevelt had overcome fear. And the confidence in his strong voice and earnest delivery gave the people hope for the first time in four long, disastrous years. They were inaugurating a president, but from the beginning the people were looking to Roosevelt to be their savior. From the perspective of history, it is easy to understand why a nation might grant a single man so much power over its future.

"Rulers of the exchange of mankind's goods have failed through their own stubbornness and their own incompetence." The new president boldly accused past leaders of the public and private sectors.

"Practices of the unscrupulous money changers stand indicted in the court of public opinion, rejected by the hearts and minds of men." Listeners responded with enthusiastic nods and wild applause.

"The money changers have fled from their high seats in the temple of our civilization." Roosevelt was addressing millions of common people who had lost their entire life savings, retirement and pension funds, jobs or farms, homes, and even families. And they cheered his good news and hopefulness.

"Our greatest primary task is to put people to work. This is no unsolvable problem if we face it wisely and courageously. It can be accomplished in part by direct recruiting by the government itself, treating the task as we would treat the emergency of a war." Roosevelt struck the vital chord. Loud applause and growing roars of approval continued to interrupt the president and echoed from millions of radios into homes across the land. "If we are to go forward we must move as a trained and loyal army willing to sacrifice for the good of a common discipline, because, without such discipline, no progress is made, no leadership becomes effective . . . . This I propose to offer, pledging that the larger purposes will bind upon us all as a sacred obligation with a unity of duty hitherto evoked only in time of armed strife."

For more than three years the people had been at war, battling for their own survival. They had been fighting on various fronts: unemployment, financial loss, humiliation, homelessness, hunger, broken dreams, a breakdown of family life, almost daily disappointment, and rising despair. They had been fighting a host of enemies: bankers, bosses, brokers, and government officials on all levels. And it hadn't appeared as though President Hoover was even trying to help them.

Hoover didn't have Roosevelt's regal bearing or communication skills, and though he had worked in his way to save the nation from depression, to the people Hoover seemed impotent, arrogant, even detached. Suddenly, the new president was talking directly to their needs in plain words they could understand. The new commander-in-chief seemed to be on their side. If he was "calling the nation to war," the people would follow. And if he needed extreme and unconstitutional power to lead them, they would surrender that power to him.

In the very next breath the president made it clear. He would demand of Congress "broad executive power to wage a war against the emergency as great as the power that would be given me if we were in fact invaded by a foreign foe."

The War on the Old Order

At the end of that resounding address, Hoover hurried off into obscurity, and Roosevelt returned to the White House eager to begin his war "against a return of the evils of the old order." The war began the very next day.

On Sunday, March 5, 1933, President Roosevelt issued a proclamation declaring a national bank holiday for the following week. He also prohibited the export of gold or the exchange for gold of foreign currency. He ordered Congress into emergency session for Thursday, March 9, and by March 10 he had called for an immediate cut in federal expenses. And though it meant cutting such important programs as benefits to veterans of World War I, Congress enthusiastically acquiesced.

During his first week in office, while the banks were closed, Roosevelt and his closest advisors worked on a complex banking bill that restructured the nation's banking system. On Sunday, March 12, those changes were readied and Roosevelt gave his first "fireside chat," reassuring the people that the banks would reopen on Monday and that the "New Deal" he had promised them would begin immediately. On Monday, March 13, he asked Congress to legalize beer, adding a "jovial celebration" to his first ten days in office.

During those next few months in power, Roosevelt demanded and received almost total control of the government, affecting every detail of American life. Almost single-handedly, the president regulated the stock market, abandoned the gold standard, controlled banks and banking, instigated a program of public works with an accompanying maze of bureaucracies and regulating agencies, and placed the federal government in charge of aid to the needy, where the church, civic agencies, and private charities once had domain.

During those first hundred days of Franklin Roosevelt's administration, the executive office of the president attained a power unimagined by the writers of the Constitution. The powers of Congress, of the courts, and of the people were greatly diminished. Further, Roosevelt, who had earlier criticized Hoover harshly for running the federal government at such high costs and growing deficits, led the nation to its sharpest increase in bureaucractic spending in the history of the nation. In spite of his enormous popularity, Roosevelt's policies moved the nation toward a radical departure from the vision of our founding fathers, setting the foundations for a welfare state and an almost imperial presidency.

Roosevelt and the Nation's Banking System

After assuming his role as commander-in-chief for his war against depression, Roosevelt closed the banks, ordered his treasury secretary, William Woodin, to draft an emergency banking bill that gave the president control over the movement of gold and penalized its hoarding, approved the issuing of new Federal Reserve bank notes, arranged for the reopening of banks with adequate liquid assets, and began to reorganize the banks in trouble.[3]

One eyewitness to the congressional debate on that bill remembered that "with a unanimous shout, the House passed the bill, sight unseen, after only thirty-eight minutes of debate."[4]

Something needed to be done and done quickly about the growing depression; the Federal Reserve system and its member banks had misused their power and needed to have that power curbed. But Roosevelt went beyond all constitutional propriety in gaining and using presidential power. Using his executive office to control the nation's monetary system is only one example. And the Congress, almost without argument or criticism, acquiesced to his demands.

In an attempt to end deflation during those first six weeks of the New Deal, the president used his new power to place an embargo on gold and to abandon the nation's gold standard. He followed that imperious act with a similar law forbidding the issuance of bonds that would be payable in gold. Then he abrogated all existing private or public contracts obligating repayment in gold to the bearer.

Charles Hurd described Roosevelt's sudden, massive gain and almost unquestioned use of power in these words: "This single law gave Roosevelt dictatorial power over credit, money issued by the government, production and purchase prices of gold and silver, and all transactions in foreign exchange. No man at the time could even define the scope of the power involved. It was the largest single peacetime grant of power ever conferred upon a President."[5]

Roosevelt and the Growth of Federal Bureaucracy

The trend toward bigger and more powerful central government really began with Franklin Roosevelt. It all started innocently enough. The president was "at war with depression." The nation's future was threatened on many fronts. Millions were poor and unemployed. Farms and factories were bankrupt and closed down. The monetary system had nearly collapsed. People were hungry and needed both immediate and long-term relief.

Roosevelt began to create federal departments or bureaus to do the job. He was building an army, but he forgot that the Constitution had already determined the divisions of that army. Our forefathers decided the federal government would have three branches, each with checks and balances on the other. After those three branches of the federal government had met their constitutional obligations, the rest of the responsibility was left with the nation's states, counties, and cities. They were closer to the people than Washington. They knew the people's needs and could meet them more effectively and efficiently than any federal bureau. Federal monies could be used to assist the state and local sectors, but the forefathers never envisioned a time when the federal government would create endless layers of federal bureaucracies to conduct or regulate these state and local tasks. But Roosevelt wanted to handle almost everything from Washington. And the programs and monies distributed to the states would be supervised by bureaus and agencies under his control.

On March 29, 1933, Congress approved Roosevelt's plan to create the Civilian Conservation Corps, an unemployment relief program designed to provide government jobs, especially for young people, on massive public works projects. Congress allocated $500 million to supply wholesome surroundings and vocational and academic training for the young and unemployed. The newly trained youths would be mobilized to work throughout the states to help conserve the nation's resources.

On May 18, 1933, the Congress approved Roosevelt's Tennessee Valley Authority (TVA). The TVA would build multipurpose dams to create reservoirs to control floods and generate inexpensive hydroelectric power. Roosevelt had decided that the federal government would use the TVA experiment as a yardstick to see how inexpensively power could be created, and then he would force private utilities to conform to those rates. In spite of the comparisons to similar projects in the Soviet Union that competed directly with free enterprise programs, and in spite of the evidence that commercial power programs throughout the nation were more effective and efficient than such a massive federal plan, the Congress once again approved Roosevelt's program with an overwhelming majority.

During that same first year in office, the president launched the National Industrial Recovery Administration (NRA). The NRA was intended to create a nationally planned economy while protecting profit-making institutions and stimulating national recovery. Each industry in the country would make up a code of practices including wages, working conditions, prices, and production acceptable to the NRA. The government licensed industries that conformed to the code and withheld licensing from the others. As a reward, price fixing was sanctioned by the government to guarantee an assured market for goods. However, the employers, in exchange for a guaranteed price, had to guarantee minimum wage, maximum hours, improved working conditions, and prohibitions against child labor.

The attempt by government to control industry in the nation was a massive failure. Huey Long compared the plan to fascism and called it an attempt "to regulate business and labor much more than anyone did in Germany and Italy."[6] And though Roosevelt's federal attempts to manage the nation's business failed, the president asked Congress for a two-year extension of the program. Before the Congress could act, however, the Supreme Court, on May 27, 1935, declared the NRA "an unconstitutional delegation of legislative power."[7]

The Federal Emergency Relief Act of 1933 (FERA) was authorized to grant billions of dollars of federal funds to provide relief to the needy through employment. The private organizations that had been the primary source of public relief until that time were not eligible to receive or distribute funds. Only public agencies could receive grant monies. Because FERA didn't get enough people back to work immediately, Roosevelt pushed through his Civil Works Administration (CWA) to design works projects, hire and train workers, and pay union wages. By January 1934 the CWA had hired 4.26 million people. But Congress, realizing at last that government could not afford to replace the private sector as the nation's primary employer, liquidated the program in less than five months.

In May 1935 FDR responded with the creation of the Works Progress Administration (WPA). The WPA was another federal jobs program creating work projects or approving projects submitted by local and state governments. Before its extinction, 7.8 million new government workers had been hired for the WPA alone.

The Social Security Act of 1935 created old age and unemployment insurance. It established public assistance to the elderly, the blind, the disabled, and dependent children. And it attempted to guarantee health and welfare services to the nation. The plan was a sincere attempt to bring "social security" to all the people by forcing workers to save a certain portion of their incomes every month and by taxing employers to pay the rest.

During the depression, to the millions of people who had lost their life savings, pensions, and profit-sharing plans, Social Security looked like a step in the right direction. But from the perspective of history, we are discovering once again that for the long haul, no matter how well-intentioned the plan, placing the welfare of the people in the hands of a federal bureaucracy is a dangerous and risky business. One Roosevelt critic wrote, "Formerly government was the responsibility of people; now people were the responsibility of government."[8]

Roosevelt spent $10.7 billion on public works and another $2.7 billion on sponsored projects. His New Deal employed 8.5 million Americans who built 122 thousand public buildings, 77 thousand new bridges, 285 airports, 664 thousand miles of roads and highways, 24 thousand miles of storm and water sewers, and uncounted parks, public playgrounds, and reservoirs. Massive federal bureaucracies were created. The national debt skyrocketed. The private sector was saddled with a maze of ineffectual and inefficient regulatory agencies. The Wagner Act of 1935 compelled employers to accede peacefully to the unionization of their plants and gave labor an almost limitless right to collective bargaining without any reciprocal obligations on the unions.

And though the nation teetered back and forth between economic chaos and signs of recovery during those first two Roosevelt terms in office, in fact there is not much evidence that all his manhandling of

Congress, the Supreme Court, and the private sector did much to end the Great Depression. Many historians see Roosevelt's New Deal as simply a continuation of Hoover's old plans for recovery rushed through Congress with no respect for constitutional limitations on presidential power and almost no concern for the load of indebtedness that such massive federal borrowing would place on coming generations. Paul Johnson wrote: "From the perspective of the 1980s it seems probable that both [Hoover and Roosevelt] impeded a natural recovery brought about by deflation."[9]

Franklin Delano Roosevelt tried to save the country from depression by assuming presidential powers never granted by the Constitution. With single-minded determination, he tried to shape the nation in his own image. He failed. But decades later, the nation still suffers from the cost of that experiment.

The Lasting Effects

Once established, large government bureaus were slow to die. Once imposed upon the nation, the complex maze of regulations and regulatory agencies was difficult to dismantle. To grant powers to unions or to employers that did not rise out of the normal give and take basic to free enterprise left a residue of hatred and suspicion that was difficult to overcome. To borrow money by the billions to save the economy only undermined the economy further in the long run and saddled future generations with a gigantic debt. To use charismatic gifts and powerful media to overwhelm all opposition was a dangerous and undemocratic precedent that still haunts the nation.

Because of FDR, the Great Depression did more to reshape the existing framework of government policy than any other single event in recent history. Out of depression came a powerful central government; an imperial presidency; the enormous political power of newspapers, radio, and later television; an antibusiness bias throughout the country; powerful unions; a complexity of federal regulations and agencies designed to control and, in many instances, protect powerful vested interests; and, most importantly, a belief in the economic policies of British scholar John Maynard Keynes, to the end that government spending and "fine tuning" would supposedly guarantee perpetual prosperity.

Roosevelt's strategy didn't work. The crash of 1929 and the Great Depression that followed taught America that we can't trust the tinkering of a powerful, charismatic president to restore the nation's economic health. Roosevelt's New Deal experiment was ineffective and far too costly.

World War II

The real economic recovery in the United States began in September 1939 when news of war in Europe caused the stock market and the American economy to begin climbing again. But we can't trust a war to bring economic prosperity to a nation either. That tragic road to recovery cost the nation even more. During World War II, 318,374 American soldiers and airmen were killed, and 565,861 more were wounded. The Navy, including Marines and Coast Guard, reported 89,345 killed and 105,953 wounded. The total casualty list was more than a million American men and women killed or wounded. Our allies counted 10,650,000 killed, wounded, or missing in battle. The Axis powers reported another 4,650,000 military personnel dead or wounded. And the loss of innocent civilians—men, women, and children—is counted in the tens of millions.[10]

To mobilize and equip more than 10 million American military personnel cost this nation in excess of $350 billion. Before the war began, under Roosevelt's New Deal the annual federal budget grew to just over $9 billion. To "save the nation from the Great Depression," federal spending had increased the national debt by about $3.9 billion annually, or more than $325 per person in the nation. But during the war years, the federal government borrowed $98 billion annually, raising the federal debt each year by $53.9 billion (500 percent), or $1,848 per year per person. The total national debt grew from $43 billion in 1940 to $257 billion in 1945.

To help meet the budget, taxes were raised. Federal government receipts rose from $5.3 billion in 1940 to $43.9 billion in 1945, and individual income taxes from $982 million to $19 billion. What was worse, the growing debt was placed primarily on the poor. During the war years, the highest effective rate of tax increase occurred at the lowest income levels, especially on those who made under $6,000 a year.[11]

What brings about economic recovery if expensive "New Deals" don't work and world wars cost too much in human life and growing debt? The American system of free enterprise backed by a federal government that respects its constitutional limits is better able to effect its own recovery than a private sector saddled by powerful bureaucracies and regulatory agencies.

The Death of the President

On March 30, 1945, President Roosevelt traveled to his Warm Springs, Georgia, hideaway for a time of recuperation from the pressures of twelve years in the presidency. The strain of those three difficult and demanding terms in office had contributed to his broken health and lagging spirits. Whether he failed or succeeded at the task, Roosevelt gave a full measure of life to the people of this nation. On April 12, 1945, Franklin Delano Roosevelt died. His body was carried by train past millions of mourners who lined the tracks from Warm Springs to Washington and from Washington to his home at Hyde Park, New York. There, in the rose garden of his family home, he was buried.

On the day of President Roosevelt's death, Vice President Harry Truman was rushed from the office of Sam Rayburn, Speaker of the House, to the White House to receive the oath of office. In the long Cabinet Room next to the Oval Office, members of the government were waiting in various stages of shock, grief, and disbelief. Surrounded by Roosevelt's cabinet and brain trust, Truman sat in silence waiting for his wife to arrive. She hurried into the room looking tired and fearful. Harry Truman stood to greet her, smiled calmly, and placed his left hand on the Bible and his right hand in the air. With that familiar oath from the Constitution, Harry Truman became the thirty-third president of the United States.

"I do solemnly swear that I will faithfully execute the office of President of the United States and will, to the best of my ability, preserve, protect, and defend the Constitution of the United States." Truman, like his predecessors, added, "So help me God." Light applause sounded. Bess Truman held her husband's hand as the new president was led through the mass of press and spectators who had gathered near his waiting limousine.

In the lobby of the White House, Chief Justice Harlan Stone quoted the presidential oath to the swarm of newspaper and radio reporters waiting there. After repeating each word slowly, the chief justice added quietly, "It's a good oath if you live up to it."[12]

16

WORLD WAR II ENDS AND THE COLD WAR BEGINS

SEPTEMBER 2, 1945

The Loss of Life and Civil Liberties around the Globe

The battleship *Missouri* rode at anchor in Tokyo Bay. The turrets, housings, and life rafts above the veranda deck were crowded with thousands of sailors eager to view this final moment of World War II. Military representatives from all the Allied forces that had participated in the Pacific campaigns were assembled on the deck awaiting the arrival of the Japanese delegation led by Foreign Minister Namoru Shigemitsu. At 9:30 A.M. the Japanese arrived in a small gig flying an American flag. They wore diplomatic morning attire with black cutaway coats, striped pants, and silk stovepipe hats.

The representatives of the United States, the United Kingdom, Canada, Australia, New Zealand, France, the Netherlands, China, and Russia stood together on one side of a long, green-covered table. The Japanese gathered in three rows facing the Allied officers. General Douglas MacArthur, the supreme allied commander, began the historic proceedings: "We are gathered here representatives of the major warring powers, to conclude a solemn agreement whereby peace may be restored."[1]

The Japanese stood at attention during MacArthur's short address. On an elevated platform nearby, the world's press snapped pictures and adjusted microphones. Ironically, just as the Japanese began to sign the black-and-gold-bound documents signaling their nation's first military defeat in 2,600 years, the sun broke through the layer of dark gray clouds. Gold braid, silver stars, bright-colored silk, and brass decorations on the uniforms of the Allied powers glittered in the unexpected sunshine.[2]

The rain that had been pouring down on the bay since early morning was replaced by brilliant sunshine. Perhaps now the firestorm of bombs that had been raining down over a period of six long years on such cities as London, Berlin, Dresden, Rotterdam, Coventry, Stalingrad, Pearl Harbor, Hiroshima, and Nagasaki would be replaced by the sudden, unexpected light and warmth of peace. Too many men, women, and children on both sides had died. Too many lives and too many cities lay in ruin. The whole world longed for peace. General MacArthur concluded the short, formal ceremony in Tokyo Bay by expressing the dream of people everywhere: "Let us pray that peace be now restored to the world, and that God will preserve it always."[3]

On that day, September 2, 1945, history recorded the end of one war and the beginning of another. The hostilities of World War II had ended, but the Cold War between the expansionist Communism of the Soviet Union and the entire free world had begun.

The Origins of the War We Now Wage

The Soviet Union cannot be blamed for creating the atmosphere in the 1930s out of which the Cold War developed. Unwittingly, the United States was a major contributor to that terrible decade of depression immediately preceding World War II.

With the collapse of the world's economy and the Great Depression that followed came an even more serious loss of human dignity and purpose. Hunger and fear stalked the earth. And with the growing human misery came rumors of fiscal abuse and scandal, stock manipulations, blatant greed, and corruption. A handful of rich and powerful families in America and abroad had insisted on maintaining their exclusive control of much of the world's wealth. Their greed and stupidity plunged the world into chaos. And a growing number of those who suffered from the ills of the depression at home and abroad turned to the economic theory of Karl Marx for an explanation.

In the *Communist Manifesto,* Marx predicted that the working class would eventually place itself in power over the ruling class and remove from its exclusive control all capital and all instruments of production, putting it into the hands of the state. For growing numbers of people, Marx's description of the world's problems fit perfectly the current complaints against the powerful Wall Street manipulators, the owners and bosses of banks and industry, and the "lackeys and stooges" in government who had helped create the Great Depression. Marx explained:

> The theoretical conclusions of the Communists are in no way based on ideas or principles that have been invented, or discovered, by this or that would-be universal reformer.
> They merely express, in general terms, actual relations springing from an existing class struggle, from an historical movement going on under our very eyes.
> One fact is common to all past ages, the exploitation of one part of society by another."[4]

In America, sensitive young intellectuals—men like Alger Hiss and Harry Dexter White—became convinced that our free enterprise system was wrong and could not be improved. Around the world, thousands of men and women like them, sincerely longing for a utopian society in which the poor would no longer be enslaved by the rich, became easy prey for the growing Communist movement under Lenin and Stalin. But the Soviet leaders who initiated, financed, and controlled the Cold War and its bloody worldwide revolution soon proved to be more ruthless, more greedy, and more oppressive than the ruling classes they succeeded.

After eliminating the oppressive Russian rule of Czar Nicholas II in the revolution of 1917, Soviet leadership between 1918 and 1935 began to encourage and assist various other Communist revolutionary movements around the world. There was a short period between 1935 and 1940 when the Russian Communist Party seemed to be "aiming at democratic reform and resistance to fascism, rather than the one-party proletarian dictatorship" and appeared to be making a sincere effort to "suspend their revolutionary drive in international communism."[5] But that Soviet attempt at taking a responsible place in the community of free nations ended with the Russians' surprising self-serving pact with Hitler's Third Reich in 1939.

The Cold War Begins During World War II

Immediately after the close of World War II, Stalin and his cronies began again to instigate Soviet-financed revolution against established governments in Europe, Africa, Asia, and South America. There would be no need for a worldwide nuclear arms race today if we had confronted the militant global expansion of Communism when it first began.

During World War II, President Roosevelt had a naive belief that once the Nazi threat had been eliminated, the world could enter an era of justice and democracy. He believed that world peace could be established through world law and a great congress of the nations. He dreamed of peace as the crowning monument to his career. But his dreams overwhelmed his sense of history. Woodrow Wilson had had the same fantasy for the League of Nations at the end of World War I. Both dreams revealed "a profound tension between American hopes and international realities."[6]

Before World War I, Europe had been divided into "great-power spheres of influence"[7] by monarchs and their conquering armies. Realistic European leaders assumed that after World War II, powerful and victorious rulers would seek once again to establish new great-power spheres of influence.

Churchill and Stalin approached their wartime negotiations at Moscow, Teheran, Yalta, and Potsdam determined to shape those spheres of influence. From the beginning, Churchill feared the territorial ambitions of Russia. Roosevelt was more naive and hopeful. He felt certain that if he could get Russia into the United Nations, the leaders of the world would work together in peace and growing unity. In order to obtain Russia's help in the war against Japan and to guarantee Russia's cooperation in the creation of a United Nations, Roosevelt was willing to make some large compromises with the Soviets. As a result, the Russians were given a head start on their Cold War victories.

In the Teheran foreign ministers conference of November 1943, Stalin agreed to assist the Allies in the war against Japan and to establish the United Nations if Churchill and Roosevelt agreed to an expansion of Russia's postwar influence in Poland and Germany.

Churchill, anxious to limit Stalin's influence over eastern Europe, had made an earlier agreement with Stalin to allow the Soviets 90 percent influence in Rumania, 75 percent in Bulgaria and Hungary, 50 percent in Yugoslavia, and just 10 percent in Greece.

That agreement was the beginning of the Cold War division of Europe. During the next months of bloody warfare against the Nazis, the advancing Russian armies took 100 percent control of Poland, Rumania, Yugoslavia, Bulgaria, and Hungary. The war in Europe was seen as a war of liberation by the United States and its western European allies. But the Soviets were liberating eastern Europe out of Nazi control and into their own domination. Within months of Churchill's agreement with Stalin, the British prime minister realized his mistake and ordered British forces to deliver the exiled Greek government back into Athens before Russian forces attempted to claim power over Greece as well.

Roosevelt believed that the Allies needed Russia's help to end the war in the Pacific. At the Yalta Summit in February 1945, Stalin agreed to enter the Pacific war in exchange for exclusive domination of Poland and the promise from Roosevelt of a divided Germany.

Before the last Allied meeting in Potsdam in July 1945, Churchill and Truman knew that the Russian armies controlled most of eastern Europe. Still, the Western powers thought they needed Stalin to complete the war in Japan. No one was sure that the atomic bomb would work. So the Soviets traded their help in the Pacific for even more power in Germany, insisting on huge reparation payments and an exclusive Russian zone of influence in Berlin and eastern Germany. Churchill and Truman acquiesced.

The Russians began immediately to move German assets, including industrial facilities, developed and undeveloped resources, even art treasures and military equipment, to Russian soil. Since the Allies placed no limits on the Soviets, they took everything that wasn't nailed down in the name of reparations. Yet the Western powers still refused to act to limit the Soviets' incredible global ambitions.

Winston Churchill's Warning

In the euphoria of victory after the armistice was signed in Tokyo Bay, few people realized that a new world war had already begun. Churchill himself announced the Cold War realities to the free world in a speech delivered at Westminster College in Missouri on March 5, 1946: "From Stettin on the Baltic to Trieste on the Adriatic, an iron curtain has descended across the Continent."[8]

Nine days later Stalin replied, calling Churchill's speech "a mixture of libel, rudeness and lack of tact . . . absurd, untrue and a firebrand of war." The Communist dictator went on to claim that during World

War II, "millions of common people, having tried the Communists in the fire of struggle and resistance to fascism, . . . decided that the Communists deserve completely the confidence of the people."[9]

The international press and the public were getting their first real Cold War taste of the Soviets' skill at using the big lie. By 1947 the "People's Democracies" of Rumania, Bulgaria, Hungary, and Poland "had to all intents and purposes been converted into one-party Communist dictatorships closely controlled by the Soviet military and police."[10] And Germany, after years of domination by Hitler and the Third Reich, found itself at the close of World War II half-slave and half-free, with its capital divided and its free zone ringed by Russian troops.

The Cold War in Europe After World War II

On June 24, 1948, the Russians sealed off access to Berlin by rail and highway from the West, leaving the city isolated 110 miles behind the Iron Curtain. The Soviets assumed the Americans would abandon Berlin. Russia could then expand its influence over the capital and eventually over all of Germany. On June 25 a courageous and determined Harry Truman announced to his cabinet, "We are going to stay. Period!"[11]

On June 26 he ordered all United States Air Force cargo planes in Europe to begin flying supplies to the blockaded city. With British help, by April 16, 1949, nearly 13 thousand tons of supplies were being flown to West Berlin every day. The blockade failed, and the Soviets reopened Berlin.

Breaking the Berlin blockade was one of this nation's few real victories over Soviet expansionism in Europe in that decade. By 1961 more than 3.5 million Germans had fled to freedom. Unfortunately, ten years after Truman's courageous stand, the Russians moved once again to consolidate their power in Berlin, and this time they succeeded.

On August 13, 1961, just after midnight, East German police backed by East German soldiers blocked all the crossing points between free and Communist Berlin and installed barbed wire barricades and tank traps as the beginning of a new crackdown against German citizens who were trying to flee to the West. The world watched in shock and surprise as an ugly cement wall was built around Communist-occupied

Berlin during those next months. Who will forget the television coverage of those brave young Berliners who gave their lives in attempted escapes over that deadly wall even as we watched?

Once again the Russians made a bold Cold War move against the free world, and once again our officials simply stood by in silence, made empty, shallow threats, or discussed the matter endlessly in press conferences and on the floor of the General Assembly of the United Nations. But nothing of substance was done to stop Soviet expansion in Germany and throughout the world.

In February 1956, workers' riots in Posnan, Poland, were crushed by the Soviets. That same year Russian forces invaded Hungary, marched on Budapest, and placed their own man, Janos Kadar, in power. In 1968 the Soviets occupied Czechoslovakia when the hint of reform threatened their total power over the Prague regime. In 1979 Soviet forces marched into Afghanistan to prop up an unpopular Marxist regime already installed by Moscow.

A close look at the current map of Europe makes clear the extent of the Soviet Union's expansion. Western Europe was liberated from Hitler while in eastern Europe Nazi tyranny was replaced by the tyranny of the Soviet Union. And in spite of resistance movements from Poland to Afghanistan, the Soviets have maintained and increased their hold on the entire region.

The Cold War in Asia After World War II

In China, Chiang Kai-shek's Nationalists continued to wage their civil war against Mao Zedong's Communists without much significant aid from the free world. In the beginning of the struggle in China, the United States helped Chiang Kai-shek, but in 1948, citing the "corruption" of his government, the United States terminated all aid to Chiang's forces. Almost immediately, Mao's Communist armies took control of China. Chiang and his supporters retreated to the island of Taiwan.

In 1950 Mao signed a treaty of friendship and mutual support with the Soviet Union. That new friendship between Moscow and Beijing led in June of that same year to the Soviet-backed invasion of South Korea by its satellite government in the north. At the close of World War II in 1945, Korea, like Germany, had been divided into zones of occupation.

The Soviets quickly moved to consolidate their power in the north. They armed the North Korean government and sponsored the "civil war" that eventually left 34 thousand Americans and American allies dead along with a million Koreans and a quarter of a million Chinese.[12] With almost no losses of their own, the Russians had managed to retain their sphere of influence in Korea. And in spite of years of warfare, that nation remained tragically divided.

Early in the 1950s, the United States began to realize the real threat of Communist expansion. Churchill's prophecy of an Iron Curtain extending around all of eastern Europe had been realized. Now, a "bamboo curtain" seemed to threaten all of Southeast Asia as well. The Soviets worked tirelessly to expand their sphere of influence around the globe. From the very end of World War II the foreign policy of the United States was forced to focus on the containment of Soviet expansion. Under Truman, United States aid was restored to Chiang Kai-shek in Taiwan and to the French battling the Communist Vietminh nationalists in Indochina.

In 1954 the French concluded their seven-year war in Indochina with an armistice that "provisionally" partitioned Vietnam into a Communist state in the north and a national state in the south. Ho Chi Minh and his Communist forces dominated the north. Refusing to be a party to the surrender of millions of Vietnamese to Communist aggression, the United States would not sign the Geneva agreements but began instead to send military aid and advisers into the south to assist President Ngo Dinh Diem against the very real Communist threat to South Vietnam and all of Indochina.

In 1964, through the Gulf of Tonkin Resolution, Congress granted President Johnson the power to take whatever steps he needed against further Communist aggression in Vietnam. Four years later approximately 541 thousand United States troops were in South Vietnam. For twelve bloody years this nation and our allies battled against Communist forces in Vietnam, before we capitulated to the enemy, with 49,433 Americans dead and another 303,616 wounded. Our allies suffered thousands of dead and wounded; 183,528 South Vietnamese soldiers and 415,000 civilians had been killed. In North Vietnam, 924,048 soldiers had died.

It was the longest war in American history, and we lost it. At least in Germany and Korea no new ground was given up to Communist expansion. The truce Henry Kissinger signed on January 27, 1973, effectively surrendered all of Vietnam to Communist control. Immediately, the victorious Soviet-backed Vietnamese Communists stretched their power into Cambodia and Laos. Already at least 3 million gentle Asian people in those shattered nations have been slaughtered by the Communist forces that now threaten all of Southeast Asia.

The Cold War in Africa

Africa has been a primary target for Soviet expansion during the last half of this century. The African people fighting to rid themselves of European colonial rule were particularly vulnerable to Marxist-Leninist doctrine. Young African students were trained in Moscow to lead revolutions in their nations. Russian embassies and consulates in every African nation became outposts of Soviet expansionism.

Mozambique became the first "People's Republic" of Africa under the hardcore Communist Frelimo party. Their treaty of friendship and cooperation with the Soviet Union gave Russia a major voice in the formation of the new nation. Angola, Ethiopia, and Somalia have all since capitulated to Soviet-backed, Marxist-Leninist regimes. Other African Marxist states include Madagascar and Benin. African states with ties to the Soviet Union but calling themselves "socialist" states include Algeria, Libya, Guinea, and Zambia.[13] But the Soviets are working for power and influence throughout the African nations, from Morocco, Tunisia, and Egypt in the north; across the great central African region including Mauritania, Mali, Senegal, Niger, Nigeria, Chad, and the Sudan; to Namibia, Zimbabwe, Botswana, and South Africa in the south.

The Cold War in Central and South America

Although Moscow had been active throughout South and Central America since the end of World War II, the real Communist foothold in this hemisphere began in Cuba with the ascent to power of Fidel Castro in 1959. The mistakes made by the United States during and after Castro's successful war against dictator Fulgencio Batista are well known. To second-guess the evolution of Castro from a sincere freedom fighter to a full-blown Marxist-Leninist in the employ of the Soviet Union would not be helpful here. Just one fact really matters now. In their strategy to extend their sphere of influence around the globe, the Soviets have created a major Western Communist base just off the shores of Miami, and from that base they are training and supplying a revolution aimed at all of the Americas.

After President John F. Kennedy's halfhearted attempt to overthrow Fidel Castro and his Soviet advisers at the Bay of Pigs on April 17, 1961, Soviet Premier Nikita Khrushchev began to stir up real trouble in the Western Hemisphere. In October of the same year, President Kennedy announced the presence of Soviet missiles in Castro's Cuba and then blockaded the island until the missiles and personnel were removed. After four days of heart-stopping threats and rhetoric on both sides, Khrushchev gave in and the missiles were removed. But the victory seemed hollow when people realized how close the Cold War had come and how easily and effectively our nation's security had been violated.

In 1979 another dictator was replaced by a Communist-backed revolution in the Western Hemisphere. General Anastasio Somoza of Nicaragua, Latin America's most notorious strong man, was replaced by the Sandinistas, a coalition of freedom fighters that under President Daniel Ortega soon demonstrated its Marxist-Soviet sympathies. From Cuba, an island off Miami, to Nicaragua, a nation placed firmly in the heart of Central America, the Soviets are attempting to extend their sphere of influence throughout the region.

The Cold War Strategy

Stalin and the Russian leaders who have followed him use Marxist economic theory as a smoke screen to cover their strategy of Russian expansion throughout the world. They pretend to advocate an equitable redistribution of wealth while in fact they have launched an all-out war to win control of the world's depleting resources. They pretend to fight for the freedom of the oppressed while in fact they have become the world's great oppressor. They pretend to advocate peace while they bring havoc and carnage to the nations.

The Soviet leadership has engaged in excess and barbarities more ruthless, more diabolical, on a wider scale than any in history. The Russian Communist elite have made a mockery of the democratic process.

The basic human rights guaranteed Americans by the Constitution are regularly violated, if not denied altogether, throughout the expanding sphere of Soviet influence. The press is censored. Free assembly is forbidden. The right to a speedy and fair trial by a jury of peers has been eliminated. The free movement of people, dissidents and loyalists alike, is forbidden. Minorities are persecuted, many almost to extinction. And in their militant atheism, the Communists have tried to eliminate almost every significant trace of faith in God from Soviet life.

During the 1960s and 1970s Russia increased its persecution of Christians, Jews, and other religious and political dissidents. Christian churches were closed, and the clergy were sent to prison or mental hospitals. For these four decades since the end of World War II, the Soviets have trained and supplied armies of terrorists and revolutionaries for armed incursions into Africa, Asia, Europe, the Middle East, and South and Central America. Russia's invasion of Afghanistan in 1979 to place its own puppet ruler in the presidential palace in Kabul is only one example of Soviet expansion throughout the world. And the seven costly years of fighting that have followed illustrate Russia's determination to continue the fight.

In that regard, Soviet leaders can no longer call themselves true Marxists. Marx saw the end of capitalism as a historic process capitalism would bring upon itself. Marx didn't proclaim the destruction of capitalism through world revolution to be a deliberate policy or duty, but "merely a prediction of what the development of international capitalism supposedly made inevitable."[14]

Russian leaders pretend, pose, and propagandize for the naive and uninformed, but in fact the world is at war with a totalitarian, atheistic power that has ambitions to conquer the world. That bloody Cold War launched by the Soviets at the close of World War II should be renamed. The Hot War of Soviet Communist expansion has already taken the lives of an estimated 250 million people, more than all the casualties in all the wars fought in our nation's history. Friends and foes of Communism alike have been murdered on whim without trial or defense. And no one is safe. Stalin is purported to have killed more Communists himself "than all the world's right wing dictators combined."[15] And the painful and tragic necessity of building an adequate defense against Soviet aggression is costing the free world enough money every day to feed and clothe the hungry and naked of the earth.

Responding to the Cold War Threat

From the beginning of the free world's Cold War with the Soviet Union our nation has been ambivalent about the appropriate response to Communist expansion around the globe. For more than four decades the Soviets have worked tirelessly and ruthlessly to achieve their stated goal of world domination. Sometimes the United States has responded with courage and determination. Other times we have turned away in cowardice and irresolve.

Immediately following World War II, Harry Truman rushed military and economic aid to save Greece from Communist aggression. But that same president refused to let Douglas MacArthur wage an effective war against Communist expansion in Korea. In 1961 John F. Kennedy demanded that Khrushchev remove his Soviet missiles from Cuba and provided American naval forces to support his demands. Yet earlier that same year Kennedy grounded military aircraft in Key West with their engines running while Cuban freedom fighters fought and died at the Bay of Pigs for want of adequate air support. He ignored two valuable maxims from Gen. Douglas MacArthur: (1) that the United States should never involve itself in a land war in Asia, and (2) in war there is no substitute for victory.

Three American presidents vacillated about the war against Communist aggression in Vietnam while thousands of our young men died and billions of dollars were wasted. This constant policy of vacillation and gradual escalation of a seemingly insane war left an entire generation confused, angry, and cynical about the Cold War threat. In the sixties and early seventies our young people took to the streets to protest. They burned draft cards, desecrated the flag, and hanged the president in effigy. The cities echoed with their cry, "Better Red than dead!" The vacillation gave way to a kind of national paralysis. A counter-culture grew up that threatened to replace traditional American values with hedonism, drug abuse, isolationism, and immorality.

And in that momentary vacuum, the Soviets moved quickly to build the largest and most powerful military machine in the history of warfare. While we wasted our national resolve, the Communists used force and cunning to expand their sphere of influence to every continent. Now the sun never sets on the Cold War that the Soviets are waging against liberty around the earth.

Ironically, during these past forty-one years of conflict, Marxist-Leninist ideology has been proved false. The ruthless tactics of the Soviet hierarchy, their blood baths at home and abroad, the loss of civil liberties for their own countrymen and in the nations they subdue, their economic policy failures, and the cold, drab, hopeless lives of millions of Communist victims revealed to the world the failure of the Communist promise.

The Soviets began this Cold War promising "a classless society with new freedom and opportunity for the downtrodden people of the earth." Now, the entire world sees that claim as laughable. The Soviet lies have been exposed. The Kremlin leaders have proved themselves no better than any other ambitious oligarchy mouthing false hopes to cover their ruthless determination to control the people and to dominate the resources of the earth.

There is no free movement anywhere by any people to embrace the Communist cause. Fear and force are the only ways the Soviets can increase and maintain their sphere of influence. Those tactics leave the free world no option. We can afford to vacillate no longer or we, too, will become victims of the Cold War. Our national policy against Soviet expansion must be simple and decisive.

First, we must stand resolutely for liberty and against Communist aggression whenever and wherever it appears. The Soviets have a proven regard for American military power. Historically, they have shown no real will to stand up against us when we use our power quickly and forcefully against their acts of global expansion. If we confront their aggression with tough resolve, they will back down.

Second, we must assist the victims of Soviet domination wherever we find them. For too long we have believed that once a country fell to Communism, it was Soviet territory and off-limits to the free world. It is our responsibility to assist victim nations in their attempts to overthrow their Communist captors and to roll back Soviet expansion. Wherever indigenous freedom fighters volunteer to fight and die to establish liberty and democracy, we must come to their aid with money and arms.

Third, the only real way to guarantee peace on this earth is through military and moral strength. We must be vigilant. The Soviets continue to build their military machine. They spend a shocking 20 percent of their Gross National Product on armaments. To maintain the peace while containing Soviet ambition for world hegemony, we must maintain our own military preparedness. Only through strength—not weakness—is peace possible.

But moral strength, too, is necessary to guide us in the control and proper use of our own military might. At the heart of moral strength is spiritual renewal. A KGB major who recently defected from the Soviet Union told me of the spiritual renewal the Russian people, too, are experiencing. "The religious revival in the Soviet Union is the only long-range hope for undermining and ultimately overthrowing the corrupt and ruthless Kremlin leadership," he said. He reported that thousands of Soviet young people are gathering secretly in forest hideaways to pray and worship. In the face of our current nuclear arms race, America, too, must continue to seek God's wisdom and guidance.

Yet even as we pray, we must work to maintain our military strength. The free world looks to the United States for leadership against the threat of Soviet domination, and the victims of Communist aggression everywhere still hope that we will help them find freedom once again.

President Kennedy summarized best this nation's promise to the waiting world in these words from his Inaugural Address:

> Let every nation know, whether it wishes us well or ill, that we shall pay any price, bear any burden, meet any hardship, support any friend, oppose any foe, to assure the survival and the success of liberty!

17

THE ASSASSINATION OF JOHN F. KENNEDY

NOVEMBER 22, 1963

The Loss of Personal Rights and Safety

Just seconds before 12:30 P.M. on Friday, November 22, 1963, three shots were fired at the open limousine carrying America's thirty-fifth president through the streets of Dallas, Texas. The president had just turned to his right to wave at the small but friendly crowd of Texans and tourists when the first bullet struck him, penetrating two or three inches into his back. His hands jerked involuntarily toward his throat as he slumped down in the back seat toward his wife. The second shot caught Texas Governor John Connally in the back as he looked over his shoulder toward the president. That bullet passed through the governor, penetrating his wrist, and finally lodging in his thigh. The third bullet hit the back of the president's head above eye level as he was bowed forward. Jacqueline Kennedy, spattered with her husband's blood, cried out, "Oh, my God, they killed my husband! Jack! Jack!"[1]

In roughly five seconds, Lee Harvey Oswald had mortally wounded the president and plunged the world into a time of anguish, fear, and self-doubt from which we have not yet fully recovered. The events that followed were witnessed on television simultaneously by the largest worldwide audience in media history. An amateur photographer even captured the bloody instant of the president's assassination on 8-millimeter film, and the terrible, unforgettable moment was played and replayed by the television networks. Through that grainy, five-second, nightmarish blur and through the media coverage of the days and nights that followed, the entire world became an eyewitness to one of the nation's most crippling tragedies, and to the horror and heartbreak that followed.

No one who watched television that day will forget it: the Secret Service man flinging himself into that bloody limousine; the motorcade speeding toward Parkland Hospital; the crowd of horrified dignitaries, police, Secret Service agents, hospital personnel, and patients wandering about the hospital entrance reflecting the nation's looks of shock and disbelief; two Catholic priests hurrying up the crowded hallways to give the young president the last rites of his church; the nurses' room filled with media representatives at a hastily assembled press briefing hearing those words of Malcolm Kilduff of the White House press staff— "President John Fitzgerald Kennedy died at approximately one o'clock."[2]

What happened that day changed the modern world forever. The charismatic young president had captured the imagination of the world. Whatever history will say about his actual accomplishments during his one thousand days in office, no doubt exists that John F. Kennedy had managed to convey the spirit of hopefulness for the future to his country and to men, women, and children around the earth. When he died, something of that hope died with him.

Assassination and the Presidency

November 22, 1963, wasn't the first time an American president had been attacked by an assassin.[3] On January 30, 1835, a mentally unbalanced house painter, Richard Lawrence, fired two pistols at President Andrew Jackson in the rotunda of the Capitol. Although the would-be assassin was standing only six feet from the president, both pistols misfired and the president's life was spared. On October 14, 1912, President Theodore Roosevelt, en route to a campaign speech in Milwaukee, Wisconsin, was shot in the chest by an insane saloon keeper, John Schrank. Roosevelt refused to be hospitalized until the speech was over, at which time he told the astonished crowd, "Please excuse me from making a very long speech . . . . You see, there is a bullet in my body."[4] On November 1, 1950, two Puerto Rican nationalists killed a White House guard as they tried to shoot their way into President Truman's temporary residence at Blair House. The president escaped injury.

Four other presidents were not so fortunate. On April 14, 1865, President Abraham Lincoln was gunned down by John Wilkes Booth in Ford's Theater in Washington, D.C. President James Garfield was shot on July 2, 1881, at the Baltimore and Potomac Railway Depot in Washington, D.C., by a disappointed office seeker. After a two-month period of recuperation, President Garfield died of blood poisoning contracted from his wounds. President William McKinley was shot and killed on September 6, 1901, by Leon Czolgosz, an anarchist, as the president visited the Pan-American Exposition in Buffalo, New York.

The growing list of recent assassinations in the United States includes names from politics and government, education and industry, even the arts. In 1968, Martin Luther King, Jr., civil rights leader and Nobel Peace Prize winner, and Robert Kennedy, the attorney general of the United States, were murdered just three months apart by James Earl Ray and Sirhan Sirhan, respectively.

In 1981 John Hinckley, Jr., tried to assassinate President Ronald Reagan on the sidewalk outside the Washington Hilton Hotel. The president, his press secretary, James Brady, a Secret Service agent, Timothy McCarthy, and policeman Thomas Delahanty were all seriously wounded, though all survived this most recent assassination attempt in a spate of ever-increasing violence in the nation.

"When Will the Shooting Stop?"

The editors of the *New Republic* headlined the question that everyone was asking: "When Will The Shooting Stop?" A subsequent editorial claimed more than twenty thousand "ordinary murders" had occurred in the United States in the previous twelve months.[5]

The editors were trying to discriminate between the assassination of a famous national leader and the murder of an average citizen; but no murder is ever "ordinary." No act of violence is more or less acceptable because of its victim's fame or influence. In fact, when a president is assassinated or when a gas station attendant, the owner of an all-night market, or a policeman on a lonely stretch of highway is gunned down, the nation suffers. When just one person among us loses his or her right to life, liberty, and the pursuit of happiness, the rights of each of us are threatened. Those rights granted by our Creator and guaranteed by the nation's Constitution are threatened today as never before in the history of our nation.

The United States Department of Justice created a "Crime Clock" in 1984 to help us understand the growing frequency of crime in our land.

Every three seconds, around the clock, a crime is committed some-where in the United States. If you break those crimes into individual units against persons or property, you discover the following:

One violent crime is committed against persons every twenty-five seconds:

> One murder every twenty-eight minutes
> One forcible rape every six minutes
> One robbery every sixty-five seconds
> One aggravated assault every forty-six seconds

One crime against property is committed every three seconds:

> One burglary every eleven seconds
> One larceny-theft every five seconds
> One motor vehicle theft every thirty-one seconds[6]

Lewis H. Lapham, an editor of *Harper's* magazine, in introducing a panel of experts on the problem of crime in the United States, claimed, "Our nation spends approximately $40 billion every year for the various forms of police protection, but nobody feels safe."[7]

The Problem of Crime Is Growing

In his introduction to a wide-ranging discussion of the growing problem of crime in America, Editor Lapham reminded his readers that crime had increased steadily over the past centuries; but during the 1960s, when the economy was surging and Americans were enjoying huge gains in their standards of living, crime rates soared. From 1965 to 1970 homicide increased by 55 percent, aggravated assault went up 48 percent, and robbery shot up by 124 percent. And these figures are adjusted for the rise in population![8]

During the 1970s and into the early 1980s, the crime rate continued to increase steadily. In 1983 and 1984 there was a measurable though temporary decline, but "crime is still drastically greater today than it was even in the 1950s."[9] Our allies in Great Britain are experiencing a similar rate of increase. As late as March 1985, Scotland Yard reported that crime in London, for example, had risen 9 percent (over the previous year's crime rate), with record high numbers of muggings and robberies in that city.[10] Still, we in America lead all our allies in every kind of crime. The United States has eight murders per capita for every two in England, and thirty-six assaults per capita for every two in Japan or one in Italy. And in holdups per capita, America leads the rest of the world by as many as ten to one.[11]

Twenty-six percent of all American households experienced a crime of violence or theft in 1984.[12] A total of 35.5 million incidents of crime were reported.[13] And though the Justice Department claimed a 4.1 percent decline in household crimes that year, FBI Director William Webster announced that serious crimes rose at a 3 percent rate during the first six months of 1985,[14] and Bureau of Justice statistics experts warned that only 35 percent of all crimes were reported to the police.[15]

The most recent crime figures are clear. Though there was a slight decline in crimes committed in 1984, in 1985 and 1986 the rate soared once again. Murder, down 3 percent in 1984, went up 1 percent in 1985. Robbery, down 4 percent in 1984, went up 3 percent in 1985. Assault, burglary, and car theft are all on the increase.[16]

One in ten women will be seriously assaulted (hit, kicked, bitten, or worse) by her husband during the course of a marriage. Those who finally press charges will have been attacked an average of thirty-five times.[17]

Crimes against minority citizens of all ages in the United States are increasing at a much faster rate than crimes against the white population. For example, black males stand a six times greater risk of being murdered than do white males,[18] and the resurgence of the Ku Klux Klan (with 10 thousand members reported in 1980)[19] and other white supremacist groups like the Aryan Nations (or Church of Jesus Christ Christians) in western Washington and Idaho is linked to the increase of racial violence and crime sprees in the Northwest.[20]

America's teenagers are the most likely victims of current crimes. Other reports note that violent crimes against persons, especially rape,[21] gang killings,[22] bombings (not traceable to terrorism),[23] racial violence, and vandalism[24] are increasing rapidly. The growing reports of child abuse, abuse of the elderly, and battered women only scratch the surface of a population that seems to grow more violent and destructive every day.

The Eisenhower Foundation noted in 1985 that its 1969 warnings about the decay of United States cities and the sharp increases in crime rates have come true, and it claimed that harsher sentencing has had little or no deterrent effect on the rise of crime nationwide.[25] One expert, Professor Gilbert Geis, who minimizes the slight decline in crime reported by the Justice Department, warned that the incidence of crime in America "still remains among the highest in the world."[26]

Crimes Against Children

During this past decade, the media have drawn attention to the growing number of crimes against American children. The Department of Health and Human Services estimated that between 1.3 million and 1.8 million children and young people disappear from their homes each year. Most of these children and teenagers are runaways or "throwaways," but estimates of the number abducted by strangers range from 25 thousand to 500 thousand every year. Many of those children are murdered. Every hour more than two hundred boys and girls may be reported missing in the United States. Perhaps the ugliest dimension of this growing scandal of America's missing children is the estimate that 60 to 70 percent of today's runaway children come from homes in which they have been abused.[27]

The Relationship of Crime to Alcohol and Drug Abuse

The correlation between violent crimes and the use of alcohol and drugs by criminals has been well established. At least 54 percent of those committing violent crimes in 1985 had been drinking alcohol just prior to committing the crime. Alcohol and drugs lower a person's inhibitions against antisocial behavior, and the desperate need for drugs on the part of addicts has led to an ever-increasing wave of crime against persons and property, especially in the major population centers.[28]

Crime and the misuse of alcohol and drugs in the nation have become two sides of the same problem; therefore, it is necessary to consider them together. A recent national forum on America's growing drug problem claimed that last year Americans spent $30 billion on illegal drugs, while our government spent $1.5 billion trying to shut down their sources of supply. The facts regarding alcohol and drug misuse in this nation are staggering.[29]

Professor Arnold S. Trebach of American University reported these helpful statistics about alcohol and drug misuse in 1985:

> Alcohol—Out of a total population of 240 million Americans . . . more than 100 million use alcohol, and 10 to 13 million are probably addicted to it.
>
> Tobacco—Roughly 56 million Americans are addicted to tobacco; and almost all tobacco users are addicts.
>
> Marijuana—Twenty million Americans smoke marijuana occasionally and between 35 and 40 million smoke it at least once a year. Three million smoke it every day. And 1.5 million are compulsive marijuana users—smokers who would suffer great discomfort if forced to stop using the drug. One in every twenty pot users is truly addicted, while roughly one in ten alcohol users is addicted.
>
> Cocaine—Twelve to fifteen million Americans probably use cocaine at least once a year. Of those, perhaps 500,000 to 750,000 use it every day.
>
> Heroin—Another 3 to 5 million Americans may use heroin at least once a year, and about 300,000 to 500,000 are addicts.
>
> Other Drugs—A couple of million Americans are addicted to Valium and to other, more obscure drugs that aren't much talked about.[30]

A special agent in charge of the Drug Enforcement Administration's New York field division claimed that throughout the nation there is a "surge in cocaine use, accompanied by the increasingly younger age of its users." He quoted a carefully documented study of high school students in Massachusetts to illustrate his point: "26 percent of high school seniors there use cocaine occasionally or have at least tried it." Stating that "cocaine is one of the most addictive illegal drugs available in the country," he warned that if one of four high school seniors now use it occasionally, "we will have a devastating problem five years down the road."[31] Now a new and vastly more potent free-based cocaine called "crack" has indeed been devastating the youth of our major cities.

There are several hopeful signs. Alcohol and drug education have made some difference in the nation's high schools, where daily marijuana use among seniors has dropped from 10 percent in 1979 to 5 percent in 1985.[32] And the use of heroin, PCP, and Quaaludes is also dropping slightly. Still, alcohol and drug addiction and the resulting personal and public tragedies are on the rise. Fear of addiction or disease (including fear of AIDS) has not worked as an adequate preventative against drug or alcohol misuse. The strict fines and jail sentences being handed out against drug misuse aren't working either.

And as any high school student could tell you, all kinds of illegal drugs are available and within easy reach of America's schools, homes, and playgrounds. The government has tried to stop or at least slow the flow. In 1986 the governments of Bolivia, Colombia, and Peru were negotiating for the use of American military helicopters and personnel to support governmental drug raids to close farms and drug factories there.[33] Even so, only an estimated 5 to 10 percent of all drugs entering the United States are intercepted.[34]

Even while you are reading, tons of illegal drugs are passing over or around the wall of drug enforcement officers at our borders, through the hands of crime organizations and their networks of drug dealers, and into the bodies of innocent children and desperate, jaded addicts alike.

"Designer drugs" began to surface in 1985 and are already becoming a great new menace in the illegal drug culture. These synthetic narcotics, variations of legal drugs, are easily and cheaply made almost anywhere, and are being sold on the street like cocaine or heroin. Their street names include "Ecstasy," MPPP, and PEPAP, but United States Senator Paula Hawkins calls them "chemical roulette." At least one hundred overdose deaths were reported in the first months of 1985. The drugs have a poison potential one thousand to six thousand times stronger than heroin.[35]

Illegal drugs from whatever source threaten vast and permanent damage to our nation and its people. Because of drugs, the equal rights to life, liberty, and the pursuit of happiness will be denied to tens of millions of crime victims in the next twelve months. These people will be robbed, raped, beaten, or murdered by Americans high on drugs or alcohol. And millions of other Americans in various stages of addiction to these poisonous substances will surrender their own rights to life, liberty, and the pursuit of happiness as they light up, drink up, or shoot up to the destruction of their bodies and minds.

No Easy Solution

I wish we knew an easy solution to the growth of crime and the misuse of alcohol and drugs within the nation. We don't. Millions of dollars must continue to be spent to educate young adults and children especially about the dangers of alcohol and drug abuse. Millions more will be used in the attempt to close our borders to the tons of illegal drugs that flow across them daily. We must continue to lend practical support to the other countries within whose borders the illegal drugs are produced and refined. Only together will we ever close down the growers and the dealers hidden away in mountains, forests, and isolated fields preparing death for our children in their secret laboratories.

It is obvious that more effective laws must be passed and enforced against crimes of every sort. Law enforcement agencies must be better funded, and law enforcement officers need to be more adequately trained and supported for their difficult and dangerous tasks. Court systems must be made to work more efficiently. The electronic and print media must become more effectively self-regulated to minimize their contribution to the problem of crime and substance abuse. The churches, schools, and homes of the nation must be aided to increase their effectiveness in education and prevention.

The list is endless and the task overwhelming. We already know that most solutions will fall short. Under President Reagan, important steps have been taken to prevent crime and stop the rise of drug use in the nation. He declared all-out war against America's organized crime families and sent major criminals to prison. He launched a major enforcement effort to prosecute white-collar criminals who have been robbing the nation of an estimated $200 billion annually from their expensive office suites in the banks, businesses, brokerage houses, and board rooms of the nation.

More than 700 thousand Americans were behind bars in December of 1985, double the total of just fifteen years ago. Each cell costs the taxpayer between $50 and $100 thousand just to build. And the costs of keeping each prisoner amount to more than $20 thousand a year. New prison construction over the next ten years will cost the nation more than $7 billion. The police feel helpless to stem the flow of crime. The courts are bogged down in cases. The prisons are filled to overflowing. And still crime mounts.[36]

Perhaps it is time to remember again the warnings of our forefathers. The trend toward anarchy in the nation; the increase in assassination attempts against our leaders; the rising rate of crime against our people; the rush to inject, swallow, or inhale poisonous substances for recreation and escape—all lead to more personal and public tragedy. Our nation itself is threatened. Our forefathers warned us this might happen. And they gave us the ultimate answer for its prevention. I quote again John Adams, second president of the United States, who said it this way:

> We have no government armed with power capable of contending with human passions unbridled by morality and religion. Avarice, ambition, revenge or gallantry would break the strongest cords of our Constitution as a whale goes through a net. Our Constitution was made only for a moral and religious people. It is wholly inadequate to the government of any other.[37]

With the irreligion, cultural relativism, and militant humanism deeply entrenched in our nation's schools and universities, with the incredible strains on our nation's families produced by the Great Depression, a World War, a population explosion, and two smaller wars, with the pervasive influence of motion pictures, television programming, and periodicals that continually hammer at our long-established moral values, it is not difficult to understand what has happened to our culture. In truth unless there is a profound religious revival to bring us back to our roots, the long-range future of our democratic institutions is clearly in doubt.

18

LYNDON JOHNSON'S GREAT SOCIETY LAUNCHED

MAY 22, 1964

The Loss of a Manageable Federal Budget

The University of Michigan's football stadium was packed with more than 80 thousand people, mainly parents, relatives, and friends of the students graduating that afternoon in Ann Arbor. According to eyewitness Merle Miller, the day was sunny and hot. The black-robed and colorfully vested members of the university's faculty sat on a special platform that extended across the north end of the stadium. The University of Michigan Marching Band played a rousing trumpet fanfare and processional as the 4,943 graduates marched in caps and gowns to their rows of chairs set up in the middle of the field.

Secret Service agents, state police, and campus security officers ringed the stadium and cleared the entrance through which President Lyndon Baines Johnson would move toward the platform. Upon his arrival, the president was given a standing ovation. Occasional placards were raised denouncing the war in Vietnam, and several of the students wore black armbands in protest. But the crowd was generally enthusiastic and supportive of the man who had been sworn to the presidency just six months before on that tragic emergency flight returning the body of John F. Kennedy from Dallas, Texas, to Washington, D.C.

Johnson's speech that day had been written originally by staff writer Dick Goodwin after an informal conference beside the White House swimming pool with the president, press secretary Bill Moyer, and other presidential aides. The president wanted a phrase that would symbolize the goals of his administration. President Kennedy's "New Frontier" had captured the imagination of the nation. Roosevelt had his

"New Deal," and Truman his "Fair Deal." Johnson wanted a catch phrase of his own. Somewhere between that poolside conference and the speech at the largest graduation in history, the notion of Johnson's "Great Society" was born. In a colorful honorary hood and gown, the president introduced his dream to the nation:

> Your imagination, your initiative, and your indignation will determine whether we build a society where progress is the servant of our needs, or a society where old values and new visions are buried under unbridled growth. For in your time we have the opportunity to move not only toward the rich society and the powerful society, but upward to the Great Society.[1]

Twenty-seven different times, the audience interrupted President Johnson's twenty-minute address with enthusiastic applause. "Join in the battle to build the Great Society," Johnson invited the students and their families. "There are," he warned, "those timid souls who say this battle cannot be won, that we are condemned to a soulless wealth." Warming up to his dramatic finale, the president concluded: "So let us from this moment begin our work so that in the future men will look back and say: It was then, after a long and weary way, that man turned the exploits of his genius to the full enrichment of his life."[2]

The crowd of students, faculty, and friends stood and cheered. The president was euphoric. On Air Force One, the press pool remembered him as "sweaty and exuberant." He joined the reporters in their cabin and reread his favorite portions of the speech to them. "That was the unveiling of the Great Society," one reporter remembers, ". . . his own program, the program he was going to run on the next fall."[3]

The primary goal of Johnson's Great Society program had been announced five months earlier, in his first State of the Union address on January 8, 1964: "This Administration today, here and now, declares unconditional war on poverty." Upon signing his first antipoverty bill (the Equal Opportunities Act) on August 20, 1964, Johnson made his overall goal perfectly clear: "Today, for the first time in the history of the human race, a great nation is able to make and is willing to make a commitment to eradicate poverty among its people."[4]

After defeating conservative Republican candidate Barry Goldwater in the November 1964 election and winning the presidency on his own,

Johnson expanded on his Great Society and war on poverty themes in the January 4, 1965, State of the Union address. He asked for federal funds to assist the elderly, the poor, black Americans, immigrants, needy children, and the mentally ill. He asked for immediate legislation to improve education, to provide scholarships and loans, to increase mental and physical health care services, to raise Social Security benefit payments, to double the war against poverty, to improve the inner city, to provide housing, to fight crime and delinquency, and to preserve and protect our environment. Johnson proposed to use government "to keep our nation prosperous . . . to open opportunity to all our people . . . and to improve the quality of American life."[5]

A River of Legislation

The first session of the eighty-ninth Congress took the president seriously. The election had delivered to the new president solid majorities in both houses of Congress. House and Senate leaders seemed determined to give the newly elected President exactly what he wanted. In the words of historian Paul Johnson, "The bills came rolling out: the Elementary and Secondary Education Act, the Medicare Act, the Rent Supplement Act, various poverty acts."[6] Johnson quoted *New York Times* journalist Tom Wicker as exulting, "They are rolling the bills out of Congress these days the way Detroit turns super-sleek, souped-up autos off the assembly-line."[7] No one questioned the president's good intentions, and almost no one, at least not at the beginning, added up what those good intentions would cost or asked if the government could afford them.

Already, the war in Vietnam was grinding down the nation's will and the nation's pocketbook. In 1966 the war was expected to cost the taxpayer almost $6 billion. During earlier wars in American history, the government had to shortchange domestic programs in order to finance war efforts. Johnson had decided, however, in the words of one correspondent, on "guns *and* butter."[8] Johnson defended his decision with these words: "We have enough to do it all . . . . We're the wealthiest nation in the world. And I cannot see why, if we have the will to do it, we can't provide for our own happiness, education, health, and environment. . . . . We need to appeal to everyone to restrain their appetite. We're greedy but not short on the wherewithal to meet our problems."[9]

First Steps Toward the "Great Society"

The president began his domestic programs on two primary fronts. Simultaneously the nation would end poverty and clean up the cities. The war on poverty would be launched by the Office of Economic Opportunity (OEO), and the massive attempt "to save our cities" would be titled the "Model Cities" program. It was an ambitious plan, but in their enthusiasm to pursue it, neither the president nor the Congress took time to add up what that plan would cost immediately, let alone what it would cost over the next ten, twenty, thirty, or one hundred years.

During the Eighty-ninth Congress alone, Johnson's programs had a 68 percent rate of passage, the highest record for successful legislation by a president in the history of the nation as 207 of his proposed bills were adopted into law. By 1966 there were twenty-one different programs to promote health (including the historic Medicare act), seventeen for education, fifteen for economic development, a dozen dealing with urban crises, four for manpower training, seventeen for preserving national resources, and two new cabinet positions created to tackle the growing problems of transportation and urban development.[10] "We have tried to do a great deal in a short time," admitted Johnson's budget director, Charles Schultze, "and the federal system has been hard put to digest so much so quickly."[11]

The Continued Growth of Federal Bureaucracy

Each Great Society program seemed absolutely necessary and worthwhile on the surface, but just below the surface were serious flaws from the beginning. The Great Society with its all-out "war on poverty" had produced a maze of agencies, funds, offices, bureaus, departments, and regional representatives within the Johnson administration. At the end of 1966 the federal government had more than $15 billion in aid and grants available to state and local governments, but it was almost impossible to find one's way to the money source through the tangle of 170 separate programs, funded by four hundred different appropriations, administered by twenty-one different departments and agencies, assisted by 150 different bureaus.[12]

"It became an exercise in grantsmanship," said Jack Flynn of the Department of Housing and Urban Development. "In the end, those that got the money were the ones that wrote the best grant applications and had the best connections in Washington."[13]

The programs looked better in design than in execution. The human factor was often discounted in the planning stages. Senator Abraham Ribicoff, once a supporter of the Great Society programs, said in 1980, "One of the great problems that we had was that the ideas of planners look good on paper and sound good. But when you deal with people, you realize that it becomes another proposition entirely."[14]

The Exclusion of the Private Sector

The Great Society determined that the federal government could by itself eliminate poverty and transform the nation. It couldn't be done. Indeed, one of Johnson's greatest mistakes was to minimize the role of real employment through free enterprise as the major factor in bringing lasting quality. The Reverend George E. Riddick of Operation PUSH in Chicago explained, "social equality is dependent upon real opportunity, and that can be conferred only by economic equality."[15]

One New York banker complained, "My business friends tell me that many Government officials tend to look upon them as rivals in competition rather than partners in progress."[16]

All too often, federal programs were administered from the top down. The opinions of people close to the actual scenes of battle were disregarded or minimized. The programs of state and local government were often undermined by this sudden flood of federal funding and its army of federally paid and appointed staff. The patient, painful work of local and national charities was often undone and replaced by federal bureaucrats who moved into towns and states like carpetbaggers with no regard for those generous, loving volunteers who had preceded them.

The Confusion in the Public Sector

The Great Society moved too quickly, creating confusion and misunderstanding. A Senate hearing in 1966 asked President Johnson's attorney general how much federal aid was available to cities. He answered, "$13 billion." The very next day, the same Senate committee asked the very same question of a second Johnson cabinet member, Bob Weaver of Housing and Urban Development. He replied, "$28 billion."[17]

Confusion reigned on every level. The city of Oakland in 1966, for example, had 140 federal grant programs, each with separate books, offices, and staff.

And in the rush, leaders were not adequately selected or trained, students were unmotivated, and final goals were confusing or missing altogether. Watts, a black ghetto area of Los Angeles, started job training classes, but the dropout rate was almost 50 percent.

The bureaucratic bottleneck in Washington often delayed programs past their useful startup times. When Watts looked as if it might erupt into racial violence a second time in the summer of 1966, $262 thousand in Great Society funds was allocated for "Operation Cool It," a plan to shift 50 thousand sweltering young people from the inner city to the beaches. But the funds weren't released until September, by which time the weather was cool and the young people had returned to school.

The Growing National Debt

The programs were top-heavy, benefiting staff more than the poor they were to assist, and that top-heaviness grew until the federal government became the nation's largest single employer. The Community Action Program, for one example, grew quickly to employ more than 180 thousand people in 907 different agencies spending about $1.2 billion every year.[18]

Gradually, the experts began to add up the immediate and longer range costs of these new programs. One city planner estimated at the beginning of the Model Cities program that making even a small impact on the problems of the cities would cost more than $2 trillion in the next twenty years alone.[19] To bring the average family income up to $3 thousand—the poverty level at the time—would cost an additional $12 billion a year. Black leaders were requesting $100 billion in designated grants. Ecologists guessed that $50 billion more would only begin to clean up the polluted rivers and lakes; more would be required to clean the smog-laden air. Nobody even dared to guess how much money would be required to improve the schools as Johnson's Great Society had envisioned.

In 1966 the cost of the Great Society, excluding Social Security programs, was estimated at $106.4 billion. The estimated cost in 1967 was $112.4 billion. As the programs grew, the costs continued to escalate. The Office of Economic Opportunity launched dozens of expensive new programs with great fanfare and high hopes: the Job Corps, the Neighborhood Youth Corps, operations Head Start and Follow Through, Volunteers in Service to America (VISTA), Community Action agencies, legan services for the poor, neighborhood health centers, and programs for Indians and migrant and seasonal workers.

The Great Society Fails

Just ten years after Lyndon Johnson initiated his plan to create a "Great Society" for America, his successor, Richard M. Nixon, decided that much of the structure should be dismantled. "The intention" of those ambitious social programs launched in the 1960s "was laudable," he said. "But the results, in case after case, amounted to dismal failure. . . . Too much money has been going to those who were supposed to help the needy and too little to the needy themselves."[20]

In fact, after hundreds of billions of dollars were spent by government to fund the initiatives of the Great Society and their spin-offs, millions of Americans still lived in poverty. Inner cities, for the most part, remained blighted. Inadequate housing continued to be a serious national problem. The billions spent on education did not begin to solve the problem of national illiteracy. Test scores of our graduating seniors continued to decline. Adequate medical and psychiatric care was still beyond the reach of great masses of Americans.

President Johnson tried to solve these tragic human needs with massive and costly federal programs. It could not be done. During his administration the number of social-welfare programs mushroomed from forty to one hundred. There is no doubt that the Great Society left the nation a legacy of caring. Some of Johnson's programs survive as created, while others continue under different names. And the hundreds of new hospitals, health care facilities, and vocational education centers and clinics that were built still serve the people in various cities across the nation.

No One Counted the Cost

Unfortunately, the "Great Society" created by Lyndon Johnson and maintained at least in part by Richard Nixon until 1973 left another kind of national legacy as well. During those years of the Great Society and its massive domestic spending, we were also paying for a costly war in Vietnam. Neither Johnson nor Nixon raised taxes to pay the bills. Doing so would have been an unpopular and politically dangerous act. Instead, they ran up huge budget deficits creating immediate and long-term debt and ultimately inflation. In 1968, Johnson's last year in office, the deficit was $25 billion. In 1971 Nixon raised the debt by $23 billion, and in 1972 the nation added another $39 billion to the nation's debt.

The lasting legacy of that increasing national debt is staggering. In Franklin Roosevelt's twelve years in office, the national debt was increased by $197 billion. Truman raised the debt by $4.4 billion, Eisenhower by $15.8 billion, and Kennedy by $11 billion. Johnson's Great Society, coupled with the costs of the war in Vietnam, raised the debt by a total of $42 billion dollars in just six years.[21]

In 1968, looking back over his time in office, President Johnson still believed that in spite of all the costly failures, the federal government could produce a Great Society. "Yes," he proclaimed proudly, "this land will be a shining and peaceful land, where rural poverty has been conquered." The American future, he claimed, would be "a future of limitless promise . . . if we only have the vision, the determination, the stick-to-it-iveness, and do not allow the dividers among us to succeed."[22]

Months later, in a visit to Bangkok, Thailand, Johnson proclaimed grandly, "A Great Society cannot really exist in one nation and not exist in another nation."[23] Besides the billions of dollars he spent domestically, President Johnson gave billions more to foreign governments in a futile attempt to establish his Great Society in other nations around the earth as well.

The Great Society Program Is Scrapped

President Johnson loved the nation and desperately wanted to create the Great Society for all its people and the people of the world. But the Great Society program was doomed from its inception. In 1973 national headlines read, "The War on Poverty Is Being Scrapped."[24] Johnson did his best to mobilize the federal government to solve the problems of the world. He failed, and the nation will be saddled with the cost of that failure for generations.

In the meantime, we must learn from Johnson's Great Society that even the federal government has it limits. What we want for our families and for our neighbors must come from within ourselves. It cannot be proclaimed by a president, passed by the Congress, or administered by millions of federal bureaucrats. The problems of poverty, inequality, and injustice are problems of the human spirit. And federal spending, even without limits, will never create a truly great society. The great society begins in the transformed hearts of the people, and it spreads one by one among us until the entire world is transformed. Somewhere along the way, our nation has lost its spiritual direction, and no massive federal program can force upon us what does not come from within. Our only sure hope is to find that direction once again.

19

ROE v. WADE, 410 U.S. 113 (1973)

JANUARY 22, 1973

The Loss of Human Rights to America's Unborn Children

Bold headlines announced the death of America's thirty-sixth president, Lyndon Baines Johnson. He was sixty-five years old when he died on January 22, 1973, in San Antonio, Texas. During the next day, radio and television broadcasts and front-page newspaper accounts retold the story of this lifelong public servant and the two wars that he had waged during his painful term in office, the "war against poverty" and the bloody, disastrous war in Vietnam.

Few people noticed the page-two story of another war that had been lost that same day, the war to save the lives of America's unborn children from legalized abortion. That war was lost in the hallowed marble halls of the United States Supreme Court in the tragic *Roe v. Wade* decision. Actually, *Time* magazine had scooped the court by hours with the announcement that "Last week *Time* learned that the Supreme Court has decided to strike down nearly every anti-abortion law in the land."[1]

Chief Justice Warren Burger was furious that the story had been leaked. The court knew that its 7-2 decision would create a national furor by overturning all existing state laws against abortion and effectively legalizing abortion throughout the country. The chief justice had wanted to postpone the announcement of this sure-to-be-unpopular decision. On January 20 he was to administer the oath of office to President Nixon at the beginning of his second term. The president was against abortion, but the chief justice had sided with the pro-abortion majority. It would be an embarrassing inaugural moment for both men.

That the media were preoccupied with President Johnson's death when the court finally got around to announcing its decision helped obscure the importance of *Roe v. Wade* even further. And the final signing of the Paris Accords ending the war in Vietnam on January 27, 1973, helped once again to create a news diversion that kept the public from really understanding the implications of this tragic Supreme Court decision.[2]

On January 22 Chief Justice Burger and the other Supreme Court justices filed into their wood and marble chambers as the crier proclaimed the familiar "Oyez! Oyez! Oyez! God save the United States and this Honorable Court."

The courtroom was jammed with lawyers, spectators, state and national officials, and the press. It would be a historic day. The lives of millions of unborn babies were at stake. The court was about to announce its decision in the case of *Jane Roe v. Henry Wade*.

Early in 1971, a young woman in Texas decided to end her pregnancy with an abortion. Texas law forbade it. Although the courts in that state respected the young woman's right of choice, they also respected the right to life of her unborn child. In most states, including Texas, abortion was illegal unless the mother's life was threatened. The young woman, named "Jane Roe" to protect her anonymity by the United States District Court for the Northern District of Texas, sued the state to have the law revoked. The federal court declared in Jane Roe's favor.

According to the court, Jane Roe's right to decide whether to abort a child or to keep it was "protected by the 9th through the 14th Amendments of the United States Constitution." The federal court declared that the Texas laws against abortion were void because they were "unconstitutionally vague and overbroad." Texas appealed the court's decision to the United States Court of Appeals for the Fifth Circuit. Eventually, the case was accepted by the Supreme Court for the final and precedent-setting verdict.

Justice Harry Blackmun had been assigned the task of shaping the majority opinion in *Roe v. Wade* from the beginning. Blackmun's wife, Dottie, was present in the courtroom that day when her husband announced the court's decision. She knew how much time and energy her husband had spent on *Roe v. Wade* since he had been assigned the case on December 17, 1971, almost fourteen months earlier. Through the winter and spring, Justice Blackmun had spent long days and nights hidden away in his second-floor office in the Supreme Court library and in a borrowed space at the Mayo Clinic in Minneapolis, reading medical and legal texts, exchanging memos with his clerks and fellow justices, and writing and rewriting drafts of his decision.

Actually, the Constitution itself provided no specific guidelines on the abortion issue. The fourteenth amendment had been quoted in Jane Roe's trial by her ACLU lawyers to protect the young woman's right to abort her baby. But it was also quoted by lawyers for the state of Texas to protect Jane Roe's unborn child from abortion. The fourteenth amendment states simply:

"Nor shall any State deprive any person of life, liberty, or property without due process of law; nor deny to any person within its jurisdiction the equal protection of the laws."

Both sides, those who favor legalizing abortion (sometimes called "pro-choice") and those who oppose abortion (sometimes called "pro-life"), quote the fourteenth amendment when making their cases. In 1868 when the fourteenth amendment was adopted, however, at least thirty-six states or territories had laws limiting abortion. Those anti-abortion laws were not changed when the fourteenth amendment was ratified, making it clear that the framers of the fourteenth amendment did *not* originally intend to use it to keep the states from regulating abortion.

Apparently because Justice Blackmun could find nothing in the language or history of the Constitution or in the social or moral precedents of the forefathers to support his own judgment to legalize abortion, he turned to medical and social policy, not to the law, to guide him.

A primary force in shaping the current social values pertinent to the question of abortion was the National Organization of Women (NOW). Organized in 1967 with just 300 members, by 1973 NOW had grown to almost 50 thousand members with 700 chapters in the United States and around the world. Throughout American history, courageous women have taken a major role in shaping the nation's values. Often as a result of times of spiritual renewal, women have organized and worked for important social change. Women fought to abolish slavery, to promote temperance, and to win the right to vote. Long ago women established their right and responsibility to take an active, equal role in government on every level.

But the radical feminists as exemplified by the National Organization of Women had lost their spiritual directions just as surely as the nation itself had lost them. In their first national conference in 1967, NOW

255

organizers demanded that the United States Congress "immediately pass the Equal Rights Amendment to the Constitution" with its assertion that abortion was "a woman's right." NOW demonstrators took to the streets demanding the repeal of all laws governing abortion. Cut off from their spiritual heritage, modern feminists had no adequate moral guidelines. They claimed that "only women can define what it means to be a woman in a liberated society."[3] And in that spirit, they demanded that the Supreme Court protect the rights to privacy even if it cost their unborn children their right to life. The clamor in the streets of those same radical feminists echoed through the marble halls of the Supreme Court and helped to shape the majority's tragic decision in *Roe v. Wade*.

Justice Blackmun had three daughters of his own. And though he hoped that he would "never face the [abortion] decision in his own family," he "presumed that his three daughters felt that early abortions should be allowed." And though the justice "claimed to be unsure of his wife Dottie's position," she had told one of his clerks, who favored ending the restrictions against abortion, "that she was doing everything she could to encourage her husband in that direction."[4]

Justice Blackmun decided that his major responsibility was to protect the rights of choice and privacy of the pregnant woman. Here, medical science misled the Court in advising the justices that the fetus was not a person and had no rights to be protected, at least not in the first three months after conception. During the first trimester, the fetus was seen as no more than tissue, a nonperson without constitutional rights or privileges. Most medical authorities saw the unborn child as "not very much a person" up through the sixth month of pregnancy. Many medical experts even claimed the fetus was a nonperson through the entire pregnancy. To these authorities, the fetus only became a "viable" person when delivered out of the mother and into the world, free from the mother's life support systems and able to survive on its own.

If Justice Blackmun had regarded the fetus as a person, that person, though unborn, would be protected by the Constitution. He did not. But to avoid the controversy he knew would follow, the justice left out any direct discussion of the viability of the fetus and tried to dodge the issue in a complex discussion of the three trimesters of pregnancy. However, before Justice Potter Stewart would add his signature to the majority decision, he insisted that Justice Blackmun say more clearly that a fetus wasn't a person. Justice Blackmun consented to his colleague's request.

"A fetus," wrote Justice Blackmun, "is not a person under the Constitution and thus has no legal right to life."

Finally, after fourteen months of professional and personal struggle, on January 22, 1973, Blackmun and the other eight justices filed into their Supreme Court chambers. Before a capacity courtroom crowd, Blackmun announced the decision. The 1856 Texas law restricting abortions in that state was struck down. The majority claimed that the unborn are not included within the definition of "person" protected by the fourteenth amendment and that prior to the end of the first three months of pregnancy, the state may not interfere with or regulate its termination.

Chief Justice Burger concurred with the majority. One of two dissenters, Justice Byron White, claimed that nothing in the language or history of the Constitution supported the Court's judgment. The Court had simply fashioned and announced a new constitutional right for pregnant mothers and had invested that right with sufficient substance to override most existing state abortion statutes. White complained that the issue of abortion should actually have been left with the people and the political processes they have designed to govern their affairs.[5]

Justice William Rehnquist also dissented. The fact that a majority of the states have had abortion statutes for at least a century indicated to Justice Rehnquist that a right to an abortion was not so rooted in the traditions and consciences of the people as to be ranked "fundamental." He also claimed that the statute should have been declared unconstitutional only as it applied to the appellant's particular situation rather than in toto.[6]

After Blackmun announced the court's ruling, it was reported that Mrs. Blackmun told her husband, "I'm very proud of the decision you made."[7] During those next few days when the news of *Roe* v. *Wade* was obscured by national and international headlines, others congratulated Justice Blackmun and the court on its decision to legalize abortion. It was a temporary calm before the growing storm of outrage that followed.

The Nation's Outrage at *Roe v. Wade*

At last, the nation began to awaken to the implications of *Roe v. Wade*. The killing of millions of unborn babies had been made legal by the nation's highest court. State laws—many of them over one hundred years old—had been arrogantly set aside by seven men. They had taken into their hands power never really granted them by the Constitution, the Congress, the president, or the people. An enormous cry of rage and disbelief soon followed.

Thousands of letters poured into the Supreme Court offices. Guards established a sorting room in the basement for the avalanche of mail. Most letters, cards, and telegrams opposed the justices' decision. According to news reports, the justice who received the second highest number of protest letters after Justice Blackmun was Justice William Brennan, the Supreme Court's only Catholic. Apparently, entire Catholic schools wrote him angry, condemning letters, and Catholics, lay and clergy alike, mailed petitions of protest. The pro-abortion majority was compared "to the Butchers of Dachau, child killers, immoral beasts, and Communists. A special ring of hell would be reserved for the Justices."[8]

In reporter Bob Woodward's investigation of this mountain of criticism, he turned up one sad yet instructive sidelight. Evangelical Christians sent over one thousand bitter letters protesting the *Roe v. Wade* decision to Justice Hugo Black. And though Justice Black had died sixteen months before the *Roe v. Wade* announcement, some of those letters and phone calls included death threats. It is a reminder that evangelical Christians, like all other concerned American citizens, must become informed before they become involved. Fortunately religious leaders protested the court's decision more effectively.

New York's Terence Cardinal Cooke asked the prophetic question: "How many millions of children prior to their birth will never live to see the light of day because of the shocking action of the majority of the United States Supreme Court today?"[9]

In Philadelphia, John Joseph Cardinal Krol, the president of the National Conference of Catholic Bishops, said, "It is hard to think of any decision in the two hundred years of our history which has had more disastrous implications for our stability as a civilized society."[10]

Justice Blackmun was stunned by the number and the fury of the personal attacks leveled against him and the Court's majority. For the first time in his life, Blackmun's speeches were picketed, his words were jeered, and his life was threatened. The nursing sisters from Saint Mary's Hospital at the Mayo Clinic, where Blackmun had researched the *Roe v. Wade* decision, wrote dozens of angry letters. And the state of Texas filed a petition requesting a rehearing of the case, comparing Blackmun's decision that a fetus was not a person to the Supreme Court's infamous decision in 1857 that Dred Scott, a slave, was not a citizen or person under the Constitution.

The *Dred Scott* Decision of 1857

Although the Supreme Court had decided three years before the Civil War began that slavery was protected by the Constitution from congressional efforts to stop its spread into new states, Lincoln himself refused to be bound by the court's ruling. "If I were in Congress," he said, "and a vote should come up on a question whether slavery should be prohibited in a new territory, in spite of the Dred Scott decision, I would vote that it should."[11]

Later, upon his inauguration as president, Lincoln repeated his opposition to those who claimed that the *Dred Scott* decision bound him as the law of the land: "If the policy of the government upon vital questions affecting the whole people is to be irrevocably fixed by the decisions of the Supreme Court . . . the people will have ceased to be their own rulers, having to that extent practically resigned their Government into the hands of that eminent tribunal."[12]

Marbury v. Madison, 1803

The Supreme Court's *Dred Scott* decision was only the second case in history in which the court declared an act of Congress to be illegal. The first case, *Marbury v. Madison,* was decided in 1803. During his last few days in office, President John Adams had appointed William Marbury a justice of the peace. Due to negligence, the commission was not delivered before Thomas Jefferson's inauguration. Once in office, Jefferson instructed his new secretary of state, James Madison, not to deliver Adams's commission to Marbury.

To get his job, William Marbury directly sued the Supreme Court instead of the lower district court for a *writ of mandamus* (an order by the Supreme Court to a lower court or to a person or agency in government commanding that a specified thing be done). The Congress had granted the Supreme Court the power to offer such a writ with the Judiciary Act of 1789. In *Marbury v. Madison,* however, the Court decided Congress had acted unconstitutionally. It declared that Congress could not grant the Supreme Court original jurisdiction over such a writ. Marbury lost his appointment, while the Supreme Court gained a dangerous new power. It had granted itself the right of judicial review, the power to declare an act of Congress illegal.

In the Constitution, our forefathers had instructed the Supreme Court to settle disputes on the basis of "this Constitution, the Laws of the United States, and Treaties made" (Art. III, Sec. 2). In other words, the Court was established to determine which disputing party had most accurately interpreted a given law; the Constitution gave the courts no express grant to judge the legality of an act of Congress. The Supreme Court took that right in such cases as *Marbury v. Madison* and *Dred Scott.*

Thomas Jefferson disputed the constitutional legitimacy of judicial review. In fact, he clearly stated that *Marbury v. Madison* was "not law." He never agreed that judicial review made "the judges . . . the ultimate arbiters of all constitutional questions." He described it as "a very dangerous doctrine indeed, and one which would place us under the despotism of an oligarchy. [The] Constitution has erected no such single tribunal, knowing that to whatever hands confided, with the corruptions of time and party, its members would become despots."[13]

The Problem of Judicial Review

Jefferson's warning was prophetic. What began innocently with *Marbury v. Madison* has evolved into a notion of judicial review that gives the Supreme Court power over all branches of the government. In the past fifty years, the Supreme Court has declared numerous acts of the president and laws of the Congress to be illegal. And in a growing number of cases, the Court is throwing out laws made by federal, state, and local legislatures and creating its own new laws to replace them.

Suddenly, the power of the people to elect lawmakers who in turn make the law has been overthrown by a handful of nonelected Supreme Court justices who have decided to grant themselves the power to make laws on their own. How did this shift of power from the people to the Supreme Court take place?

Once again, historians look back to that dangerous period of prosperity and hopefulness between the Civil War and World War I to find the answers. Once again, we find the teachings of Darwin's evolutionary theory at work, this time shaping the notion of judicial review. Woodrow Wilson himself concluded, "living political constitutions must be Darwinian in structure and practice."[14]

To modern jurists, the words, phrases, sentences, and paragraphs of the Constitution had no definite, absolute meanings. The Constitution is alive, said the Darwinians. It changes as people's ideas about it change. Little by little, the actual words and values of the Constitution were replaced by the words and values of the jurists who were interpreting it. What our forefathers had in mind when they wrote those words seemed out of reach or unimportant by comparison to the interpretations placed upon them by the modern courts.

Justice William Brennan, of the pro-abortion majority in *Roe v. Wade,* explained the dangerous notion of judicial review in a speech at Georgetown University: "It is arrogant to pretend that from our vantage we can gauge accurately the intent of the framers on application of principle to specific contemporary questions. We current justices read the Constitution in the only way that we can: as Twentieth Century Americans . . . . The ultimate question must be, what do the words of the text mean in our time?"[15]

In those words, Brennan made two dangerous and false assumptions. First, he stated flatly that we cannot know the original intent of the framers because we are separated from them by two hundred years of history. Second, he claimed we must interpret the Constitution in the light of our morality, not the morality of our forefathers. James A. Reichley, author of *Religion in American Public Life,* replied: "If justices do not reflect the authority of the Constitution, the public must inquire, why should their opinions count for more than those of any other citizen?"[16]

Without believing in the Constitution as our ultimate authority, we have no trustworthy standard by which a law can be judged. Without believing that we can understand the original intent of our forefathers, modern jurists give up the attempt to understand it altogether. And without acknowledging our forefathers' conviction regarding "the laws of nature and of nature's God" as the ultimate moral authority, we have no ancient moral standards by which our modern morality can be tested or informed.

Roe v. Wade, with its legalization of abortion, is just one example of the dangerous and destructive effects of this current notion of judicial review. First, with no constitutional authority, the Supreme Court struck down laws against abortion in almost every state. It was an inexcusable infringement upon the rights of the people in each state to decide that complex social issue for themselves. The state legislatures had decided against indiscriminate abortion. In one blow, the Supreme Court struck down all those decisions.

Second, in place of all those state laws, the Supreme Court created another law legalizing abortion. Seven men decided that law against the will of the majority of the American people. In every Gallup poll taken since that 1973 decision, at least 75 percent of the citizens of this nation do not agree that abortion should be allowed under all circumstances, and a solid majority would eliminate the 95 percent of abortions that are performed for social convenience.[17]

Third, the Supreme Court established a moral precedent regarding the definition and value of human life that disregards the universal laws revealed in nature and in the Judeo-Christian Scriptures. Most abortions are performed between seven and thirteen weeks of pregnancy. Yet by the seventh week, the unborn child has fingers, toes, eyes, lungs, a beating heart, and brain waves. Nature is clear. Abortions kill babies. And the revealed laws of God about such killings in both the Old and New Testaments are easily understood.

Last year approximately 1.5 million unborn babies died inside their mother's wombs, victims of the instruments and poisons of abortion. Since the Supreme Court's decision in *Roe v. Wade,* more than 18 million unborn babies have died. Legal abortion has become a primary method of birth control, and hundreds of thousands of teenage girls and young women are returning to abortion clinics for second and third abortions—many times within the very same year. Abortion clinics have become a multibillion-dollar industry, while millions of qualified families applying each year for babies to adopt must be turned away because there just aren't babies available.[18]

In 1765, John Adams wrote these words: "You have rights antecedent to all earthly governments; rights that cannot be repealed or restrained by human laws; rights derived from the Great Legislator of the Universe." In its 1973 decision in *Roe v. Wade,* the United States Supreme Court decided to exclude the unborn from their God-given rights, and the nation still suffers the tragic consequences of that immoral and unconstitutional decision.

20

AMERICA DEFEATED IN VIETNAM

APRIL 29, 1975

The Loss of Honor and the Will to Win

At 4:00 A.M. the first North Vietnamese rocket slammed into a fuel truck standing beside the runway at Saigon's Tansonnhut airfield. The explosion awakened the city and sent a ball of fire into the cloudy, predawn sky. Dozens of rockets followed, bringing fiery destruction to the airbase and death and injury to the terror-stricken people who were camped around the field, hoping to escape the final collapse of South Vietnam.

Another salvo of rockets landed on the Defense Attaché Office complex in Saigon. One of the first rockets killed two young Marine guards on duty there: Lance Corporal Darwin Judge of Marshalltown, Iowa, and Corporal Charles McMahon, Jr., of Woburn, Massachusetts. Officially, these two young men were the last Americans to die in Vietnam. In the disorganized and panicked rush to leave the city that final day, their bodies were left behind in the morgue of the Seventh-Day Adventist Hospital.

North Vietnamese General Van Tien Dung and 100 thousand North Vietnamese troops were moving on Saigon. The rockets and 130-millimeter artillery shells were slamming into military and civilian targets in and around the city every minute. South Vietnamese forces were fighting bravely against overwhelming odds, but the fall of Saigon was just a few hours away.

Only weeks before, on Easter Sunday, Danang, South Vietnam's second largest city, had fallen to the Communist forces. Thousands of men, women, and children had waded into the South China Sea trying to escape on a small flotilla of fishing boats and barges. Children were lost in the chaos. Hundreds drowned.

During the weeks that followed, more than 50 thousand Americans and Vietnamese had been evacuated from the capital. Still, America's last ambassador to South Vietnam, Graham A. Martin, refused to give the orders to evacuate Saigon. He was determined to support the South Vietnamese in their struggle against the advancing Communist forces. His determination was noble, but it came too late. In fact, America had already abandoned its allies in Vietnam. The war was over, and the skeleton force that remained was simply waiting for the inevitable Communist victory.

Operation Frequent Wind[1]

Operation Frequent Wind had been thoroughly planned for an evacuation of the American forces, our allies and their families, and tens of thousands of Vietnamese military and civilian personnel. The American radio station in Saigon was to play "I'm Dreaming of a White Christmas." Then the announcer would report, "The temperature in Saigon is 105 degrees and rising." At that signal, all those on the evacuation lists were to head for zones around the city where they would board buses, trucks, and cars for their last journey to the airbase and evacuation to Guam and the Philippines by C-130 military aircraft.

"White Christmas" was never played. The announcer never gave his signal. Frantic messages raced back and forth between Ambassador Martin and Secretary of State Henry Kissinger in the White House situation room. Finally, after an eleven-hour delay, at 3:06 P.M., President Ford ordered Operation Frequent Wind to begin. Less than four hours of daylight was left, and fierce battles were raging in the suburbs of Saigon.

It was too late for fixed-wing aircraft to transport the thousands of men, women, and children we had promised not to abandon. The airport runways had been blasted into moonscapes by Communist rocket and artillery fire. Finally, the ambassador activated Option IV, the largest helicopter evacuation in history. A wave of CH-53 and CH-46 helicopters was launched toward Saigon from the carrier *USS Coral Sea* and the small fleet of American ships waiting for the rescue signal just off the coast of South Vietnam.

In those next frantic hours, more than 6,236 people were flown by helicopter from the Defense Attaché Office alone. Thousands more were helicoptered from the perimeter of the Tansonnhut airbase. Only one hundred evacuees were scheduled to be flown from the American embassy. In fact, between 2,000 and 3,000 Americans and Vietnamese were waiting inside the lightly guarded compound with another 3,000 to 4,000 desperate people trying to climb the walls and force their way into waiting lines.

With the darkness came heavy rains. Only a few helicopters had landed and departed from the embassy. The crowd was growing more and more fearful. The North Vietnamese armies were approaching. The sound of artillery fire mixed with thunder, and the flames of burning buildings lit up the lightning-streaked skies above the city. Someone found a 35-millimeter slide projector to illuminate the embassy's helicopter landing pad. Ambassador Martin was still promising that nobody would be left behind, and he refused to be evacuated until his promise had been kept. President Ford finally had to command Martin to leave on the next available helicopter flight. Carrying the folded American flag that had hung above the embassy, Ambassador Martin obeyed. It was 4:58 A.M.

The Marines assigned to guard the embassy quickly retreated inside. Barricading the doors against the frightened, angry crowd, they rode the elevator to the sixth floor and climbed the stairway to the roof. The Marines locked the doors behind them. People who had been promised flights to safety panicked when they saw the Marines depart. In desperation, they stormed the embassy. A fire truck was driven through the front-door barricades. A mob surged through the building toward the roof top. At the last possible moment, the final rescue helicopter arrived to evacuate the Marines. From the open helicopter those last young Americans to leave Vietnam looked down on thousands of abandoned allies they had promised to protect.

A German priest, a large group of officials from the South Korean embassy, and 420 Vietnamese who had worked for the embassy were still waiting patiently in the embassy courtyard, not realizing that Operation Frequent Wind had ended without them. Tens of thousands of others who had risked their lives and the lives of their families to directly assist the American forces were also abandoned. Two billion dollars worth of military equipment, $16 million in South Vietnamese gold reserves, and at least $3.5 million in American currency were among the nonhuman assets lost or left for the enemy.

Just four hours after the Marine guards were airlifted from the roof of the American embassy, a Communist tank smashed through the wrought-iron gates of the presidential palace in central Saigon. One hundred thousand Communist troops ringed the city. South Vietnam's 18th Division had fought bravely before disintegrating in the face of much larger and better equipped Communist forces. That morning, the war in Vietnam ended. After a lightning-quick advance toward Saigon to capture the city before the summer rains began, the Communists had won their victory, and the South Vietnamese and American forces were left to count their losses.[2]

The Cost of the War in Vietnam

Fifty-eight thousand Americans died in Vietnam. Another 300 thousand were wounded. At last count 2,441 Americans were still regarded as missing in action. Vietnamese casualties added into millions. At least 1.7 million Vietnamese soldiers had died. More than 3.2 million were wounded. Almost 100 thousand Vietnamese were amputees, and at least 800 thousand children had been orphaned by the war. Somewhere between 13 thousand and 18 thousand Amerasian children—children with one American and one Vietnamese parent—remained in Vietnam, subject to various forms of discrimination. No price tag could be placed on the human suffering and loss of America's nineteen-year involvement in Vietnam, but the United States government had spent at least $150 billion to conduct and lose the tragic conflict.

And with the fall of Saigon to the Communist North Vietnamese, the tragedy in Indochina seemed only to begin. In the months that followed, an estimated 1 million Vietnamese tried to flee their homeland by boat across the South China Sea. Thousands of these "boat people" were killed braving Communist patrols, violent storms at sea, attacks by pirates, and leaking, unseaworthy boats that filled with water and left hundreds to drown, to die from heat and exposure, or to be eaten by the sharks.

Tens of thousands who did not escape were rounded up by the conquering Communist forces and shot, imprisoned, or placed in "re-education camps." Thousands more just disappeared. Buddhist and Christian clergy, intellectuals and artists, former politicians, military leaders, and police were murdered, tortured, humiliated, or imprisoned. Hundreds of thousands of ordinary citizens were uprooted and forced from their hometowns and villages to live in rural outposts and barren farm areas in the name of resettlement of unproductive urban zones. Even the most elementary human rights were denied the 24 million people of the South who became victims of the new Communist totalitarian state.[3]

In neighboring Laos, the government quickly fell to Communist Laotians who were loyal to Hanoi. Sixty thousand Meo tribesmen were murdered or exiled by the occupying Vietnamese forces. And as in Vietnam, Laotians experienced mass arrests, murders, imprisonments, and relocations.

In Kampuchea (Cambodia), after the 1975 takeover by Pol Pot, the Khmer Rouge forcibly evacuated whole cities, performing mass executions in their attempt to eliminate all traces of Western influence. During those three years before the Communist North Vietnamese takeover of Cambodia, between 1.2 and 3 million gentle Cambodian people were murdered or starved to death.

Greatly assisted by the 550 American tanks, 1,200 American armored personnel carriers, 1,330 American artillery pieces, and at least 1,000 American aircraft abandoned in Vietnam, the Communist Vietnamese extended their influence and the influence of their close friends, the Soviet Union, through much of Indochina.

The Loss of Honor and the Will to Win

Just five days before Saigon fell, President Gerald Ford addressed the student body at Tulane University in New Orleans. Already, he had consigned to history the American tragedy in Vietnam: "Today, Americans can regain the sense of pride that existed before Vietnam. But it cannot be achieved by refighting a war that is finished . . . . These events, tragic as they are, portend neither the end of the world nor of America's leadership in the world."[4] The president was right to try to give the nation hope during that time of failure and disgrace, but he was kidding himself if he actually believed that America could so easily "regain the sense of pride that existed before Vietnam."

The United States had suffered its first major military defeat. On television almost every night for an entire generation, 240 million Americans had witnessed the bungled war effort with growing incredulity. Together the people shared the grief and humiliation of the daily body count, the public contradictions by presidents and generals, the growing confusion about the purpose of the war, and the eventual sense of impending defeat. Then, on that last day, the nation watched together the final frantic retreat up a crowded stairway to a helicopter pad on the roof of an American embassy under siege.

Precious human and financial resources had been drained away. The country was painfully divided. Memories of the angry, sometimes violent demonstrations against the war and the tragic student deaths at Kent State were fresh and hurtful to recall. Vietnam (coupled with Watergate and the resignation of Richard Nixon) had crippled the American presidency. The War Powers Resolution weakened the president's ability to conduct foreign policy. Hundreds of thousands of servicemen and women who had risked their lives in Vietnam returned to public humiliation and painful, private suffering.

And, though President Ford spoke hopefully, in fact, "America's leadership in the world" seemed damaged almost beyond repair. The nation had abandoned almost 30 million people to Communist tyranny. The Soviets had extended their sphere of influence throughout Indochina without the loss of a single soldier, sailor, or airman. Our retreat created a dangerous vacuum in leadership for the entire free world, and the Soviets moved quickly to take advantage of their opportunity. Almost unhindered, the Communists moved into Angola, Ethiopia, South Yemen, and Afghanistan. And from their base in Cuba, the Soviets increased support for terrorism and revolution throughout Central and South America.

The Iranian Captivity

"America's leadership in the world" had reached its lowest level in modern history when on November 4, 1979, several hundred Iranian militants seized the United States embassy in Teheran. Ninety people were taken hostage, including sixty American citizens. The terrorists demanded that the deposed shah be returned for trial from the New York hospital where he was then being treated. President Carter refused. He retaliated by reviewing the visas of 45 thousand Iranians in America. He cut off purchases of Iranian oil. He froze all Iranian assets in the United States. But the militants refused to budge, and the captivity of our embassy and its personnel continued.

On February 11, 1980, Iranian President Bani-Sadr insisted that the captives would be released only if the United States "confessed past crimes," delivered the shah and his assets to Iran, and promised never again "to interfere in Iran's internal affairs." After five months of humiliation before the world at the hands of the extremist Muslim terrorists, on April 7, President Carter severed all diplomatic relations with Iran and imposed an embargo on American exports to that country. Again, the tactics proved unsuccessful. Finally, on April 24, President Carter tried to rescue the hostages by helicopter from a secret base in Iran's eastern desert. The attempt failed. The American rescue forces couldn't even communicate with each other. Three American helicopters suffered mechanical breakdowns. In the ensuing chaos a helicopter crashed into a transport, and eight young American servicemen died.

The Iranians rushed members of the world's press to the site of America's most recent humiliation. Pictures of twisted wreckage and burned American bodies were sent by satellite around the globe. The national humiliation of that one final day in Vietnam was relived in Iran on an almost daily basis as terrorists bullied and threatened their American prisoners before the television cameras. For 444 days the world watched and waited while the United States was held captive in its own embassy. That Iranian captivity symbolized a growing sense of the nation's helplessness before her enemies. America, the once mighty world power, had been defeated in Vietnam; outwitted and outmanuevered by Soviet expansion in Africa, Asia, and Latin America; and humiliated by terrorists and fanatics around the globe.

And in Teheran, while cameras recorded the scene, fifty-two American captives were herded into secret locations throughout the city. The streets echoed with the mob's loud cry, "Death to America!" And while the world watched, friends and foes of the United States wondered if in fact the mob was right. Had the nation's moral and military wounds been fatal? Was America's leadership of the free world over and done?

The once proud and mighty nation had lost its way, and the world wondered if it would find it again.

At the beginning of the century, America had turned from her spiritual and political foundations. As a result, the nation had suffered great loss. Her spirit had been broken. Her will to win had been crippled dangerously. But life was left in her, and as the decade of the 1980s began, that new life stirred.

New Winds Blowing

In early 1980, 500 thousand people were preparing to march on Washington in the largest demonstration of religious and moral conviction in the history of the land. Tens of millions of Americans had been praying that God would lead the nation back to her spiritual roots. A former California governor who liked to quote Washington, Jefferson, and Lincoln was running a close race for the presidency. And new religious and political coalitions were forming to bring about a peaceful transfer of power from those who had misled the nation to those who would bring the nation back on course again.

PART THREE

FINDING
OUR WAY
AGAIN

21

A SPIRITUAL MARCH ON WASHINGTON

APRIL 29, 1980

A Mandate to Return to Our Judeo-Christian Roots

The morning dawned damp, gray, and cold. For days heavy rain had been falling on Washington, D.C., and more was predicted. It didn't matter. By 4:00 A.M. the wet grass and slippery sidewalks of the twenty-three-block-long Mall between the Capitol Building and the Washington Monument were alive with people. Hundreds had spent the night in sleeping bags or wrapped in blankets on park benches, hoping to get front-row positions near the speakers' stand. By 5:00 A.M. thousands of excited men, women, and children were piling out of church buses and vans, station wagons, and sedans, balancing umbrellas and Bibles in their hands. Before the 6:00 call to worship, cabs and city buses, cars, and even open trucks would deliver tens of thousands more from hotels, motels, private homes, and assembly points across the city.[1]

Carrying banners, wearing colorful badges and T-shirts, singing, praying, and lifting their arms in praise, they gathered by the thousands before the giant stage that had been erected in the middle of the Mall directly in front of the Smithsonian Institution. The historic, red-brick building with its regal towers and turrets stood like a great cathedral behind the scene. Red, white, and blue bunting draped the platform. A white circular banner suspended above the massed choirs read, "Washington for Jesus, April 29, 1980."

Reporters with cameras and recorders interviewed the early arrivals. Speakers and musicians assembled on the stage. A mass of people from every state in the Union assembled quietly on the Mall. Spontaneously, before the rally even began, someone began to sing "He Is Lord."

Thousands of voices joined in. Eyes were damp with tears. Hands were stretched heavenward.

Exactly at 6:00 A.M., John Gimenez stepped up to a clear plastic podium and said quietly, "Let's pray."

No trumpet fanfare. No laser lights or exploding fireworks lit up the predawn sky. No timpani rolled to call the growing crowd to worship. A short, dark-haired man whose face had never been on the cover of *Time* or *Newsweek* walked to the microphone and without a word of explanation called the crowd to prayer.[2]

With those two little words, "Let's pray," John Gimenez launched one of the great days in American history. The moment his voice echoed out across the Mall to the steps of the Capitol itself, 50 thousand people bowed their heads and raised their hearts together. Before the day ended, an estimated 500 thousand people had joined in that prayer. This was no token prayer as one might pray before a political rally, a football game, or a club luncheon. This was the first prayer of the twelve straight hours of serious praying that would follow. To pray for the nation and her people was the only reason 500 thousand people had come to Washington that day. Between 6:00 A.M. and 6:00 P.M. they would hear their biblical theme repeated dozens of times: "If My people who are called by My name will humble themselves, and pray and seek My face, and turn from their wicked ways, then I will hear from heaven, and will forgive their sin and heal their land."[3]

For nineteen months, hundreds of volunteers had worked in cities and states across the country, mobilizing this great army to pray. And the roughly 500 thousand who drifted on and off the Mall during those twelve great hours of praying represented tens of millions of people who were watching the event live on television. The three primary Christian television networks, CBN, PTL, and TBN, had joined their broadcast staffs and facilities to saturate the nation live from Washington. Through that unprecedented act of cooperation, millions of Americans were called to pray for this nation and for our world that day.

The idea of calling the nation to prayer through a great rally and march on Washington originated with John Gimenez, pastor of Rock Church in Virginia Beach, Virginia. In Oakland, California, in October 1978, the dream was born in John's heart as he preached from the words of the prophet Isaiah.

At the time Isaiah wrote, the people of Israel, like the citizens of America, had departed from their spiritual roots. They were in deep trouble. They had forsaken the ways of God and were living in immorality and corruption. Their treasury was bankrupt. Their military might had ebbed away, and they found themselves surrounded by a powerful enemy. The end was in sight for their once proud and prosperous nation. And John remembered the promise God had given Solomon at the building of the temple: "If My people who are called by My name will humble themselves, and pray and seek My face, and turn from their wicked ways, then I will hear from heaven, and will forgive their sin and heal their land."

The only hope for Israel was a return to righteousness. The prophet demanded that

". . . every knee shall bow,
Every tongue shall take an oath."[4]

John Gimenez heard the prophet's ancient call and began to dream of what might happen to America if her people, too, were called to return to righteousness. He pictured a mass of people assembling in the nation's capital to pray, to confess, and to call the nation back to her spiritual roots.

In November 1978 John shared his dream with me over lunch at a motel restaurant in Virginia Beach. If you have read the first chapter of this book, you will know why I suggested April 29 as the target day for his great march on Washington. On that same day in 1607, members of the first permanent English settlement in the New World planted a cross on the beach at Cape Henry, Virginia, and dropped to their knees in the sand to ask God's blessings on this new land. What better day could there be to remember the nation's spiritual heritage and to call the people to pray that God might renew His blessings upon us?

John's dream captured me, and together we began to tell others about our emerging plan for an April 29, 1980, mass rally and march on Washington. Bill Bright, the founder and director of Campus Crusade, joined me as co-chairman of "Washington for Jesus," serving with our national chairman, John Gimenez.

Within weeks, Demos Shakarian, founder and president of the Full Gospel Businessmen's Fellowship International, and Bishops J. O. Patterson and Jesse Winley confirmed our vision, and together we called for volunteers from across the nation to join us. An illustrious and faithful group of co-sponsors volunteered their staffs and facilities to help us. Protestant and Catholic clergy; presidents and executives of major denominations; officials of Christian colleges, universities, and seminaries; founders and officers of major American corporations; radio and television evangelists; publishers; authors; artists; and lay men and women joined the team.

John took his dream to Jim and Tammy Bakker at PTL and to Jan and Paul Crouch at TBN. They immediately volunteered to join the CBN in the first experiment by the Christian television networks to promote an event jointly and broadcast it simultaneously.

Ted Pantaleo was appointed national coordinator for "Washington for Jesus" to create teams of volunteer organizers in every state and in most major American cities. Loren Cunningham, founder and president of Youth with a Mission, volunteered hundreds of his young people to distribute tons of literature across the nation and in the nation's capital. The national steering committee decided on a simple strategy:

Keep it scriptural—because the Bible is our only trustworthy source of authority.

Keep it simple—because there is only one issue, to humble ourselves and pray.

Keep it spiritual—because the weapons of our warfare are not political or social, based on man's doing, but spiritual and entirely dependent upon God.

Keep it serious—because the glory of God's kingdom and the future of our nation are at stake.[5]

The logistic plan for the march and rally had been developed by the National Capital Parks Service and the city of Washington for the visit of Pope John Paul II in the fall of 1979, when 179 thousand Catholics assembled for the papal mass. We had no idea how many Protestant and Catholic Christians would gather for "Washington for Jesus."

The press was skeptical. At first it simply ignored our plans for the prayer march and rally. Then it accused the organizers of gathering this large crowd of Christian believers to apply "right-wing political pressure" to national officials during the election year. A *New York Times* reporter called John Gimenez "a former drug addict who was born in Harlem."[6] And when the reporter pushed John to admit our "reactionary agenda," John answered, "It's almost as if no one believes that a group of Christians would come here and pray for their country."

And though our agenda was spiritual and not political, significant portions of the media boycotted the event. It was easy to forgive the press for its absence. We understood that print and broadcast journalists had trouble comprehending why so many people would go to so much effort "just to pray." Even the organizers of "Washington for Jesus" were surprised by the size and enthusiasm of the huge crowd that began to arrive in Washington on April 28, just one day before the rally.

On the evening just preceding the big day, four thousand women packed Constitution Hall to be challenged to pray by actress Dale Evans Rogers, singer Sarah Jordan Powell, and the event co-chairmen's wives, Anne Gimenez, Dede Robertson, and Vonette Bright. At the same time, Christian clergy were assembling from across the nation to share with each other the power and promise of prayer to change their churches as it changed the nation. And in RFK Stadium, 30 thousand young people had assembled to sing and pray in preparation for the long day ahead. Thousands of young people spent the night on their knees and then walked through the early-morning darkness to the Mall.

The Capitol dome was still ablaze with light when the rally began. A red beacon flashed on top of the Washington Monument. People walked quickly and quietly in the semi-darkness. Never in the history of the nation had the people gathered in such great numbers in the capital to pray. The agenda was simple and clear: "From the rising of the sun to its going down the LORD's name is to be praised."[7]

With the sun still low in the sky and blocked by thick, gray clouds, John Gimenez asked the great and growing throng, "Why have we come to Washington?"

"To pray," they answered as one voice.

"We're here because we need healing," he continued. "We need healing in the church first of all. . . . Then, we'll get healing for the land."

Nancy Honeytree began to play her guitar and sing quietly the first verse of "The Old Rugged Cross." Almost immediately the crowd joined in singing. At that moment, Arthur Blessit carried a rough, wooden cross onto the Mall. Arthur has carried the cross on walks across the nation and in countries around the earth to remind the world of the story of Jesus and the meaning of His suffering.

Nicky Cruz, whose dramatic conversion story was told by David Wilkerson in his best-selling book *The Cross and The Switchblade,* gave his moving testimony. He knew the consequences of drug abuse in his own life, and he called on the people to pray for millions of Americans, rich and poor, who are still enslaved by drugs.

Demos Shakarian, whose family had immigrated to America to escape the bloody persecution and pogrom of his people in Turkey, told of his love for this country and then warned prophetically: "I love America. She's been good to me. But America is in trouble, and we have come to Washington to pray."[8]

Josh McDowell, the popular campus lecturer, warned the nation that the suicide rate among high school and college students had risen by 300 percent in just the past decade. He spoke of the joy that Christ had brought to his own life and led the crowd in prayer for the millions of American students who found their lives to be empty and futile.[9]

The massed choirs sang. The orchestra and brass ensemble played. America's greatest gospel singers led the crowd in songs of testimony and praise. And prayers were played, sung, read, and spoken in various languages by guests of every color and race. Hundreds of thousands of people joined their voices in singing together a moving version of the Lord's Prayer: "For thine is the kingdom and the power and the glory forever. Amen."

Before and after every testimony, every challenge, every song of faith, the people prayed. They stood hand in hand, thousands of them, asking for God's forgiveness. They clustered in small groups praying sentence prayers for friends and family; for national and world leaders; for nations torn by flood, famine, terrorism, revolution, or war. And they knelt on the still-damp grass and prayed together for a great spiritual awakening in the land.

During the past century, in spite of the nation's move toward secular humanism and away from our Judeo-Christian roots, there have been signs of spiritual awakening and renewal with every decade. The nineteenth-century voices of Charles Finney, Dwight L. Moody, and Billy Sunday have had their twentieth-century counterparts. The radio voice of evangelist Charles Fuller crackled out across the still-primitive Old Fashioned Revival Hour radio network, calling the nation to repentance in 1931. From an auditorium in Long Beach, California, the Fullers' weekly radio network call to repentance and faith remained constant through the Great Depression and World War II.

During the war and postwar years came such lay evangelistic organizations as Youth for Christ, Inter-Varsity, the Navigators, Young Life, Campus Crusade, the Christian Businessmen's Committees, the Full Gospel Businessmen's Fellowship International, the Gideons, the Fellowship of Christian Athletes, and the Yokefellows.

Dr. Billy Graham's mass evangelism ministry began in Los Angeles in 1948. His "Hour of Decision" radio broadcasts and television specials launched the modern era of electronic evangelism.

The next few decades brought a new and wondrous miracle. The Holy Spirit fell upon the lives of millions of American Christians and on believers in every nation. This modern Pentecost has contributed to the growth of the church and to the hope for spiritual renewal in our nation and around the earth.

And on April 29, 1980, all the great spiritual streams flowed together into Washington, D.C. Catholics and Southern Baptists prayed side by side with Presbyterians and Nazarenes. Charismatics and noncharismatics grasped hands or knelt beside each other to lift their voices to God on behalf of this nation and its future. Red and yellow, black and white, the Christians gathered to talk to God and listen to His servants.

Dr. Adrian Rogers, pastor and soon-to-be-elected president of the Southern Baptist Convention, cried out: "It is not the sins of the world holding back revival. It is the sins of the saints."[10] Then he quoted from the Old Testament book of Proverbs, "Righteousness exalts a nation, but sin is a reproach to any people."[11]

Thousands of young people were wearing blue T-shirts with those words emblazoned around an American flag: "Righteousness exalts a nation!" They cheered and applauded each speaker. They joined hands and sang with Pat and Shirley Boone, John Hall, and the massed choirs. Those young people were from every state, but they loved the same Lord, studied the same Bible, and carried the same burden for their nation. And when it was time to pray, the young people were in the front lines praying sincere, intelligent prayers for their churches, for their friends and families, and for the country they loved.

Two dozen congressmen greeted us that day. Mark Hatfield, the senior Republican senator from Oregon, spoke words of wisdom in a live, on-the-scene television interview. He welcomed the people to Washington. On behalf of all the government officials in the nation's capital, he thanked them for their prayers. Then he paraphrased the ancient biblical words of the prophet Amos, who warned the people that "religious and spiritual meetings are despised by God unless they are backed with acts of mercy, justice and reconciliation."[12]

Mark Hatfield is a devout Baptist layman. He knows the people gathered on the Mall that day. He knows the hundreds of millions of dollars they give to feed the hungry, dress the naked, heal the sick, and care for the needy at home and around the earth. He has visited their missions in the inner city. He has worked with their volunteers in life-saving programs in his home state and across the country. He knows that no one cares about this nation in ways more generous and practical than the people who gathered on the Mall that day; yet he was right to remind us. Prayers for the nation combined with loving works on the nation's behalf will make all the difference.

At 12:00 noon the great crowd gathered on Constitution Avenue for a march through the city. Drums rolled. Trumpets sounded a fanfare that echoed through the capital. Hundreds of thousands of voices sang together, "God's truth is marching on." For that moment, Washington stopped its business and looked down from open windows and out of open doors at that parade of Christians in the street. Uniformed policemen from Washington and other cities and states marched behind a banner reading, "Cops for Christ." Arthur Blessit carried the cross at the front of the moving sea of faces. Delegations from each state marched behind colorful banners. I stepped out of the front row of marchers at one point and climbed a stairway to look back on long streets filled with my brothers and sisters. The prophet Joel described this same army more than three thousand years ago: "Every one marches in formation,/And they do not break ranks. / They do not push one another; / Every one marches in his own column. . . . / They are not cut down."[13]

While we marched, other, smaller groups moved toward the White House, the steps of the Capitol Building and the Supreme Court, and even across the Potomac to the Pentagon to kneel in fervent prayer for the men and women inside each building who helped to guide the nation's destiny. Then, from across the city the crowds reconverged on the great Mall to complete the day of prayer.

Pat Boone said, "Today, we're having the Sermon on the Mall. The eyes and ears of the world are on us."[14]

Bishop J. O. Patterson, national executive of the Church of God in Christ, stood before the huge crowd and exclaimed: "Our trouble began when we turned our back on God and His Word. And I know that it may look dark and dismal, but God's hand is not short nor His ear deaf. And as true as I stand here, I believe God has begun the process of healing America now and today!"[15]

Bill Bright added this warning: "This is the most important day in the nation's history apart from its founding, because unless God does something supernatural to intervene in the affairs of this nation, I believe that we shall lose our freedom to a foreign power."[16]

CBN co-host Ben Kinchlow asked the crowd to point their hands toward the building that houses the Senate and House of Representatives. "Stretch out your hand toward that building," he said prayerfully. And immediately half a million hands were raised toward the Capitol. "Loose our nation's capital, all our leaders," he prayed, "and let the power of God flow into that nation, and let this day mark a day of return to the principles of God."[17]

All through the program the skies had remained gray and ominous. A storm threatened. Then Dr. E. V. Hill, a Baptist minister from Los Angeles, a charter member of the Southern Christian Leadership Conference and a board member of the Billy Graham Evangelistic Association, stood to pray: "We come here today not seeking power from the government, but we're asking that Thy Holy Spirit, which is the power, will fall upon us afresh and anew." As Dr. Hill began to pray, the sun started to break through the clouds. "We believe You're going to save us from the wrath that is sure to come unless we repent. We acknowledge our weaknesses and our wickedness," he prayed.

The people lifted their faces toward the sunshine even as they prayed with Dr. Hill. He continued, "We acknowledge that we have strayed far from Thee, but we know that Thou art a loving God."

Suddenly, the sky above us turned blue. The clouds just rolled back and gave us a quick glance of heaven. It was a strange and wonderful experience to see and feel the sun for the first time in three long, dark days.

"Thou art a tender God," Dr. Hill prayed. "Thou art a merciful God and so we say, in the name of Jesus, save us, Lord; restore us, Lord; bless us, Lord." Half a million people broke the silence with a thunderous "Amen" as Dr. Hill concluded his prayer.[18]

Many times during that incredible day, I sat on the platform watching men and women of faith from all across the nation as they prayed. They were every color, every class, every denomination imaginable. They were chief executive officers of large corporations, and they were unemployed, blue-collar workers. They were old and young, rich and poor, well-dressed and shabby. But they were one, and their prayer for the nation was one prayer. And God was hearing and would answer their prayer. April 29, 1980, was the beginning of a spiritual revolution. And I joined with the 500 thousand people in the Mall and the millions watching on television in praying that one day this same spiritual revolution would sweep the nation.

22

THE INAUGURATION OF RONALD REAGAN

JANUARY 20, 1981

A Mandate to Return to Our Conservative Roots

On a balmy, 68-degree day in January 1981, Ronald and Nancy Reagan stood in the open doorway of their ranch-style home on San Onofre Drive in the Pacific Palisades suburb of Los Angeles. After saying good-bye to their daughter Patti and to a friendly crowd of neighbors who had gathered on the lawn, the Reagans walked to their limousine. A few minutes later, a band from Palisades High School played "Hail to the Chief" as the Reagans boarded Air Force One for their flight to Washington, D.C., and to Ronald Reagan's gala inauguration as the fortieth president of the United States.

"This will be a new beginning," the president promised after taking the oath of office on his battered family Bible, ". . . an era of renewal."[1]

Seventy thousand people had gathered for the inauguration ceremonies on the west front of the Capitol, the side overlooking the Mall and its monuments. Previously, inaugurations had been held on the Capitol's east front, which looks out on the Supreme Court and the Library of Congress. President Reagan was the first to be sworn into office overlooking the Mall, the place where just nine months before 500 thousand of us had gathered to pray for a return by this nation to its spiritual and political roots. Never before in her history had this nation been in such drastic need of "an era of renewal."

Domestically, the national economy was in chaos. The inflation rate had reached 15 percent, and the prime interest rate hovered at 15 percent and higher. The 1981 budget deficit the newly elected president had inherited was mounting weekly to at least $50 billion. The presi-

dent had promised in his campaign speeches to halt this "great inflation" and to stabilize the economy once again.

Abroad, America had become the world's laughingstock. The defeat
in Vietnam; the collapse of most of Indochina to the Soviet-backed Vietnamese; the Soviets' recent invasion of Afghanistan; and the loss of
Angola, Mozambique, Ethiopia, South Yemen, and Nicaragua to Communist governments left the United States looking powerless and afraid.
The Soviets were expanding their atheist-Marxist sphere of influence
around the globe with impunity. And in Teheran, fifty-two American
hostages were spending their 444th day in captivity. The new president
had promised to end this era of Soviet expansionism and to bring the
captives home.

After the inaugural ceremonies on that cold, snow-sprinkled morning
in the nation's capital, President and Nancy Reagan hosted the traditional luncheon for congressional leaders. At the close of the luncheon,
an aide hurried to the president's side. Reagan smiled, whispered something to his wife, and stood to address his guests and the world's press:
"Some ten minutes ago, the planes bearing our prisoners left Iranian
airspace, and they're now free of Iran."[2]

Apparently, the Ayatollah Khomeini and his terrorist friends sensed a
new mood in Washington. This president had promised "an era of renewal," and on his first day in office, at least one tyrant half a world
away took him seriously.

At the heart of his program for renewal would be the president's un-
flagging optimism. He hated the word "inevitable." On the campaign
trail, he had expressed time and again his sincere belief that human
beings have the strength to stand against their "fates" and reverse them.
"I've always believed a lesson my parents taught me," he told a *Ladies'
Home Journal* reporter. "In America, there's no such thing as 'inevitable.' We have the freedom and opportunity to meet great challenges and
to better our lives."[3]

Reagan's refusal to give in to the "inevitable" reflected a return to
the spirit of the Pilgrims, the spirit of 1776, and the spirit of Washington, Jefferson, and Lincoln. That belief would help shape the president's domestic and foreign policy as he began on that first day in office
to keep his promise for renewal. One Reagan observer said it this way:
"In simple terms, his 'can do' attitude stands in stark contrast to the
recent sense of helplessness, fatalism, or malaise that has permeated so
many ideas about government. Reagan's 'can do' attitude, however, re-

fers not to leaving it to government to do it alone, but to letting people solve their problems in their own way."[4]

The new president ended his first inaugural address with these words: "The crisis we are facing today requires . . . our best effort and our willingness to believe in ourselves and to believe in our capacity to perform great deeds, to believe that together with God's help we can and will resolve the problems which now confront us. And after all, why shouldn't we believe that? We are Americans."[5]

Reagan's Stand on the Domestic Issues

The Family. During his campaign for the presidency, Reagan spoke of his concern for the erosion of the American family. The growing divorce rate; the abuse of children and the elderly by family members; the increase in family violence; the rate of family suicides, especially among women and children; the misuse of alcohol and drugs within the family; the decreasing rate of church and synagogue attendance by family members—all pointed to the gradual disintegration of the most important and influential unit of traditional American society.

Immediately, Reagan would initiate legislation to assist in the renewal of the American family by decreasing the economic hardship and stress experienced by middle- and lower-income families. These measures included lower taxes, reducing the so-called marriage penalty, increasing the child-care credit, and virtually eliminating the inheritance tax on a family farm or business for the surviving spouse.

Nancy Reagan joined her husband in working for an era of family renewal by sponsoring an all-out attack on drug and alcohol abuse through private and public agencies, and through creative education regarding drugs and the terrible consequences of their misuse.

Saving the American family became a primary item on President Reagan's agenda for renewal. "I've always believed," he said early in his presidency, "[that] families and family values are the foundation of America's goodness and strength."[6]

Abortion. Even before his election, Ronald Reagan took a clear pro-life stand. "Interrupting a pregnancy is the taking of a human life," he said in Boston in 1980.[7] "Everybody that is for abortion has already been born,"[8] he said with a knowing grin in one debate with John Anderson. And in the president's State of the Union address five years later, he asked Congress "to move this year on legislation to protect the unborn."[9]

Women. The president expressed clearly his opposition to the Equal Rights Amendment, yet he worked diligently to help create greater economic independence for American women. During his first term in office he was glad to announce: "Among adult women, employment has risen to an all-time high. And the kind of jobs women hold are improving. In 1983, women filled two-thirds of all the new jobs in managerial and professional fields . . . . And the number of businesses owned by women is growing four times faster than the number of those owned by men."[10]

Education. At the close of the president's first term in office, he could report verifiable gains in his promised "return to excellence" in education. "We're stressing basics of discipline, rigorous testing and homework," he said, "while helping children become computer-smart as well. For 20 years, Scholastic Aptitude Test scores of our high-school students went down. But now they have gone up two of the last three years."[11]

School Prayer. Ronald Reagan was committed to the renewal of the spiritual life of the nation from the beginning of his first term. He thanked the Congress "for passing equal access legislation giving religious groups the same right to use classrooms after school that other groups enjoy." Then, in his 1985 State of the Union address, he added, "No citizen need tremble, nor the world shudder, if a child stands in a classroom and breathes a prayer. We ask you again," he said to the joint session of Congress, "give children back a right they had for a century and a half or more."[12]

Crime. Immediately after taking office, the president called the Congress and the courts to "reaffirm common-sense values: that say right and wrong matters, that say individuals must be responsible for their actions, and that say, yes, punishment must be swift and sure for those who prey on the innocent."[13] The president urged the Congress "to feel more compassion for the victims of crime than for those who commit crime," and "to use the death penalty where necessary."[14] After Reagan's first three years in office, crime rates in the United States experienced their sharpest drop in the history of crime statistics. Obviously we cannot relax our prayerful vigilance against crime. Already, the crime rate is beginning to climb again. What began in 1980 with the march and the election of President Reagan must be continued in 1988 or all that we have gained as a nation may be lost.

Church and State. The president was well acquainted with the Judeo-Christian values upon which the nation was founded. In his presidential debates in 1980, Reagan told what he had been experiencing in his travels around the country: "I have felt a great hunger in America for a spiritual revival, for a belief that a law must be based on a higher law, for a return to traditions and values that we once had."[15]

Though Ronald Reagan is a Christian himself, and though he has advocated throughout his administration a return to the nation's spiritual roots, he has been a staunch advocate of pluralism within the nation and a defender of the rights of each individual to worship God as he or she desires.

Civil Rights. During his debates with Jimmy Carter, Reagan took a clear stand for "total equal opportunity for all people."[16] As president, he believed that the best way to build racial equality was to build economic equality. He fought to renew the economy, to help the private sector create jobs, and to get people of every color back to work again. The president's stand against "affirmative action programs becoming quota systems" and his work to end expensive government programs that were ineffective or "had outlived their usefulness" was misinterpreted by some as action against racial or economic equality. In fact, by renewing the private sector, by slowing or even ending inflation, by lowering interest rates, and by getting people back to work, President Reagan has moved the country toward an era of real civil rights renewal.

Economic Policy. From the day he announced his candidacy, Ronald Reagan was clear on economic matters: "The people have not created this disaster in our economy; the federal government has. It has overspent, overestimated, and overregulated. In the thirty-four years since the end of World War II, it has spent 448 billion dollars more than it has collected."[17]

Immediately upon assuming office, he proposed legislation to reduce the growth in government spending and taxing to reform or eliminate unnecessary and unproductive (or even counterproductive) regulations, and to encourage a consistent monetary policy. All these measures were aimed at balancing the budget, ending the increases in the national debt, and maintaining the value of our currency.

President Reagan's economic solutions would not be easy or immediate. And if those presidents who succeed him are not similarly committed, all the nation's economic gains could be lost again. Still, the debate regarding Ronald Reagan's economic policies can be informed by two facts. First, he entered the presidency with the inflation rate at 15 percent. After twenty-five straight months of economic growth, the three-year inflation average was just 3.9 percent, the lowest in seventeen years. And second, he entered the presidency with the prime interest rate soaring to 21 percent. As of this writing, the prime interest rate has retreated to 7.5 percent and is falling to levels not seen in decades.[18]

The president's economic policies have achieved amazing and rapid results. After just five years in office, the country has experienced its strongest economic growth in thirty-four years. Seven and three-tenths million new jobs have been created. In the last two years alone, more of our citizens have been working than ever in history.

Unfortunately, the president did not achieve all his economic goals. The balancing of our nation's budget still eludes us. The growing national deficit still hangs menacingly overhead. But Ronald Reagan has turned the country in the right direction, and we must be certain that in 1988 we continue on that path to economic sanity, a balanced budget, and a radically decreased national debt.

Social Programs. In 1980 Ronald Reagan made clear his views on welfare. "If welfare were truly successful," he claimed, "government would be boasting each year of how much it has reduced the welfare rolls, how many less people there were in need of assistance." Then he added, "Now remember, we're not talking about those people who are invalid and through no fault of their own cannot provide for themselves. We have always taken care of those people—and always will. We're talking about those people who are able-bodied and who, for whatever reason, have not been able to make their way out there in the competitive world. The idea of welfare should be to put those people back on their feet, make them self-supporting and independent."[19]

Reagan was also the first president to warn the nation clearly regarding the serious problem basic to the Social Security system: "It is trillions of dollars out of balance," he said in 1980, ". . . based on a false premise with regard to how fast the number of workers would increase and how fast the number of retirees would increase."

Immediately, President Reagan began a thorough study to bring renewal to the Social Security system while promising still "that no one presently dependent on Social Security is going to have the rug pulled out from under them and not get their check."[20]

States' Rights. In the first announcement of his candidacy, Ronald Reagan reminded the nation that "the 10th Article of the Bill of Rights is explicit in pointing out that the federal government should do only those things specifically called for in the Constitution. All others shall remain with states or the people." He claimed rightly that "we haven't been observing that 10th Article of late." He accused the federal government of taking on functions that "it was never intended to perform and which it does not perform well. There would be a planned, orderly transfer of such functions to states and communities, and a transfer with them of the sources of taxation to pay for them."[21]

Reagan's Stand on Foreign and Defense Issues

National Defense. In an interview just prior to his election, Ronald Reagan made clear the skeleton of his views on national defense. "Our defenses," he said, "must be whatever is necessary to ensure that the potential enemy will never dare attack." Then, to help discourage the escalating arms race he added: "If you strive for an obvious superiority then you may tempt the other side into being afraid and you continue escalating on both sides."[22]

From the beginning of his presidency, Reagan worked for peace. He shared his dream "to see that day when nuclear weapons are banned from this earth forever."[23] But he refused to disarm unilaterally or to take lightly the Soviet threat.

The Soviet Union. The President proposed a Strategic Defense Initiative "aimed ultimately at finding a non-nuclear defense against [the Soviets'] ballistic missiles." When critics said his SDI would bring war to the heavens, Reagan replied, "Its purpose is to deter war, in the heavens and on the earth." And when they claimed his defense proposals would only force the Soviets to develop new programs of their own, he answered: "The Soviets have strategic defenses that surpass ours; a civil-defense system, where we have almost none; and a research program covering roughly the same areas of technology that we're now exploring."

And when the critics claimed the president's Strategic Defense Initiative would take too long to develop, he answered, "Then let's get started."[24]

Communist Global Expansion. In a news conference just after his first inauguration, President Reagan made clear his views on the threat of Communist expansion. He pointed out that every leader of the Soviet Union since the revolution has made clear "their determination that their goal must be the promotion of world revolution and a one-world socialist or Communist state." From the beginning of his presidency, Reagan has refused to believe that the Soviet-backed violent extension of Communism was "inevitable."[25]

And where genuine national liberation movements sought to recapture their country from a Communist tyranny imposed from without, the president's policy was clear: "America reserves the right—and may indeed have the duty—to support those people."[26]

"We must stand by all our democratic allies," the president affirmed in an address to Congress, "and we must not break faith with those who are risking their lives—on every continent, from Afghanistan to Nicaragua—to defy Soviet-supported aggression and secure rights which have been ours from birth."[27]

Terrorism. On January 27, 1981, in a White House ceremony welcoming home the Americans held hostage in Iran, the president made clear his views on terrorism: "Let terrorists be aware that when the rules of international behavior are violated, our policy will be one of swift and effective retribution. We hear it said that we live in an era of limits to our power. Well, let it also be understood there are limits to our patience."[28]

World Peace. Immediately after his inauguration, President Reagan made it a national priority to re-establish cordial relations with the nations and peoples of Africa, Asia, Europe, the Middle East, and the Americas. Under Reagan this nation has regained its role as a respected leader of the free world and a determined enemy of tyranny and terrorism wherever they may appear.

Reagan announced this in his first debate with Jimmy Carter:

I believe with all my heart that our first priority must be world peace, and that use of force is always, and only, a last resort when everything else has failed. And then only with regard to our national security . . . . I have seen four wars in my lifetime. I'm a father of sons. I have grandsons. I don't ever want to see another generation of young Americans bleed their lives into sandy beachlands in the Pacific or rice paddies and jungles in Asia or the muddy, bloody battlefields of Europe.[29]

President Reagan's Re-election

On February 6, 1985, President Reagan was escorted into the Capitol for his annual State of the Union address to the joint houses of Congress. Senators and congressmen, distinguished visitors in the galleries, and even members of the world's press who were assembled there stood to their feet and gave the president a rousing welcome.

Just five years before, 500 thousand people had gathered on the Capitol Mall, and millions more had joined them through television, to pray for a time of public and private renewal. The president had kept his inaugural promise to begin an era of renewal for the nation and her people. As President Reagan stood to speak, millions were thanking God for hearing and answering their prayers.

Through Ronald Reagan the nation has begun its return to those spiritual and political ideals upon which it had been founded. The legislators gathered beneath the dome of the Capitol and the tens of millions watching on television or listening on radio had high hopes that during the president's second term in office he would bring that goal of national renewal another step closer to fulfillment.

"I am pleased," the president began, "that after four years of united effort, the American people have brought forth a nation renewed— stronger, freer, and more secure than before. . . ."

"Tonight," he continued, "America is stronger because of the values that we hold dear. We believe faith and freedom must be our guiding stars, for they show us truth, they make us brave, they give us hope and leave us wiser than we were. Our progress began not in Washington, D. C., but in the hearts of our families, communities, work places and voluntary groups, which together are unleashing the invincible spirit of one great nation under God."[30]

23

ANOTHER DATE WITH DESTINY

ELECTION DAY, 1988

A Mandate to Take Our Place as Responsible Citizens
in Every Level of Government

On election day in November 1988, my wife, Dede, and I will drive our Ford Bronco from our home on the CBN University campus down a country lane ironically named the Centerville Turnpike. We will pass a CBN University housing area and a large cluster of dark brown, cedar townhouses and duplexes en route to Brandon Avenue. Just ahead on Pope Street will be a huge school parking lot filled with yellow buses that will have transported many of the 2,500 Brandon Junior High School students to their classrooms from their neighborhoods around Virginia Beach.

We will turn right into the circular, weathered asphalt driveway, park near the school's entrance, and walk thirty paces to the multipurpose gymnasium, where precinct workers will be waiting with ballots for the presidential election. We will wait in line with our neighbors from Virginia Beach while workers search their lists for our names and addresses.

After we sign the official voting list, volunteer election officials will hand us a white ballot in a dark gray, folded envelope and point us to the nearby stage where three-sided voting booths will have been assembled for this election. Inside the booth, we will slip our punch-card computer ballots into a Voteamatic-3 punch machine, with each ballot option described in large letters on easily turned metallic pages. We will pick up the steel stylus and poke tiny holes into our ballots beside each person or issue that we favor.

After removing the punched ballots from the Voteamatic-3, we will walk back across the gym, place our ballots in the PBC-3 computerized vote-counting machine, and we will watch while the little marvel tabulates our votes and issues each of us our own voter's number. The totals remain a secret inside the machine until the end of the day, but instantly we know our votes have been counted. At that moment, we will have exercised our right to vote as citizens of this free nation. It will have taken fifteen minutes of our busy day, but we will have helped to shape the future of our country with the most powerful tool at our command, the right and the responsibility to vote.

When you exercise your right to vote in 1988, you are celebrating a uniquely significant American date with destiny. Nineteen hundred and eighty-eight is the bicentennial of our nation's determination to create a government of the people, by the people, and for the people. In 1787 the Constitution that described this experiment was ratified. Exactly two hundred years ago in 1788 the nation's first elections were held to select the president and the Congress. In 1789 George Washington was inaugurated first president of these United States.

When you vote in 1988 you will be celebrating two hundred years of American freedom. Millions have died to secure and protect your right to vote and billions of people now living have never once experienced such freedom.

Are you a registered voter? On Election Day, 1988, will you vote? In the presidential election of 1984, were you one of the 92,653,000 Americans who voted? Or were you among the 81,283,000 men and women who disenfranchised themselves? Forty-seven percent of the nation's eligible citizens did not vote in 1984.[1] It was another American date with destiny; yet almost half of the nation's potential voters missed their opportunity to share in the excitement of that day.

Every time you vote (or refuse to vote), you are making history. This coming presidential election is no exception. The very act of voting is a dramatic and nation-shaping event. Most of the world watches in wonder as Americans decide their destiny freely at the polls. To ignore or forget that opportunity is to lose a place in history and to risk losing the right to vote forever.

In Most Nations, Free Elections Do Not Exist

What a privilege it is to vote freely when in most nations, including the Soviet Union, free, democratic elections do not exist! One official party candidate suffices for each position in the 1,500-member Supreme Soviet. And though a 100 percent voter turnout is expected and enforced, the only political party is the Communist Party and the only candidates are the Party's candidates.

A Russian citizen may cross out the approved candidate's name and write in his or her own choice for a position, but the act is futile and seldom tried. In the Soviets' 1979 election, for example, 99.99 percent of the electorate (174,734,459 voters) voted the party line, while just 185,422 people dared write in a second choice.[2]

In the 1986 election in the Philippines, the news media gave firsthand evidence of what often happens in other nations where free elections are supposed to be taking place. Thugs intimidated, injured, and even killed voters before stealing ballot boxes and destroying ballots. Officials, supposedly banned from the polling places, bribed voters with cash or paid voters to stay away from the polls altogether. Whole neighborhoods of people found their names eliminated from the voting lists. Counterfeit ballots were printed. The vote-counting process was marred with haggling, death threats, and acts of violence. Seeing that the free election was being undermined, angry, determined voters held their ground and guarded the remaining ballot boxes with their lives. Many brave men and women in the Philippines died or were seriously injured while exercising or defending their right to vote.[3]

The Price of Voting Freely in America

Even in America, the right to vote freely had to be won with blood, sweat, and tears. At the Constitutional Convention in 1787, determining the qualifications of voters for electing members to the House of Representatives was left to the states; the right to vote was restricted to men who owned property and paid taxes, and even they couldn't vote directly for the president.

After seventy-three years, in 1860, the voting privilege was extended to men without property who paid little or no tax. Thirty years later, in 1890, Wyoming became the first and only state to grant suffrage to women. Another thirty years would pass before the nineteenth constitutional amendment forbade states' denying the right to vote on the basis of sex.

In 1870 the fifteenth amendment made it unconstitutional to deny the right to vote on the basis of race, color, or previous condition of servitude, but black and brown Americans were still effectively disenfranchised by a combination of poll taxes, rigged literacy tests, whites-only primaries, violence, and fear. Ninety-six years after the fifteenth amendment was ratified, the twenty-fourth amendment (1964) ended poll taxes and the Voting Rights Act (1965) gave adequate protection to black voters.

And though American young people eighteen to twenty-one years of age could fight and die in wars across the world, it wasn't possible for them to vote until the twenty-sixth amendment was passed in 1971.

This country struggled almost two hundred years to open the doors of those polling booths to every adult American. Yet in every presidential election in modern history, almost half the nation's eligible voters neglected to vote. In recent presidential elections, 47 million American voters did not bother to exercise their hard-won right. Only about 38 percent vote in off-year congressional elections, and a substantially smaller number cast ballots in state and local elections or in primaries of any kind.[4]

If the Nation Is Destroyed, It Will Be by Our Indifference

Admit it. You aren't really convinced that your one vote can make a difference. Out of 92 million voters, what chance do you have of influencing an election? Plenty!

In 1976, for example, just eight thousand votes cast differently in Ohio and Hawaii could have swung the presidential election from Carter to Ford.[5] And in 1986 in Illinois, two followers of extremist Lyndon LaRouche actually won the Democratic nominations for secretary of state and lieutenant governor because the handful of voters who did vote in the primary neglected to take the responsibility seriously enough to check the backgrounds and beliefs of their candidates.

In fact, getting more voters to vote is less important than getting those voters who do vote prepared to vote the issues. In Germany, for example, in 1933, 88.8 percent voted in the Assembly election swept by the Nazis. *Newsweek* commentator George Will asked, "Did that high 1933 turnout make the Nazi regime especially legitimate?"[6]

In a post-election poll after that Illinois primary, a number of voters admitted they *voted for* the LaRouche cult candidates because their names had "an Anglo-Saxon ring" and their opponents' names, George Sangmeister and Aurelia Pucinski, "were foreign-sounding."[7] Others apparently *voted against* a mainline Democratic candidate because he refused to select a woman as his running mate.

Few voters took time to investigate Hart and Fairchild, those La-Rouche cult candidates with the Anglo-Saxon names who proposed "to hang Henry Kissinger and Katherine Graham for treason and to arrest and try the Queen of England for pushing heroin."[8] In that Illinois primary, 79 percent of eligible voters neglected to vote, and too many of the 21 percent who did vote had no idea for whom they were voting. Anyone who has studied this country's election patterns knows that thousands of local and state elections are won or lost every year by a handful of votes and by voters who may or may not bother first to understand the issues.

In 1988 the presidential election promises to reverse those unhappy voting trends. Great segments of the American electorate are awaking to a new sense of patriotism and political concern. Led by evangelical Christians determined to bring about a new era of spiritual and political renewal, more people will vote and vote wisely than in any other presidential election in the nation's history.

We must end forever the growing sense of apathy and disinterest that has recently plagued our democratic process. Each of us must become a responsible, active citizen once again. We must vote and vote thoughtfully, for the future of our nation is at stake.

Let America's dates with destiny help guide you. Remember our ancestors kneeling in the sands of Cape Henry seeking God's guidance and strength. Remember our forefathers meeting in Philadelphia to create a Declaration of Independence on behalf of life, liberty, and the pursuit of happiness. Remember George Washington leading an army of farm boys, traders, and immigrants against the crack troops of George III to win and secure those rights for each of us. And remember President Lincoln in the bloody ruins of Gettysburg asking if a nation "conceived in liberty and dedicated to the proposition that all men are created equal . . . can long endure."

Now, more than a century later, we must ask ourselves again, can such a nation as ours endure the troubled times ahead? Can we endure if we forsake the God of our fathers and strip from our national consciousness the teachings of the Holy Bible? Can we endure if we continue such profligate waste in government, the accumulation of such an unsupportable debt, and the amassing of power in the central government with the resulting loss of freedom and individual initiative by the people? Can we endure as a free nation when over 50 percent of our people receive some payment or subsidy from the federal government? Can we endure if we lose the understanding that the source of our wealth is the individual initiative of our people rather than the largess of various government bureaucracies? Can we endure if we refuse to declare acts of our citizens either right or wrong and if we accept as part of our lifestyle blatant immorality, adultery, drunkenness, and drug abuse?

America stands at the crossroads. A moral and spiritual renewal of historic proportions is underway. People across the land are crying out for leadership by statesmen and stateswomen who care about future generations instead of politicians who care only about the next election.

Either we will return to the moral integrity and original dreams of the founders of this nation, and from that renewal to a future filled with technological advance, increasing prosperity for all our people, and a new birth of freedom on the earth that will insure our triumphant entry into the twenty-first century, or we will give ourselves over more and more to hedonism, to all forms of destructive anti-social behavior, to political apathy, and ultimately to the forces of anarchy and disintegration that have throughout history gripped great empires and nations in their tragic and declining years.

This book is written to show what was, what is, and what might be the story of our nation and its people. That choice is ours!

POSTSCRIPT

A Word *about* My Evangelical Christian Friends

A recent Gallup poll suggests that 70 million Americans consider themselves to be evangelical Christians. They come from a rich variety of backgrounds and experiences. They are white, black, yellow, red, and brown. They are wealthy and they are poor. They are educated and they are self-taught. They are top executives, and they are laborers, farmers, and auto mechanics. Their ancestors were nobles and slaves, peasants and great landowners. They have Anglo, European, Latin, African, and Asian roots. And they live in ghettos from Bedford-Stuyvesant to Watts and in elegant, guarded neighborhoods from Park Avenue to Beverly Hills.

These evangelical Christians may all look alike to the press, but in fact they are very different from each other. They attend great cathedrals and tiny storefront churches. Some shout and weep and lift their arms in praise. Others kneel in ordered, liturgical silence. Their biblical translations vary. They celebrate the Lord's Supper in dozens of different ways. They are scattered across the nation in great cities and tiny villages. They represent an amazing cross section of the total American culture and experience. And though these evangelicals love each other as their Lord commanded, they remain independent from each other in a thousand different ways. Evangelicals are not one uniform, homogeneous group as their critics fear. In fact, they are as wonderfully diverse from each other as they are from their unbelieving

298

neighbors and as deeply committed to freedom, pluralism, and individuality as any people in the nation.

But in recent months evangelicals are finding themselves more and more united in their concern for the nation's spiritual and political renewal. When they pledge their allegiance to "one nation, under God," they really mean it. They are committed to the basic truths upon which this nation was founded and to the Creator who is their source and sustenance. "We hold these truths to be self-evident," they reaffirm sincerely, "that all men are created equal, that they are endowed by their Creator with certain unalienable Rights, that among these are Life, Liberty and the pursuit of Happiness."

With the nation's forefathers, they quote the Bible, the Declaration of Independence, and the Constitution as trustworthy guidelines in the lives of individuals and government. They agree with President John Adams that "our Constitution was made only for a moral and religious people. It is wholly inadequate to the government of any other." They have rediscovered the central significance and ultimate necessity of spiritual renewal to this nation's strength, and they are committed to a speedy and wholehearted return by America to her Judeo-Christian heritage.

The newly active evangelicals are also discovering that millions of other men and women in America support similar spiritual and political ideals even though they are members of other religious traditions or are uncertain of their personal faith.

Fortunately it didn't take long for these newly awakened evangelicals and their allies to learn that they have to change their political ways before they can change the ways of the nation. In the past they have boycotted or ignored the political process altogether. And when or if they voted, they often voted as irresponsibly as those Illinois Democrats who nominated cult members for two major state offices.

Editors of the popular evangelical journal *Christianity Today* claim that "if only half of the unregistered evangelical voters in the United States had registered and voted, they could have reversed every presidential election in the last 100 years."[9] For too long the evangelical Christian has complained about not being heard in the highest levels of government. According to *Christianity Today,* if the principles that we evangelical Christians hold dear have been ignored by winning candidates in past elections, it has been our own fault.

Those editors quote one politician who put it bluntly: "We can vote as we please without losing the support of the evangelical vote because (1) evangelicals don't vote! They aren't even registered to vote. (2) Evangelicals don't know who voted for what, so they can't possibly punish any legislator for not taking their wishes seriously. And (3) even if they do know how we voted, and disapprove of our votes, they aren't deeply enough committed to do anything about it."

As a result, summarizes *Christianity Today*'s editorial board, "politicians have tended to ignore evangelical wishes."[10]

This election year will end forever the isolation and inactivity of evangelicals and their allies. At this moment, there is a growing determination among clergy and laity alike to register evangelical voters in every state of the union. Already, millions of new evangelical voters have been registered since the last presidential election. No longer will the evangelical Christian voter neglect his or her right to vote. Nor will the evangelical Christian voter be ignorant and uninformed about the issues.

A Word *to* My Evangelical Christian Friends

I have written *America's Dates with Destiny* to summarize briefly just a few of the major moments in American history that shaped our past for good or evil. I have written to every American, regardless of his or her religious or political background. But I have especially written to my fellow evangelicals, trying to review the spiritual truths that gave this nation birth and the political blunders that led us off the pathway. I want to direct these last few words to you, my brothers and sisters in Christ.

During the last two years, I have visited your homes and churches in every state across the nation. I have talked and listened to your clergy and your laity. I have addressed your conventions, your rallies, and your citywide meetings. I am excited about your new commitment to the nation's spiritual and political renewal. You are coming to life as a political force, and already you are making a difference.

Register New Voters

Congratulations to you evangelical volunteers responsible for registering millions of new voters. If your church has no campaign to register voters, make it your goal to register every eligible voter in your congregation. Call city hall or your voter registration office. Equip ushers and other volunteers to register people on the church lawn, in the Sunday school classes, or after a mid-week prayer meeting or Bible study.

Remember, the average American family moves every three years. Because the nation has no universal registration system, every time a family moves, the voters in that family need to renew their registration. And if you do nothing else before the 1988 election, at least be sure to register yourself.

Study and Discuss the Issues

Congratulations to the churches whose pastors and teachers are bringing the important spiritual and political issues before their congregations. If you haven't already begun to study the issues together as a church family, begin soon. These are biblical issues, too, you know, worthy of consideration in your adult education department, in your mid-week study groups, and even in your Sunday morning services.

You pastors and teachers are right to be concerned that your sermons and lessons not be reduced to political propaganda. Your people will be on different sides of many issues, and they will sometimes support opposing parties and candidates. Good! That's the way it should be. But major issues that we have ignored all too long face the nation and the world. And those issues have roots in our Old and New Testament heritage.

Preach those issues! Teach those issues! Get your people to study and discuss those issues! The first eleven chapters of this book represent just a few of the major political themes with biblical and spiritual significance to your congregation. Each theme has a biblical text. Each historic moment has its spiritual heritage.

America's second president, John Adams, gave us good advice when he said: "It is the duty of the clergy to accommodate their discourse to the times; to preach against such sins as are most prevalent; and to recommend such virtues as are most wanted. . . . If the rights and duties of Christian magistrates and subjects are disputed, should they [the clergy] not explain them, show their nature, ends, limitations and restrictions?"

For too long, church leaders have been silent in the name of freedom and fairness or doctrinal purity. Now, whole generations are ignorant of our nation's Judeo-Christian heritage. We must eliminate that ignorance or be destroyed by it. Our people are brainwashed by candidates with huge television and billboard budgets. The real issues are drowned in political rhetoric and bumper sticker solutions. Don't be afraid to take a stand. It doesn't mean you have to publicly support a candidate or a ballot issue. But where the candidate or the issue requires a moral decision, help your people make that decision wisely, guided by biblical truth and the wisdom of our nation's forefathers.

Join Together with Other Churches

Congratulations to you pastors and lay volunteers who are working together with other churches in your city and state to speed spiritual and political renewal to the nation. In the past year, I have been invited to address many of your large inter-church rallies. You are succeeding in your task to encourage evangelical Christians to become more responsible citizens. Your enthusiastic and inspiring programs are educating and motivating a whole evangelical generation to take a more active role in the political process.

If you have not tried it yet, I encourage you to join with other churches in your city for a rally or meeting dedicated to bringing the issues and candidates before concerned Christian voters. When it is appropriate, invite both sides to address you. Insist that the candidates, their representatives, and the spokespersons who stand for various issues leave time for your people to ask honest questions and get honest answers. Use the gym or the classroom if the sanctuary seems inappropriate, but don't be afraid to open the doors of your church to political controversy. You will be amazed at the growing interest and expertise that evangelicals are acquiring in their new determination to practice responsible Christian citizenship.

Get Involved at the Precinct and Primary Level

In the past, most evangelical Christians have waited until Election Day to get involved in the political process—if they got involved at all. Now they are beginning to discover that waiting until it's time to vote is waiting too long. On Election Day, it is too late to help select a candidate that represents or even understands your views. On Election Day it's too late to understand, let alone influence, the issues that will decide your future. The time to influence the candidates and issues is months and even years before the election, and the place is at the level of the precinct and the party primary.

Picture America as a large patchwork quilt divided into 175 thousand neighborhood pieces. The real work of the American political process goes on in those tiny precinct divisions. Yet evangelical Christians have seldom, if ever, been involved on a precinct level. If you want to really help the nation find spiritual and political renewal, start in your local precinct.

Imagine what could happen in America's 175 thousand precincts if just ten evangelical Christian volunteers could be mobilized to assist in each one. The American political process would be revolutionized, and the future of the nation would be changed forever. And believe it or not, such a great and generous pool of evangelical volunteers would be welcomed with open arms by the skeleton crew of Republican and Democratic workers who have faithfully manned their posts these many long years.

Precinct workers go door to door to register voters. They help to mobilize their community to political action, and they help their neighbors to understand better the issues and candidates. Precinct volunteers represent their precincts in the statewide party caucuses where delegates are selected for the national conventions and where party candidates and issues are chosen for every level of government.

Evangelicals are already beginning to discover that real power lies with the precinct volunteer. Look what happened in 1960, for example. Richard Nixon would have beaten John F. Kennedy if he had managed to get just one vote more per precinct across the country. When Governor Carter was seeking the Democratic presidential nomination in 1976 in Virginia, a state with over 5 million people, only 20 thousand showed up for the Democratic precinct caucuses that selected him. And in 1984, former Vice President Walter Mondale was nominated to be the Democratic presidential standard-bearer with only 6 million voters involved in all the primaries in all the states.

As has been the case throughout the nation's political history, a tiny minority working faithfully in each precinct usually determines the nation's political platforms and party candidates. That tiny minority could be reshaped by evangelical Christian volunteers and our allies, with lasting positive results for the nation.

Your Date with Destiny Is Now

The nation stands at another crossroads. During the twentieth century, America wandered off the course established by her forefathers. In this past decade we have been finding our way again. But we must not relax our vigil. It was not enough that 500 thousand Americans prayed for the nation's renewal on the Capitol Mall in Washington, D.C. We must continue to pray for the nation in small groups and in huge rallies all across America. It is not enough that Ronald Reagan has begun the journey back toward our spiritual and conservative roots. We must continue and advance the work he has begun.

And it is not enough to wait for that date with destiny in November 1988 before you act. Get involved now. Be sure you're registered to vote. Volunteer to work on the precinct level for your political party. Call your pastor and suggest an evening to discuss and pray about the issues that confront the nation and the world. Organize an interchurch "Concerned Christian Voters" rally. Meet the candidates. Study the platforms. Understand the propositions. Get your family involved. Cut out newspaper stories and pass them around the table and discuss them after dinner. Watch for special television programs that inform you about the issues. View and discuss them together with your family and friends. Volunteer to register voters. Give a gift to support a worthwhile candidate or issue. Send a card or letter to the White House, to the Congress, or to the Supreme Court making your opinions known. Share this book with a friend. Collect signatures to get the important issues on the ballots. Run for office. Work in the campaigns of those who run. Above all else, pray for the nation that we might truly find our way again.

And please, don't be overwhelmed by all the jobs still waiting to be done. Just select one that is interesting and possible for you. Then try your best to do it! Don't worry about your inexperience. Don't worry about making a mistake or being criticized unfairly. Don't worry about success or failure, winning or losing. Just choose one goal and work to accomplish it. And while you are deciding whether you will or will not act, remember these simple words from Edmund Burke: "The only thing necessary for the triumph of evil is for good men [or women] to do nothing."

NOTES

Introduction

1. New York Times News Service, June 13, 1986, Washington, D.C., quoted in *Daily News,* June 14, 1986, 1.

2. Ibid.

3. Genesis 1:27.

4. John 3:3.

5. *Daily News,* June 4, 1986, 2.

Chapter 1

1. Genesis 1:26.

2. Matthew 28:19-20 NIV.

3. First Charter of Virginia, in Richard L. Perry, ed., *Sources of Our Liberties: Documentary Origins of Individual Liberties in the United States Constitution and Bill of Rights* (Chicago: American Bar Foundation, 1978), 39-40.

4. Mayflower Compact, in Perry, 60. See also Herbert W. Titus, "America's Colonial Charters: Seedbed for a Christian Nation" (unpublished ms., CBN University). Dr. Titus is Provost and Dean of the School of Law and Public Policy at CBN University. I am indebted to him for his insight and assistance in preparing *America's Dates with Destiny.*

5. Charter of Massachusetts Bay, in Perry, 94.

6. Charter of Maryland, in Perry, 105.

7. Charter of Rhode Island and Providence Plantation, in Perry, 169.

8. Charter of the Carolinas, in Francis N. Thorpe, ed., *Federal and State Constitutions* 5 (reprint, 1905, n.p.), 2743.

9. Charter of Pennsylvania, in Thorpe, 3036.

Chapter 2

1. For two fascinating and differing accounts of the "massacre at Henrico," see Robert Hunt Land, "Henrico and Its College," *William and Mary Quarterly* 18 (October 1938): 453-498; and George J. Cleaveland, "At Henrico," *Alumni Gazette* 37:3 (March 1970): 4-10.

2. Land, 498.

3. Pauline Pearce Warner, *The County of Henrico, Virginia: A History* Published by the country in 1959. Now available through CBN University.

4. Alexander Whitaker, "Good News from Virginia," ms. sermon held at Sargeant Memorial Room, Norfolk Public Library.

5. Ibid.

6. James I to Archbishop of Canterbury, in Peter Walne, "The Collections for Henrico College: 1616-1618," *The Virginia Magazine of History and Biography* 80 (July 1972): 258.

7. George Newman to ministers and wardens, ibid.

8. David J. Geyertson, "God's Work Stands" (unpublished Historical Perspective of CBN, Virginia Beach, Virginia, 1980), 6.

9. Ibid.

10. John S. Flory, "The University of Henrico," *Southern History Association Publications* 8 (Jan. 1904): 41-52.

11. Edward D. Neill, ed., "The Earliest Efforts to Promote Education in English North America," Macalaster College *Contributions*, 64-65. See Dr. David Geyertson's personal files of archival journals and manuscripts, CBN University.

12. Warner, "The County of Henrico," 27.

13. W. Gordon McCabe, "The First University in America: 1619-1622," *The Virginia Magazine of History and Biography* 30 (April 1922): 149-150.

14. Ibid., 147.

15. William Crashaw, "Introduction" to the Reverend Alexander Whitaker's sermon, "Good News from Virginia," op. cit.

16. "New England's First Fruits in Respect to the Progress of Learning in the College at Cambridge in Massachusetts Bay," in Verna M. Hall, comp., and Rosalie J. Slater, developer, *Teaching and Learning America's Christian History* (San Francisco: Foundation for American Christian Education, 1975), frontispiece. For more information write Foundation for American Christian Education, Box 27035, San Francisco, CA 94127. See also Peter G. Mode, ed., *Sourcebook and Bibliographical Guide for American Church History* (Menasha, WI: G. Banta Publishing Company, 1920), 73-74.

17. Mode, 75.

18. Ibid., 109.

19. Ibid., 109-110.

20. David A. Lockmiller, *Scholars on Parade: Colleges, Universities, Costumes and Degrees* (New York: MacMillan, 1969), 70.

21. Ibid., 78.

22. Ibid., 81.

23. Nathaniel B. Shurtleff, ed., *Records of the Governor and Company of the Massachusetts Bay in New England* (Boston: William White, 1853), 2:203.

24. Gerald L. Gutek, *Education and Schooling in America* (Englewood Cliffs, NJ: Prentice Hall, 1983), ch. 2.

25. Paul Leicester Ford, ed., *The New England Primer: A History of Its Origin and Development* (New York: Dodd Mead, 1897).

26. Noah Webster, *An American Dictionary of the English Language* (1828; reprint, San Francisco: Foundation for American Christian Education, 1967), s.v.

Chapter 3

1. Jonathan Edwards, "Sinners in the Hands of an Angry God," quoted in *The World's Great Speeches,* ed. Lewis Copeland (New York: Dover, 1958), 227-228.

2. Alexander V. G. Allen, *Jonathan Edwards* (Boston: Houghton Mifflin, 1891), 126.

3. Edwards, 227-228.

4. Edwards, 227-228.

5. Elisabeth D. Dodds, *Marriage to a Difficult Man: The "Uncommon Union" of Jonathan and Sarah Edwards* (Philadelphia: Westminster, 1971), 92.

6. Nehemiah Strong, as related in Timothy Dwight, *Travels in New England and New York,* in Ola Elizabeth Winslow, *Jonathan Edwards 1703-1758: A Biography* (New York: Macmillan, 1940), 193.

7. Edwards, 227-228.

8. Stephen William, *Diary,* in Winslow, 192.

9. Rene Descartes, *Discourse on Method,* quoted in John A. Garraty, "The Colonial World," *The American Nation: A History of the United States to 1877* 1 (New York: Harper & Row, 1975), 54.

10. For background material on Jonathan Edwards and the Great Awakening, see op. cit. See also Edward H. Davidson, *Jonathan Edwards: The Narrative of a Puritan Mind* (Boston: Houghton Mifflin, 1966); Edwin Tunis, *Colonial Living* (Cleveland, OH: World, 1957); Perry Miller, "The Garden of Eden and the Deacon's Meadow," in *A Treasury of American Heritage: A Selection from the First Five Years of the Magazine of History* (New York: Simon and Schuster, 1960); Perry Miller, *Jonathan Edwards* (New York: W. Sloane, 1949).

11. C. H. Fause and T. J. Johnson, eds., *Jonathan Edwards: Representative Selections* (New York: American, 1935), 75-84.

12. Ibid.

13. Ibid.

14. Ibid.

15. Ibid.

16. Charles Chauncy, "Seasonable Thoughts on the State of Religion in New England" (Boston, n.p., 1743), 35-109, passim.

17. Ibid.

18. Edwards, 73-84.

Chapter 4

1. *Oxford Companion to American History* (New York: Oxford University Press, 1966), 236.

2. Jim Bishop, *The Birth of the United States* (New York: Morrow, 1976), 230.

3. Resolution for Independence, in Henry Steele Commager, ed., *Documents of American History* (Englewood Cliffs, NJ: Prentice-Hall, 1973), 100. All citations to the Declaration are taken from this source.

4. Leviticus 25:10.

5. A. James Reichley, *Religion in American Public Life* (Washington, DC: The Brookings Institution, 1985), 94.

6. Cited by Reichley, op. cit., from Robert M. Healey, *Jefferson on Religion in Public Education* (New Haven, CT: Yale University, 1962), 26, 27, 34; Walter Berns, *The First Amendment and the Future of American Democracy* (New York: Basic Books, 1970), 31.

7. Quoted by Rousas John Rushdoony, *This Independent Republic: Studies in the Nature and Meaning of American History* (Fairfax, VA: Thoburn, 1978), 6.

8. A. Koch and W. Peden, eds., *The Life and Selected Writings of Thomas Jefferson* (New York: Modern Library, 1944), 567.

9. Quoted by Norman Cousins, in *In God We Trust* (New York: Harper and Brothers, 1958), 117.

10. Henry S. Randall, *The Life of Thomas Jefferson* (New York: Derby and Jackson, 1958), 3:451.

11. John Locke, *Second Treatise On Civil Government* 77 (n.d.: Liberal Arts Press, 1952). Quoted by Dr. Herbert W. Titus in an unpublished work titled "The Christian Legacy of America's Declaration of Independence," CBN University.

12. I. W. Blackstone, *Commentaries on the Laws of England* (39; reprint Chicago: University of Chicago, 1979).

13. Ibid.

14. Henry Jaffa, "Are These Truths Now, Or Have They Ever Been, Self-Evident? The Declaration of Independence and The United States of America on their 210th Anniversary" (unpublished essay), 1-2.

15. Perry Miller, "The Garden of Eden and the Deacon's Meadow," 119-121.

16. Genesis 1:27.

17. Genesis 2:7.

18. 2 Corinthians 3:17.

19. Ecclesiastes 3:13.

20. Numbers 22:19.

21. Matthew 24:35.

22. 1 Samuel 8:18.

23. 1 Samuel 8:22.

24. Deuteronomy 17:19-20.

25. Romans 13:1, 4.

26. S. E. Forman, ed., *The Life and Writing of Thomas Jefferson*, 2nd ed. (Indianapolis: Bobbs, Merrill Co., 1900), 255-256.

27. John Calvin, *Institutes of the Christian Religion*, ed. John T. McNeill, trans. Ford Lewis Battles, Library of Christian Classics (Philadelphia: Westminster, 1960), 4. Quoted by Dr. Titus in "Legacy."

28. 1 Samuel 15:17, 26.

Chapter 5

1. Bill for Establishing Religious Freedom, in William Taylor Thom, *The Struggle for Religious Freedom in Virginia: The Baptists*, Johns Hopkins Studies in Historical and Political Science, Herbert B. Adams, ed. (Baltimore: Johns Hopkins, 1900), 79.

2. Charles F. James, *Documentary History of the Struggle for Religious Liberty in Virginia* (1899; reprint, New York: Da Capo, 1971), 19. This reprint is the only source for many of the pertinent perspectives and studies.

3. Thom, 11.

4. Bishop of London, Bishop Meade, "Old Parishes and Families of Virginia" (1743), and F. L. Hawks, "History of the Protestant Episcopal Church of Virginia," in James, 28.

5. Thom, 40.

6. William Fristoe, "History of the Ketocton Baptist Association," in James, 31.

7. Robert B. Semple, "History of the Baptists of Virginia" (1810), in James, 30.

8. F. L. Hawks, in James, 31.

9. Semple, in James, 38.

10. James, 36.

11. Ibid, 33.

12. James, 52.

13. Thom, 40.

14. From John S. Barbour, "Oration on the Life, Character, and Services of James Madison, delivered at Culpeper Courthouse, July 18, 1836," in James, 60.

15. Bill of Rights, Constitution of Virginia, in Perry, *Sources of Our Liberties*, 312.

16. General Assessment Bill, in James, 129.

17. *The Papers of James Madison*, ed. Robert A. Rutland, et al. (Chicago: University of Chicago, 1973), 8:299.

18. Thom, 79.

19. Ibid.

20. Ibid., 79-80.

21. Ibid., 80.

22. Hawks, in James, 141.

23. John Leland, in Thom, 40.

24. Bancroft, in James, 14.

25. James, 14; see also Lewis Peyton Little, *Imprisoned Preachers and Religious Liberty in Virginia* (Lynchburg, VA: 1938).

26. George Washington, letter in Thom, 9.

Chapter 6

1. Clinton Rossiter, *1787: The Grand Convention* (New York: Macmillan, 1966), 179.

2. Ibid., 235.

3. Ibid., 236.

4. Ibid., 237.

5. Ibid., 237-8.

6. Samuel Adams, "Rights of the Colonists" (1772), in Verna M. Hall, *The Christian History of the Constitution of the United States of America* (San Francisco: Foundation for American Christian Education, 1976), xiii.

7. Washington's Farewell Address, in Commager, 173.

8. John Adams, in *The Works of John Adams, Second President of the United States* collected by Charles Francis Adams (Boston: Little, Brown, 1854).

9. The Constitution of the United States, in Commager, 138. All quotations from the Constitution are from this source.

10. *Documentary History of the Constitution of the United States of America,* derived from the records, manuscripts, and rolls deposited in the Bureau of Rolls and Library of the Department of State (Washington, DC: Department of State, 1900), 3:236.

Chapter 7

1. Douglas Southall Freeman, *George Washington: A Biography* (New York: Scribner's, 1954), 6:187. The description of the first inauguration day is derived from Freeman's account.

2. Ibid., 187-93.

3. Washington's First Inaugural Address, in Commager, 151. All quotations from the Address are from this source.

4. Freeman, 196.

5. *Encyclopaedia Britannica,* s.v. "Washington, George."

6. Henry Lee, in "Resolution in the House of Representatives on the death of Washington," December 26, 1799, in *Encyclopaedia Britannica,* loc. cit.

7. Paul F. Boller, Jr., *George Washington & Religion* (Dallas: Southern Methodist University, 1963), 27.

8. Reichley, *Religion in American Public Life,* 102.

9. Ibid.

10. Quoted in Hall, *The Christian History of the Constitution,* 573.

11. Reichley, 99.

12. Anson Phelps Stokes and Leo Pfeffer, *Church and State in the United States,* rev. ed. (New York: Harper & Row, 1964), 35.

13. Hall, *The Christian History of the American Revolution,* frontispiece.

14. Reichley, 102.

15. *Basic Writings of George Washington,* ed. Saze Commins (New York: Random House, 1948), 356-57.

16. Baptist General Committee to President Washington, in James, *Documentary History of the Struggle for Religious Liberty in Virginia,* 171-2.

17. Washington to the General Committee, in James, 173.

18. Stokes and Pfeffer, 87.

19. In Hall, *The Christian History of the Constitution,* 68.

20. Ibid., 56.

21. Ibid., 13.

22. Peter Wiernik, *History of the Jews in America from the Period of Discovery of the New World to the Present Time* (1931; reprint, Westport, CT: Greenwood), 99-101, in Stokes and Pfeffer, 243.

23. Reichley, 87.

24. Wiernik, in Stokes and Pfeffer, 243.

25. Douglas Southall Freeman, *Washington,* an Abridgment in One Volume by Richard Harwell of the Seven-Volume *George Washington* (New York: Scribner's, 1968), 707.

26. Ibid., 708.

27. Ibid.

28. Washington's Farewell Address, in Commager, 173.

Chapter 8

1. Paul Russell Cutright, *Lewis and Clark: Pioneering Naturalists* (Urbana: University of Illinois, 1969), 47-8. See also Bernard DeVoto, ed., *The Journals of Lewis and Clark* (Boston: Houghton Mifflin, 1953); Donald Barr Chidscy, *Lewis and Clark: The Great Adventure* (New York: Crown, 1970).

2. Jefferson to Lewis, in *The Original Journals of the Lewis and Clark Expedition,* ed. Reuben Gold Thwaites (New York: Dodd, Mead, 1904-5), 7:248. Hereafter cited as *Journals.*

3. Cutright, 48.

4. Merrill D. Peterson, *Thomas Jefferson and the New Nation: A Biography* (New York: Oxford University, 1970), 653.

5. John Bartlett, *Familiar Quotations* (Boston: Little, Brown, 1982), 891:7.

6. Thomas Jefferson, First Inaugural Address, in Commager, 187.

7. Jefferson to Rush, Bartlett, 388:15.

8. Peterson, 762.

9. Ibid., 764.

10. Lally Weymouth, ed., *Thomas Jefferson: The Man . . . His World . . . His Influence* (New York: Putnam's, 1973), 115.

11. Jefferson to William Stevens Smith, November 13, 1787.

12. *Journals,* 7:249.

13. Cutright, 394-5.

14. Ibid., 397.

15. Psalm 8:1-3.

16. *Journals,* 7:248.

17. Ibid., 7:250.

18. Jefferson to the Republican Citizens of Washington County, Maryland, March 31, 1809.

19. Thomas Jefferson, "Syllabus of an Estimate of the Merit of the Doctrines of Jesus, Compared with Those of Others," quoted in Peterson, 957.

20. Dale L. Morgan, *Jedediah Smith and the Opening of the West* (Lincoln, NE: University of Nebraska, 1953), 311.

21. Jefferson to Charles Willson Peale, August 20, 1811.

Chapter 9

1. Charles G. Finney, *Memoirs* (New York: A. S. Barnes, 1876), 185.

2. Ibid., 185-6.

3. Ibid.

4. Ibid., 186-7.

5. Ibid., 186.

6. Kenneth Scott Latourette, *A History of Christianity* (New York: Harper and Row, 1953), 1229.

7. Finney, 19-20.

8. Ibid., 20.

9. Williston Walker, *A History of the Christian Church* (Cleveland, Ohio: Case University Press, 1969), 510.

10. Ibid., 509.

11. Bertram Wyall-Brown, *Lewis Tappan and the Evangelical War Against Slavery,* quoted by William G. Shade in essay, "Anti-Slavery," source unknown, 134.

12. Rossiter, *1787,* 267.

13. Nathan Schachner, *Thomas Jefferson: A Biography* (New York: Appleton-Century-Crofts, 1951), 1:154.

14. Finney, 324.

15. Harriet Beecher Stowe, "Uncle Sam's Emancipation," in Noel B. Gerson, *Harriet Beecher Stowe: A Biography* (New York: Praeger, 1976), 104, 79.

16. Edward Wagenknecht, *Harriet Beecher Stowe: The Known and the Unknown* (New York: Oxford University, 1965), 244-5.

17. Stowe, in Gerson 104.

18. Forrest Wilson, *Crusader in Crinoline: The Life of Harriet Beecher Stowe* (Philadelphia: Lippincott, 1941), 284.

19. Luke 10:1.

20. Shade, 138.

21. Ibid., 136.

22. Blanche Glassman Hersh, *The Slavery of Sex: Feminist-Abolitionists in America* (Urbana: University of Illinois, 1978), 138.

23. Ibid., 14-15.

24. Ibid., 39-40.

25. Elizabeth Cady Stanton, in Alice Stone Blackwell, *Lucy Stone: Pioneer of Women's Rights* (Boston: Little, Brown, 1930), 940.

26. Hersh, 83-84.

27. Ibid., 86.

28. Ibid., 89.

29. Ibid., 84.

30. Ibid., 140.

31. Finney.

Chapter 10

1. Carl Sandburg, *Abraham Lincoln: The War Years* (New York: Harcourt, Brace, 1939), 2:466. The description of the delivery and reception of the Gettysburg address is derived from Sandburg's account, pp. 466-477.

2. Ibid., 466.

3. Ibid., 468.

4. Ibid., 469.

5. Ibid., 472.

6. Ibid., 472-3.

7. For further information on Lincoln or the Civil War, see Sandburg, *Abraham Lincoln: The War Years,* vols. 1-4; Don Congdon, ed., *Combat: The Civil War* (New York: Delacorte, 1967; Paul M. Angle, *The Civil War Years* (New York: Doubleday, 1967); Edgar DeWitt Jones, *Lincoln and the Preachers* (New York: Harper and Brothers, 1948); James A. Rawley, *Race and Politics: "Bleeding Kansas" and the Coming of the Civil War* (Philadelphia: Lippincott, 1969); Charles Morrow Wilson, *The Dred Scott Decision* (Philadelphia: Auerbach, 1973).

8. Abraham Lincoln, First Inaugural Address, in Commager, 386, 388. All quotations from the Address are from this source.

9. For further references to underlying issues behind the Civil War, see Harry V. Jaffa, *Crises of the House Divided* (Chicago: University of Chicago, 1982).

10. Lincoln to Greeley, August 22, 1862, in Commager, 418.

11. Abraham Lincoln, "Reply, The Seventh Joint Debate," in Commager, 355. All quotations from the Reply are from this source.

12. Jaffa, 53.

13. Bartlett, 522:6.

14. Lincoln to Stephens, in T. Harry Williams, *Abraham Lincoln: Selected Speeches, Messages, and Letters* (New York: Holt, 1957), 135.

15. Jaffa, 316-17.

16. In Bartlett, *Familiar Quotations,* 15th ed. (Boston: Little, Brown, 1980), 520. All quotations listed under date and circumstance are from this source, pp. 520-524.

17. Charles A. Beard and Mary R. Beard, *The Beards' New Basic History of the United States,* rev. by their son, William Beard (Garden City: Doubleday, 1968), 268.

Chapter 11

1. Richard H. Schneider, *Freedom's Holy Light* (Nashville: Thomas Nelson, 1985), 86.

2. Mary Virginia Fox, *The Statue of Liberty* (New York: Messner, a Simon & Schuster company, 1985), 37.

3. Beard and Beard, *New Basic History,* 274-302.

4. Oscar Theodore Barck, Jr., and Nelson Manfred Blake, *Since 1900: A History of the United States in Our Times* (New York: Macmillan, 1959), 2-4.

5. John F. Kennedy, *A Nation of Immigrants* (New York: Harper & Row, 1964), 69.

6. Ibid.

7. Ibid., 70.

8. *Statistical Abstracts of the United States, 1986,* 83.

9. Ibid., 84ff. Appendix A offers an excellent summary of immigration statistics.

Chapter 12

1. Woodrow Wilson, Speech for Declaration of War Against Germany, in Commager, 2:128. All other quotations from the speech are from this source.

2. Josephus Daniels, *The Wilson Era* (Chapel Hill: University of North Carolina, 1946), 34.

3. J. Wesley Robb. *The Reverent Skeptic: A Critical Inquiry into the Religion of Secular Humanism* (New York: Philosophical Library, 1979), 58.

4. John Durant, *Darwinism and Divinity* (New York: Oxford University Press, 1985), 17.

5. *Encyclopaedia Britannica,* s.v. "Nietzsche, Friedrich."

6. Lawrence A. Cremin, *The Transformation of the School: Progressivism in American Education, 1876-1957* (New York: Knopf, 1961).

7. Paul Johnson, *Modern Times: The World from the Twenties to the Eighties* (New York: Harper and Row, 1983), 4.

8. *Great Events from History: America Series,* ed., Frank Magill (Englewood Cliffs, NJ: Salem, 1975), 1195.

9. Paul Kurtz, ed., *Humanist Manifestos One & Two* (Buffalo, NY: Prometheus, 1973), 7-10.

10. Arthur S. Link, *Woodrow Wilson* (New York: World, 1963), 92.

11. Hanson W. Baldwin, *World War I: An Outline History* (New York: Harper and Row, 1962), 156ff.

12. *Academic American Encyclopedia* (Danbury, Conn.: Grolier, Inc., 1985), 245.

13. 2 Corinthians 4:8-9.

14. Link, 173-4.

Chapter 13

1. Peggy Lamson, *Roger Baldwin: Founder of the American Civil Liberties Union* (Boston: Houghton Mifflin, 1976), 90.

2. Ibid., 91-2.

3. Ibid., 93.

4. Ibid., 95.

5. Ibid., 6.

6. For other Roger Baldwin biography, see *Current Biography,* 1940, 43-44, s.v. "Baldwin, Roger"; "Profile," *The New Yorker,* July 11, 1953, 18; "Obituary," *The New York Times,* August 27, 1981, D18.

7. Lamson, 6.

8. Ibid., 125.

9. Ibid., 67.

10. Ibid., 103.

11. *Current Biography,* loc. cit.

12. Barbara Habenstreit, *Eternal Vigilance: The American Civil Liberties Union in Action* (New York: Messner, 1971), 17.

13. Ibid., 16-17.

14. Arthur M. Schlesinger, Jr., *The Almanac of American History* (New York: Bison, 1983), 441.

15. Ibid., 438.

16. Lamson.

17. Lamson, 229.

18. Ibid., 51.

19. "Creation Goes to Court," *Newsweek,* Dec. 21, 1981, 57.

20. Jack Weatherly, "Creationists Concerned About Court Test of Arkansas Law," *Christianity Today,* Sept. 18, 1981, 40.

21. From *The New York Times,* Aug. 29, 1982, as reported in Richard A. Baer, Jr., "They Are Teaching Religion in Public Schools," *Christianity Today,* Feb. 17, 1984, 12.

22. "Away with a Manger," *The New Republic,* Oct. 31, 1983, 4.

23. Baer, loc. cit.

24. Ibid.

25. Whittacker in Bernard Schwarts, *Inside the Warren Court* (Garden City, NJ: Doubleday, 1983), 181.

26. 42nd Annual Report of the American Civil Liberties Union, July 1, 1961–June 20, 1962, 22.

27. Bernard Schwarts, *Super Chief* (New York: New York University, 1983), 261.

28. Ibid., 441.

29. Ibid.

30. Lamson, 291.

Chapter 14

1. Gordon Thomas and Max Morgan-Witts, *The Day the Bubble Burst: A Social History of the Wall Street Crash of 1929* (New York: Doubleday, 1979), 347-68.

2. Edward Robb Ellis, *A Nation in Torment: The Great American Depression, 1929-1939* (New York: Coward-McCann, 1970), 68-91. See also chapter 16, "What the Depression Did to People," 229-54.

3. From a four-column headline published on the front page of *The New York Times,* Oct. 25, 1929.

4. Ellis, 89.

5. Robert S. McElvaine, *The Great Depression: America, 1929-1941* (New York: New York Times, 1984), 27-8.

6. W. W. Kiplinger, quoted in McElvaine, 26.

7. Benjamin Franklin, *Poor Richard: The Almanac, 1733-1758* (New York: Paddington, 1976), 7.

8. Ibid., 231.

9. Ibid.

10. Johnson, 233.

11. From Federal Reserve Annual Report, 1933, cited in Johnson, 233.

12. Ibid., 234.

13. McElvaine, 42.

14. Johnson, 236.

15. Ibid.

16. Ibid.

17. McElvaine, 25-51.

18. Ellis, 256.

19. Ibid., 232.

20. Ibid., 231.

21. Franklin, 99.

22. John Kenneth Galbraith, quoted in Ellis, frontispiece.

Chapter 15

1. Walter Lippmann, *Interpretations: 1933-1935* (New York: Macmillan, 1936), in *The Roosevelt Era,* Milton Crane, ed. (New York: Boni and Gaer, 1947), 10.

2. Franklin D. Roosevelt, First Inaugural Address, in Commager, 2:238. All quotations from the Address are from this source.

3. William E. Leuchtenburg, *Franklin D. Roosevelt and the New Deal: 1930-1940* (New York: Harper and Row, 1963), 43.

4. Ibid.

5. Charles Hurd, 107.

6. McElvaine, *The Great Depression,* 161.

7. Paul Johnson, 256.

8. Garet Garrett, *The People's Pottage* (Caldwell, ID: Caxton, 1958), 9-10.

9. Johnson, *Modern Times,* 256ff.

10. *Encyclopaedia Britannica,* s.v. "World War II."

11. Melvyn Dubofsky, Athan Theoharis, and Daniel M. Smith, *The United States in the Twentieth Century* (Englewood Cliffs, NJ: Prentice-Hall, 1978), 319.

12. Jonathan Daniels, "Thursday Afternoon," in *The Roosevelt Era,* 626.

Chapter 16

1. Douglas MacArthur, *Reminiscences* (New York: McGraw-Hill, 1964), 274ff.

2. Dale Kramer, ed., *Yank: The Story of World War II as Written by the Soldiers* (New York: Greenwich House, 1984). 180ff.

3. Ibid.

4. Saul K. Padover, ed. and trans., *Karl Marx on Revolution* (New York: McGraw-Hill, 1971), 91ff.

5. Robert V. Daniels, *Russia: The Roots of Confrontation* (Cambridge, MA: Harvard University, 1985). xx.

6. Ibid., 210.

7. Ibid.

8. Robert V. Daniels, *A Documentary History of Communism* (London: University Press of New England, 1984), 140-41.

9. Ibid.

10. Daniels, *Russia*, 222.

11. *A Pictorial Biography: H.S.T.* (New York: Grosset-Dunlap, 1973), 83.

12. Johnson, 450.

13. See Political Map of Africa, in David Ottaway and Marina Ottaway, *Afrocommunism* (New York: Africana, 1981), 1.

14. Daniels, *A Documentary History of Communism*, xix.

15. Daniels, *Russia,* 175.

Chapter 17

1. Keith Fuller, ed., *The Torch Is Passed: the Associated Press Story of the Death of a President* (Seattle: Western Printing and Lithographing, 1963), 13.

2. Merriman Smith, "Eyewitness Account," in *Four Days* (New York: American Heritage, 1964), 32-33.

3. Joseph Nathan Kane, *Facts About the Presidents* (New York: H. W. Wilson, 1974), see Index, s.v. "Assassinations" and "Attempted Assassinations," 401.

4. Ibid., 176.

5. "When Will the Shooting Stop?" *The New Republic,* April 11, 1981, 5.

6. U.S. Justice Department, *Crime in the United States, F.B.I.* (Washington, DC: General Printing Office, 1984), 5. Note: "The mode of display should not be taken to imply a regularity in the commission of crimes; rather it represents the annual ratio of crime to fixed time intervals."

7. Lewis H. Lapham, ed., "Images of Fear: On the Perception and Reality of Crime," *Harper's,* May 1985, 40.

8. Ibid., 41ff.

9. Ibid., 41.

10. *Los Angeles Times,* Mar. 14, 1985, H:2:1.

11. John Borden, "The Crackdown on Organized Crime," *Scholastic Update,* Mar. 21, 1986, 27.

12. *Los Angeles Times,* June 10, 1985, I:1:2.

13. *Los Angeles Times,* Oct. 7, 1985, I:2:1.

14. *Los Angeles Times,* Oct. 13, 1985, I:5:1.

15. *Los Angeles Times,* Dec. 2, 1985, I:5:1.

16. Ted Gest, "A Crime Rise That Stumps the Experts," *U.S. News & World Report,* May 5, 1986, 24.

17. Elizabeth Carpenter, "Traumatic Bonding and the Battered Wife," *Psychology Today,* June 1985, 18.

18. *Los Angeles Times,* May 6, 1985, I:4:1.

19. David Chalmers, *Hooded Americanism: The History of the Ku Klux Klan* (New York: Watts, 1980).

20. *Los Angeles Times,* Jan. 21, 1985, I:1:3.

21. *Los Angeles Times,* Apr. 8, 1985, I:1:3.

22. *Los Angeles Times,* Jan. 7, 1985, I:2:6.

23. *Los Angeles Times,* May 19, 1985, I:2:1.

24. *Los Angeles Times,* April 4, 1985, I:2:5.

25. *Los Angeles Times,* Mar. 4, 1985, I:11:1

26. *Los Angeles Times,* Apr. 28, 1985, IV:3:1.

27. Margaret O. Hyde and Lawrence E. Hyde, *Missing Children* (New York: Watts, 1985), 1.

28. *Los Angeles Times,* Nov. 4, 1985, I:6:5.

29. "What Is Our Drug Problem?" a forum convened by Mark D. Danner, *Harper's,* Dec. 1985, 39-46ff.

30. Ibid., 41.

31. Ibid., 41.

32. Ibid., 41.

33. *Los Angeles Times,* July 17, 1986, 1.

34. "What Is Our Drug Problem?", 44.

35. *U.S. News & World Report,* Aug. 5, 1985, 14.

36. Ted Gest, "NO VACANCY Signs Go Up at the Nation's Jails," *U.S. News & World Report,* Dec. 23, 1985, 39.

37. John Adams, *The Works of John Adams.*

Chapter 18

1. Merle Miller, *Lyndon: An Oral Biography* (New York: Putnam's, 1980), 375ff.

2. Ibid., 375.

3. Ibid., 377.

4. Johnson, *Modern Times,* 638.

5. Howard B. Furer, ed., *Lyndon B. Johnson* (Dobbs Ferry, N.Y.: Oceana Publications, Inc.), 89.

6. Johnson, 639.

7. "LBJ's Decision: Guns and Butter," *New York Times,* Aug. 10, 1965.

8. *U.S. News & World Report,* Jan. 24, 1966.

9. Doris Kearns, *Lyndon Johnson and the American Dream* (New York: Harper and Row, 1976), 213.

10. "The Dimming of the Dream," *Time,* Dec. 9, 1966, 25.

11. Ibid.

12. Ibid.

13. Ibid.

14. William L Chaze and Benjamin M. Cole, "After 15 Years of 'Great Society,'" *U.S. News & World Report,* June 30, 1980, 38.

15. Ibid., 36.

16. *Time,* op. cit., 26.

17. *Time,* Dec. 9, 1966, 25.

18. "Why 'War on Poverty' Is Being Scrapped," *U.S. News & World Report,* Mar. 5, 1973, 11.

19. "GREAT SOCIETY and Its Future," *U.S. News & World Report,* Dec. 19, 1966, 32ff.

20. Richard M. Nixon, quoted in *U.S. News & World Report,* Mar. 5, 1973, 11.

21. "Budget Deficits: The Endless River of Red Ink," *U.S. News & World Report,* Feb. 7, 1983, 24-5.

22. Vaughn Davis Bornet, *The Presidency of Lyndon Baines Johnson* (Lawrence, KS: University Press of Kansas, 1983), 250.

23. Ibid.

24. "Why 'War on Poverty' Is Being Scrapped," *U.S. News & World Report,* 11.

Chapter 19

1. Bob Woodward and Scott Armstrong, *The Brethren* (New York: Simon and Schuster, 1979), 237.

2. This brief summary of Justice Blackmun's decision in *Roe v. Wade* is based on Woodward and Armstrong, 166-235; and Jerry Falwell, *If I Die Before I Wake* (Nashville: Thomas Nelson, 1985), 31-48.

3. Judith Papachriston, *Women Together* (New York: Knopf, 1976), 220ff.

4. Woodward and Armstrong, 183.

5. Summaries, 35 L Ed 2d 147, JANE ROE v. HENRY WADE, 410 US 113, 93 S ct 705, pp. 119ff.

6, Ibid.

7. Woodward and Armstrong, 238.

8. Ibid., 239.

9. Ibid., 238.

10. Ibid.

11. Quoted in Herbert W. Titus, "The Supreme Court Isn't Supreme; The Constitution Is," *The Washington Post,* July 14, 1986, A11.

12. Ibid.

13. Ibid.

14. Woodrow Wilson, in *Constitutional Government in the United States,* quoted in Jerry Ralph Curry and Jay V. Garriss, *Our Orwellian Court* (Chesapeake, VA: National Perspectives Institute, 1986), 13.

15. Justice William J. Brennan, in "Intent of the Framers," *Newsweek,* Oct. 28, 1985, 97.

16. Reichley, *Religion in American Public Life, 160.*

17. David O'Steen, *USA Today,* Dec. 1, 1982.

18. "America's Abortion Dilemma," *Newsweek,* Jan. 14, 1985, 20ff.

Chapter 20

1. Arnold R. Isaacs, *Without Honor: Defeat in Vietnam and Cambodia* (Baltimore: Johns Hopkins University, 1983), 295ff.

2. Stanley Karnow, *Vietnam: A History* (New York: Viking, 1983), 613ff.

3. George Shultz, address to the Department of State, Apr. 25, 1985, Department of State Bulletin, June 1985.

For a variety of periodical sources regarding the War in Vietnam and its aftermath see:

> *Atlantic*:
> > 257:40-41 My '86 "The War We Knew: An Oral History"
> *Commonweal:*
> > 113:239-40 Ap 25, '86 "Vietnam's American Children"
> *Life*:
> > 9:41-45 Ja '86 "Ceremonies: A year for Making the End of Two Wars"
> *U.S. News & World Report*:
> > 100:10 Ap 14, '86 "What Vietnam Should Have Taught Us"
> > 100:7 Ja 20, '86 "U.S. And Hanoi Dance a Minuet"
> > 98:60-2 My 6, '85 "10th Anniversary"
> > 98:35-41 Ap 22, '85 "Vietnam: Lasting Impact"
> *Newsweek*:
> > 107:26-7 Jan 20, '86 "The Lost Americans"
> > 105:48-9 May 13, '85 "10th Anniversary . . ."
> > 105:72-73 Ap 22, '85 "Live from Ho Chi Minh City"
> *Time*:
> > 125:38-40 My 13, '85 "10th Anniversary"
> *Foreign Affairs*:
> > 63:747-58 Spring '85 "Coming to Grips with V.N."
> > 63:722-46 Spring '85 "Lessons of Vietnam"
> *World Press Review*:
> > 32:48 Jl '85 "Rewriting History"
> > 32:48 Je '85 "Vietnam's Anniversary Battles"
> *Commentary*:
> > 81:40-3 Mr. '86 "Vietnam: How We Deceived Ourselves"
> *New Republic*:
> > 192:7-25 Ap 29, '85 "Vietnam: 10 Years After"
> *Harpers*:
> > 270:35-8 Ap '85

4. Karnow, 667.

Chapter 21

1. David Manuel, *The Gathering: Washington for Jesus* (Orleans, MA: Rock Harbor, 1980), 183ff.

2. Gordon L. Hankins and John Gilman, eds., *My People: A Pictorial History of Washington for Jesus* (Klamath Falls, OR: Craft Printers, 1980), 25. Available from One Nation Under God, P.O. Box 62524, Virginia Beach, VA 23462.

3. 2 Chronicles 7:14.

4. Isaiah 45:23.

5. Hankins and Gilman, 14.

6. Ben A. Franklin, "200,000 March and Pray at Christian Rally in Capital," *The New York Times,* Apr. 30, 1980, Al, 20.

7. Psalm 113:3.

8. Demos Shakarian, recorded live, July 21, 1986, CBN 700 Club Video Tape.

9. Josh McDowell, ibid.

10. Manuel, 40.

11. Proverbs 14:13.

12. Senator Mark Hatfield, July 21, 1986, CBN 700 Club Video Tape.

13. Joel 2:7-8.

14. Manuel.

15. Ibid.

16. Ibid.

17. Ibid.

18. Ibid.

Chapter 22

1. "President Reagan," *Congressional Quarterly,* 1981, 113-14.

2. Ibid., 35.

3. Ronald Reagan interview in *Ladies' Home Journal,* Nov. 1984, 148.

4. Wayne Valis, ed., *The Future Under President Reagan* (Westport, CT: Arlington House, 1981), 15.

5. "President Reagan," 115.

6. Ronald Reagan interview, *Ladies' Home Journal,* 179.

7. Ronald Reagan interview, *Boston Globe,* Jan. 13, 1980, in "President Reagan," 93.

8. "President Reagan," 84.

9. Quoted in *U.S. News & World Report,* Feb. 18, 1985, 79.

10. Ronald Reagan interview, *Ladies' Home Journal,* 179-80.

11. Ronald Reagan, State of the Union Address, Feb. 6, 1985.

12. Ibid.

13. Ronald Reagan interview, *Ladies' Home Journal,* 180.

14. Ronald Reagan, State of the Union Address, 1980.

15. "President Reagan," 94.

16. Ibid.

17. Ibid.

18. *U.S. News & World Report,* Feb. 4, 1985, 65.

19. Ibid., quoting interview, *Detroit News,* Jan. 13, 1980, 95.

20. Ibid., 94.

21. Ronald Reagan, Announcement of Candidacy, Nov. 13, 1979.
22. Interview, *Boston Globe,* Jan.13, 1980.
23. Ronald Reagan, State of the Union Address, Feb. 6, 1985.
24. Ibid.
25. "President Reagan," 97.
26. "A White House View," *U.S. News & World Report,* Jan. 27, 1986, 29.
27. Ronald Reagan, State of the Union Address, Feb. 6, 1985.
28. "President Reagan," 97.
29. Ibid.
30. Ronald Reagan, State of the Union Address, Feb. 6, 1985.

Chapter 23

1. "Voter Participation," *Statistical Abstracts of the United States, 1986,* 255.
2. "One Party, One Vote," *Time,* Mar. 12, 1984, 48.
3. "Marcos and the Election Mess," *Newsweek,* Feb. 17, 1986, 14-20.
4. "Democracy's Rusty Weapon," *The New Republic,* Apr. 14, 1986, 7.
5. "Our November Call to Conscience," *Christianity Today,* Sept. 21, 1984, 12-13.
6. "In Defense of Nonvoting," *Newsweek,* Oct. 10, 1983, 96.
7. "Democracy's Rusty Weapon," 7.
8. Ibid.
9. "Our November Call to Conscience," 12.
10. Ibid.